A WRITER'S WORKBOOK

An Interactive Writing Text for ESL Students

Second Edition

A WRITER'S WORKBOOK

An Interactive Writing Text for ESL Students

Second Edition

TRUDY SMOKE
Hunter College

St. Martin's Press
New York

Editor: Kathleen Keller
Managing editor: Patricia Mansfield-Phelan
Project editor: Erica Appel
Production supervisor: Alan Fischer
Cover design: Celine Brandes
Cover photo: Victor Schrager
Book design: Suzanne Bennett, Leon Bolognese and Associates
Illustrations: Alan Robbins

Library of Congress Catalog Card Number: 90–71647
Copyright © 1992 by St. Martin's Press, Inc.

Manufactured in the United States of America.
65432
fedcba

For information, write:
St. Martin's Press, Inc.
175 Fifth Avenue
New York, NY 10010

ISBN: 0–312–05021–6

Acknowledgments

"Don't Expect Me to Be Perfect," Sun Park, *Newsweek*, © 1984 by Newsweek, Inc. All rights reserved. Reprinted by permission.

"Our Good Opinion of Ourselves," from *American Educator* by Harold Stevenson. Copyright 1987. Reprinted with permission from the Summer 1987 issue of the *American Educator*, the quarterly journal of the American Federation of Teachers.

"The Extended and Conjugal Nuclear Family" from *Readings In Sociology: A Biographical Approach*, 2/ed., by Peter L. Berger and Brigitte Berger. Copyright 1972, 1975 by Peter L. Berger and Brigitte Berger. Reprinted by permission of Basic Books, a division of HarperCollins Publishers.

William Saroyan: *Madness in the Family*. Copyright © 1988 by New Directions Publishing Corporation. Reprinted by permission of New Directions Publishing Corporation. UK rights granted by the William Saroyan Foundation.

Reprinted by permission of The Putnam Publishing Group from *The Joy Luck Club* by Amy Tan. Copyright © 1989 by Amy Tan. World rights granted by the Sandra Dijkstra Literary Agency.

Acknowledgments and copyrights are continued at the back of the book on page 326, which constitutes an extension of the copyright page.

*To Alan
and to all
my students*

Contents

Chapter Two Observing the Family   21

Peter L. Berger and Brigitte Berger: "The Extended and Conjugal Nuclear Family"   21

Chapter Five Succeeding in School   90

Gary Althen: "Student-Teacher Relationships"   90

Chapter Eight **Comparing the Sexes**   154

Ian Robertson: "How Different Are the Sexes?"   154

Chapter Nine: Aging and Living   175

Pablo Casals: "Age and Youth"   175

Unit Four
Finding a Job and Working   193

Chapter Ten Working with People   195

Jolie Solomon: "Trying to Be Nice: Customer Service"   195

Chapter Eleven   Enjoying Your Work   213

Stuart Oskamp: "The Work Itself: A Social Psychologist Looks at Job Satisfaction"   213

Chapter Fourteen Establishing an Identity   272

Kurt W. Fischer and Arlyne Lazerson: "The Social Context of Identity Formation"   272

Alternate Contents

Writing Strategies

Includes: Essay Strategies • Essay Form • Suggestions for Writing • Getting Started • Student Essay • Revising

Editing Strategies

Includes: Vocabulary Development • Commonly Confused Words • Mechanics • Editing Practice

Grammar Strategies

Preface

*T*his revision of *A Writer's Workbook* was written with the needs of the college-level ESL student in mind. Guided by teachers' responses to the first edition, I have made changes that I think make this an even more effective textbook.

The emphasis on writing has been expanded in this edition. Writing improves with practice. Using this book, students will write and learn to give and receive feedback. In addition, research and common sense tell us that students write, read, and think better when teachers and texts make the connections between writing and reading clear. *A Writer's Workbook* is organized to increase student awareness of the reading/writing connections; as a result, students read about and discuss new concepts, ideas, and problems before they begin to write.

The book is organized into five units, each dealing with a different aspect of life—Family and Growing Up, Language and Communication, Society and Playing Roles, Finding a Job and Working, and Home and Finding One's Place. Each unit contains three chapters, each organized around a specific type of reading selection. The first chapter in each unit begins with a selection of journalistic writing—taken from a newspaper or a magazine, and chosen because students have found it interesting, informative, and filled with ideas about American culture. The second chapter in each unit contains an excerpt from a textbook. These selections are from required and/or commonly paired courses for ESL students in colleges across the United States;

they also introduce to students some aspect of American culture and include articles on the family, intercultural communication, sociology, psychology, and history. The third chapter in each unit features a short story, or an excerpt from a novel or autobiography. Chosen because of their themes, these literary selections exemplify high-quality writing. Moreover, the authors represented either have written about feeling like an outsider in a society or are themselves users of English as a second language. The selections are by William Saroyan, Ernest Hemingway, Pablo Casals, Han Suyin, and Nahid Rachlin.

The book also contains short excerpts by such authors as Amy Tan and Mike Rose, which also relate to the overall themes of learning a new culture and language, growing up, and learning to succeed in school. This edition also contains more than fifteen essays written by ESL students from countries all over the world, thereby exposing students to a wide variety of writing styles and approaches.

Every chapter begins with a new feature to this edition, "Prereading Activities." These are designed to help students make predictions and think about the reading topic before they read that chapter's selection.

Following each reading, "Reading and Thinking Strategies" gets students thinking about what they have read and discussing the responses and ideas it generated. Because of the positive comments from teachers, this edition also features the dialogue journal, in which students and teachers develop a written dialogue through an exchange of letters kept in student journals. Although many students rely on the journal suggestions in each chapter, the letters can be written about various subjects. Teachers respond in brief to the content, rather than to the grammar or surface errors, of each letter. Some teachers have found that modeling correct responses through the journals helps students deal with specific problems. Responding to the journals should take no more time than reading a set of student essays and, in many ways, it is more enjoyable for teacher and student. Dialogue journals are valuable for enabling students and teachers to get to know one another in a way not usually provided in the classroom.

The section that follows, "Writing Strategies," gives students the opportunity to write letters, short responses, and essays after reading and discussing each chapter selection. Although each chapter includes "Suggestions for Writing," encompassing a variety of rhetorical modes, the emphasis in the book is on description, narration, comparison, and persuasion—the most commonly taught modes in ESL writing courses. Each chapter also includes a section on revising, and teachers should encourage their students to experiment with different revision techniques to discover which ones work best for them. Each writer is unique, and each writer's process is unique as well. Students can revise their own writing or use the student essays provided in each chapter to practice particular revision strategies.

To assist students in understanding the differences between revising and editing, each chapter also contains "Editing Strategies" and related practice exercises. However, like most teacher-researchers, I am convinced that the best editing assignments involve students working on their own writing. After focusing on highlighted editing strategies, students can work alone or in pairs and apply what they have learned to their own writing. In this way, students become better editors and, as a result, more self-sufficient writers. The book also offers supplementary exercises that teachers can assign to students based on individual needs.

Editing strategies are followed by "Grammar Strategies," some designed to be presented to the entire class, and others recommended for small group or individual work. Many teachers and tutors find it useful to assign material from the editing or grammar strategies sections to students while they are working with others in writing conferences. No one student will need to do every exercise in the book. However, the wide variety of types and levels of activities should fulfill the students' individual needs.

As I revised *A Writer's Workbook*, I kept in mind teachers' comments. Most teachers supported the notion of an ESL writing textbook that would challenge and stimulate the interests of ESL students, while offering a wide variety of exciting activities requiring students to think, reason, and use English to communicate. It is hoped that this book will meet these needs.

The process of revising a textbook is a collaborative experience, involving the efforts and responses of many people. I want to express my gratitude to my friends, family, and colleagues, whose strength and goodwill kept me going throughout the writing of this edition. The continued encouragement of Andrew Robinson, Chair of the Department of Academic Skills at Hunter College, City University of New York, was most meaningful in the completion of this book. My gratitude also goes to the hundreds of students whose experiences and insights assisted me in understanding the complex process of learning a new language.

I would like to thank the following reviewers for their insights and suggestions: Frank Pialorsi, Center for ESL, University of Arizona; Amy Sales, Boston University; Joanne Leibman, University of Arkansas–Little Rock; Craig Katz, ESL Program, Camden Community College; Ellen Lipp, California State University at Fresno; Janice Baldwin, Delaware County Community College; Carolyn Abels, Capital University; Karen Scriven, East Carolina University; Jennifer McKenzie, University of Missouri–St. Louis; and Linda Hirsch, Hostos Community College/CUNY.

Above all, I would like to express my deepest thanks to Kathleen Keller, ESL Editor, who contributed her support, intelligence, and patience to this project. I am also grateful to Jennifer Doerr, ESL Editorial Assistant, for her time and organizational ability, which ensured the completion of this project. I acknowledge and appreciate all the work of Erica Appel, Project Editor, whose vision made this book elegant and attractive. It is impossible for me to complete a project such as this without thanking my husband, Alan Robbins—for his illustrations that add to the beauty of the book, and for his creativity, gentle support, patience, and love.

Trudy Smoke

A WRITER'S WORKBOOK

An Interactive Writing Text for ESL Students

Second Edition

Family and Growing Up

CHAPTER ONE

Understanding Expectations

PREREADING ACTIVITIES

1. In a small group, discuss the following question: Should parents pressure their children to do well in school? Why or why not?
2. Write "Expect nothing" at the left edge of a sheet of paper and "Expect perfection" at the right edge, and draw a line between them. Then discuss the various academic, social, personal, and physical expectations that you have had or been subject to, and position them on the line. Think about the differences in the expectations your family, classmates, teachers, and friends have had for you and your own expectations for yourself.

   What have you learned about expectations from this exercise?

Don't Expect Me to Be Perfect

This essay first appeared in a 1990 special edition of Newsweek *dedicated to teens. Sun Park, a junior who receives A's and B's in her high school in New Jersey, wrote this essay about some of the problems she has faced in trying to meet her parents' expectations.*

I am a 16-year-old Korean-American. My family has been in the United States for six years now. I'll be a junior next fall.

When I first came to the States, it took two years before I could speak English fluently. By the time I started middle school, I realized that most of my fellow students had never met many kids like me 5 before. They had this idea, probably from TV and movies, that all Asians are nerds and all Asians are smart. It's true that some are. I know many smart people. But what about those Asians who aren't so smart? Having a reputation for brains is nice, I guess, but it can also be a pain. For instance, sometimes when my classmates do not know 10 something, they come to me for the answer. Often I can help them. But when I can't, they get these weird expressions on their faces. If I were a genius, I would not mind being treated like one. But since I am not, I do.

The problem isn't just limited to the classroom. My mother and 15 father expect an awful lot from me, too. Like so many Korean parents, and many ambitious American parents, they're very competitive and can't help comparing me with other kids. Mine always say to me, "So and so is smart, works so hard and is so good to his or her parents. Why can't you be more like him or her?" Because I am the oldest kid in 20 my family, they expect me to set a good example for my younger sisters and relatives. They'd rather I concentrate on schoolwork than dating. They want me to be No. 1.

Most of the time I want to do well, too. I'm glad I take all honors classes. But now that I am at those levels, I have to be on my toes to 25 keep doing well. The better I do, the more pressure I seem to place on myself. Because my parents want me to be perfect—or close to perfect—I find myself turning into a perfectionist. When I do a project and make one little error, I can't stand it. Sometimes I stay up as late as 2 A.M. doing homework. 30

I don't think I would be like this if my parents weren't motivating me. But I don't think they know what pressure can do to a teenager. It's not that they put me down or anything. They have plenty of faith in me. But to tell the truth, sometimes I really like to be lazy, and it would be nice just to take it easy and not worry so much about my grades all 35 the time. Maybe my parents know this. Maybe that's why they encourage me to be better. Well, it still drives me crazy when they compare me with others. I wonder if those smart kids have parents like mine.

Sure, I'm proud of who I am, and I love my parents very much. But then there are times I just feel like taking a break and going far away 40 from parents and teachers. Of course that's impossible, but it's always nice to dream about it.

Reading and Thinking Strategies

Discussion Activities

Analysis and Conclusions

1. When writers write, they usually think about the people or audience for whom they are writing. Who is the audience for "Don't Expect Me to Be Perfect"? What specific words or ideas in the essay tell you who Park was writing for?

2. Based on what you have learned from reading this essay, describe Sun Park.

3. Describe Park's family. Why do you think they are so concerned about her success in school?

Writing and Point of View

1. In small groups in your class, discuss Park's essay. Does Park believe that parents should pressure their children to succeed in school?

2. What examples does Park give to support her point of view? In what ways has your position on this issue been influenced by the essay you have just read?

3. If *you* were to write an essay like this one, what position would you take on families' pressuring their children to succeed in school? What details would differ from Park's essay?

Personal Response and Evaluation

1. Park suggests that people have stereotyped Asian students. What specific examples can you cite in the media, school, and wider community that may have contributed to such stereotyping? What can you do as a college student to change these ideas?

2. Many parents expect more of the oldest child in the family. In your experience, is this true? If so, why do you think that this happens?

3. Park is concerned about turning into a perfectionist. What does the term *perfectionist* mean? Do you think that being a perfectionist is negative or positive? Is it possible to be a perfectionist in one area of your life and not in other areas?

Debate

Divide the class into two groups, one in favor of pressuring children to succeed in school and the other opposed. Debate the issues, using personal experiences and observations to support points of view. You might want to videotape or tape-record this debate and then review it and discuss what occurred.

Journal Writing

Keeping a journal will be a major part of your writing experience while you use this book. Your journal will be a place where ideas count much more than spelling or grammar. You may be able to use some of these ideas in other writing assignments; even more important, you will use them to get to know yourself better and to get to know your teacher. We will use dialogue journals in which you write to your teacher and he or she writes back to you. However, many students also keep private journals in which they write their private thoughts. Each chapter includes suggestions and questions to write about in your journal, but you may also decide to write about something else that is important to you. Sometimes the topics will simply point you in a direction, and you can explore as many or as few as you choose.

After reading about Sun Park and her family, think about your own experiences as a student. Close your eyes and think about the word *school*. Think about the word *pressure*. What thoughts come to your mind? When you are ready, write down your thoughts. Do not worry about writing complete, grammatically correct sentences. Write, and the writing itself will help you become a better writer.

Extra Reading

Harold W. Stevenson, a professor of psychology at the University of Michigan, Ann Arbor, has conducted research on child development and education for many years. He is interested in understanding the varieties of expectations and styles of learning in different countries. The following selection is excerpted from an article by Stevenson that appeared in the American Educator *in 1987. How do Stevenson's ideas correspond with Park's ideas?*

Our Good Opinion of Ourselves

If children believe they are already doing well—and if their parents agree with them—what is the purpose of studying harder? Children who have unrealistically high self-evaluations may see little reason to study hard, and this may well be the case with American children. When asked to rate such characteristics as ability in mathematics, 5
brightness, and scholastic performance, American students gave themselves the highest ratings, while Japanese students gave themselves the lowest. American children believed their parents and teachers were more satisfied with their performance and worried less about their own performance in school than did Chinese and Japanese children. 10
When asked how well they would do in mathematics in high school, 58% of American fifth graders said they expected to be above average or among the best students. These percentages were much higher than those of their Chinese and Japanese peers, among whom only 26% and 29%, respectively, were this optimistic. . . . American children had to 15
do less well than Chinese and Japanese children for their mothers to be satisfied and much worse before their mothers expressed dissatisfaction with their academic performance.

Writing Strategies

The Writing Biography

"Know thyself" is one of the basic premises of writing. The more you know and understand yourself as a writer, the better you will feel about expressing yourself in writing. The purpose of the following assignment is for you to think about yourself as a writer and to write your own "writing biography."

Because there is no neat, gradual way to learn to write and because progress *seems* so unpredictable and just plain slow, a major part of learning to write is learning to put up with this frustrating *process* itself.

PETER ELBOW

In essay form, write a "writing biography" about yourself in which you describe some of the experiences and people who have influenced your writing. Try to answer some of the following questions in your biography.

1. What is your earliest memory about learning to write in your first language? How old were you?
2. What is your earliest memory about learning to write in English? How old were you?
3. What types of writing did you do in elementary school? How did you feel about writing when you were in elementary school? What did your teachers do in elementary school that helped or did not help you to learn to write?
4. What types of writing did you do in high school or in other schools you have attended? How did you feel about writing in those classes? What did your teachers do that helped or did not help you to learn to write?
5. Do you write for any college classes other than this one? If so, which classes? What do you write for those classes?
6. Do you write letters, poems, stories, or do other kinds of writing for pleasure? What kind of writing do you prefer to do?
7. How do you feel about writing today?
8. What is the easiest part of writing for you?
9. What is the hardest part of writing for you?
10. What one aspect would you like to change about your writing?

Essay Strategies

The Paragraph

Part of learning to write in a new language is learning how readers of that language expect ideas to be organized. Most native speakers of English expect essay, text, and story writing to be divided into paragraphs. Each paragraph serves as a guide for the reader. It shows what the writer thinks is important, what belongs together, and where a new idea begins. Paragraphs help the reader digest writing, just as breaking up a meal into courses such as soup, salad, main dish, and dessert helps in the digestion of a meal. If all the food from a meal were piled on the table in front of you at once, you might not know where to begin to eat. When writers do not use paragraphs, readers often cannot understand the big blocks of sentences piled up in front of them. So a clear, considerate writer breaks up ideas into paragraphs.

A paragraph begins with an indented line. This makes it stand out from the rest of the text. A paragraph is not too long, usually not more than 250 words, but you do not have to count the number of words. You can use your judgment. When your ideas are changing or when you want to divide a general concept into smaller parts, you should begin a new paragraph. A paragraph is a group of sentences related to a single subject.

A paragraph usually has a topic sentence or main idea that tells the reader what the paragraph is about. This topic sentence can appear anywhere in the paragraph. Sometimes it is implied, which means that it is not actually stated, but the reader can find it by inferring or reading into what the author has written.

A paragraph may have different purposes in a piece of writing. It may explain a concept introduced in a topic sentence. It may illustrate a point or give support to an argument. Each paragraph works together with the rest of the paragraphs in a letter, essay, story, or book to help the reader understand the writer's point of view.

Fill in the following blanks with the seven characteristics of a paragraph discussed so far.

_____

_____

_____

_____

_____

_____

_____

☐ ☐ ☐

EXERCISE

Paragraphs make writing easier to read. They help the reader know how the writer thinks. The following piece of writing would be easier to read if it were divided into paragraphs. Read it with a classmate and decide where new paragraphs should begin. Remember that each time you begin a totally new thought, you should indent for a new paragraph. Most writers agree that there should be three paragraphs in the following exercise.

The Park essay made me think about my family and what they expect of me. I am the first child in my family to go to college in the United States, so they think I should set a good example for my younger brothers and sisters. I have tried very hard to study and to do well in my courses, although it was not easy at first. When I started 5 college, I was nervous about English. I still made a lot of mistakes and did not understand everything my teachers said in class. Since I felt nervous about raising my hand, I usually did not ask questions, and I missed some important information. The best thing that happened to me in college happened when my biology teacher required each of us 10 to join a study group. I found that I could ask my questions to the other students in my class, and some of them even knew the answers. We all share our notes, and that helps me, too. It also helps me to say the new words from biology out loud to the whole group. After I do that, I remember them better. Joining a study group has helped me 15 become a successful student in college. As a result, I suggested to a few of the students in my anthropology class that we meet to discuss the class lectures and the reading. It seems to be helping them as much as me.

Essay Form

Paragraph Development

Learning to write in English involves more than just learning new vocabulary and grammatical structures. Part of learning to write is finding out the order in which readers expect ideas to be arranged.

Some researchers have stated that readers of English expect a straight line of development. In this kind of writing, the paragraph often begins with a statement of its main or most important idea; this is called the topic sentence. This main idea is divided into connected ideas that are developed further in the paragraphs that follow the first one. Although this is the traditional approach for most English speakers, it may be different from what you learned in your first language.

For example, Fan Shen, who was born in the People's Republic of China and is now living in the United States, wrote an article in 1989 about this difference. The article states:

In English composition, an essential rule for the logical organization of a piece of writing is the use of a "topic sentence." In Chinese composition "from surface to core" is an essential rule, a rule which means that one ought to reach a topic gradually and "systematically" instead of "abruptly."

Robert B. Kaplan, like many other linguists, has studied the ways in which writers arrange their ideas. This field of study is called contrastive rhetoric. In 1965 Kaplan created a diagram to illustrate the arrangements of ideas in different language systems. Examine the following diagram carefully.

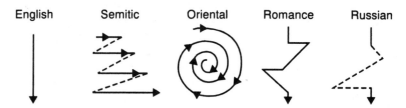

Diagram from Robert B. Kaplan, "Cultural Thought Patterns in Inter-cultural Education," *Language Learning* 16 (1966): 1–20.

In the space provided, draw a diagram of the way you think ideas are arranged in your first language.

How does your drawing compare with Kaplan's illustration? Write a paragraph in which you explain whether such diagrams are helpful or not in your understanding of the differences in the arrangement of ideas in your first language and in English. Write about the differences you have noticed in the way your first language is organized and in the way that English is organized.

□ □ □

EXERCISES

1. In some cultures, writing is organized differently from English. Discuss the answers to the following questions based on your first language or any other that you have studied other than English.

   a. In writing in your first language or any other language you have studied, do you divide your writing into paragraphs?
   b. If you do, how do you know when to begin a new paragraph?
   c. If you do not, how do you indicate to the reader that you are beginning a new thought?
   d. Is the idea of a topic sentence new to you? How are the ideas about a subject grouped in your language? What usually comes first, second, or last?

2. As part of focusing on paragraph structure, the class should divide into small groups. Each group should look at paragraph 3 in Park's essay. Copy the topic sentence of that paragraph here:

_____

List the supporting details that tell more about the topic sentence or main idea:

_____

_____

_____

_____

_____

_____

3. To help readers understand what they have written, writers connect their ideas from paragraph to paragraph. Answer the following questions about how Park's essay is connected from sentence to sentence and paragraph to paragraph.

   a. What is "the problem" in the first sentence in paragraph 3?
   b. In sentence 4 in paragraph 3, to what does *mine* refer?
   c. In sentence 1 in paragraph 4, with what in the preceding paragraph does *too* connect?
   d. In sentence 1 in paragraph 5, to what does *this* refer?
   e. In sentence 6 in paragraph 5, to what does *this* refer?
   f. In sentence 7 in paragraph 5, to what does *that's why* refer?
   g. Which of Kaplan's diagrams seems to fit Park's style of writing in this essay? If none is appropriate, draw your own diagram of the way Park seems to organize her writing.

Suggestions for Writing

Give yourself time to think before you write. If you have any difficulty beginning your writing, look in your journal or at the "Getting Started" suggestion on page 12. When you do begin to write, keep your audience in mind. Try to make your writing interesting to your readers as well as to yourself.

1. In an essay, describe the most important ideas that you learned about yourself when you wrote your writing biography. Try to

organize your writing so that it moves from your specific experience or experiences to general concepts about how students learn to write.

2. In many families, the oldest child is treated differently from the younger children. Write an essay in which you give examples of this and explain why you think this happens.

3. Some people think of success as the attainment of high grades, educational degrees, and good jobs. Write an essay in which you define the qualities that mean success to you. Illustrate the qualities you choose with your experiences, observations, and readings.

4. Many ambitious parents push their children to succeed in school. Do you agree or disagree with the idea that pushing children helps them to succeed? Support your point of view with your experiences, observations, and readings.

5. Write an essay in which you describe the differences between your own educational, social, and personal expectations and those that your family has for you. Review the prereading activities on page 3 for ideas.

Getting Started

Talking to Get Ideas

If you have any difficulty getting started, talk to a classmate about what you are planning to write. Begin by discussing each topic and the ideas on which a writer could focus. Take turns explaining to one another why you would choose or not choose a particular topic; this will help you narrow down your choices.

When you have narrowed down your choices to two or three possible topics, discuss your ideas for each topic. Then, together choose the topic that interests you the most. Before you begin to write, together make a list of ideas that you will refer to as you write your essay. When you finish your first draft, share it with the same classmate.

A Student's Writing Biography

The following writing biography is a draft written in 15 minutes in an ESL writing class. The student, Lendsa Guillaume, is from Haiti. As you read her essay, determine which of the suggested questions she focused on.

Writing is a very difficult course, mostly for the foreign students. You have to think critically and think in English. You have to know your punctuation and be careful about your grammar, plurals and more and more. But in my case, it is not the same because I love writing.

The first time I had to write was when I was seven years old. I had to write a little letter for my mother for Mother's Day. I was so happy to write it, but I was writing in my first language.

When I had to write in English I was happy too. I remember when I was in high school, the teacher asked the students to write one sen- 10 tence and I wrote "I love you" and he was laughing. He said, "That's nice." All the other students did not want to show their sentences; they were ashamed, but that was nice anyway. When I first entered college, I did not like to write about anything because I thought my writing was too poor, but I tried hard anyway. 15

The first thing I like about writing is, for instance, if one is upset with his or her friends and cannot communicate verbally, then he or she can write about what caused the upset. In other words, I like writing because it is another way to communicate.

In summary, I personally think everybody, once you are in college, 20 must like writing because that's mostly what college is about. If you do not know how to write, you'll never make it in college.

Lendsa Guillaume, Haiti

Revising

Reread this student's writing biography and answer the following questions about what she has written. You can do this on your own or with another student in your class.

1. What in her essay reveals Guillaume's attitude about writing?
2. What part of her writing biography did you like the most?
3. What would you like to know about her that she did not include in her writing biography?
4. Whom do you think she expected to read her essay, to be her audience?
5. How could she revise the essay to make it communicate better? Here is a suggested revised version of Guillaume's first paragraph:

   Writing is a very difficult course, particularly for the foreign students. All students have to think critically when they write, but foreign students also have to learn to do this in English. They also have to be aware of punctuation and grammar, plurals, and many other things. In my case, I am aware of the problems, but I am willing to try to do my best because I love writing. For me, whether I am writing in my first language or in English, my goal is the same: to communicate my ideas and feelings to others.

Apply the five questions just listed to your own writing biography. Then exchange papers with a classmate and discuss them. Writing is a very personal experience, but it is a communicative activity. One way to judge how well your writing is communicating is to share it with a peer. When you and a classmate exchange papers, it is important to show respect for each other's writing. Read slowly and carefully. Do not mark the other person's paper. After reading, ask each other questions and listen carefully to the answers. These answers can help you when you actually rewrite your paper. Here are some suggestions for questions:

1. What do you think I am trying to say?
2. What did you like best about my essay?
3. Did any part of it make you stop and read it over in order to understand what I meant?
4. What do you remember most about my essay without looking at it again?

You will certainly think of more questions, but keep in mind that the purpose is the sharing of writing. Do not evaluate or judge each other's writing, but offer support and suggestions. After discussing your essay in this way, keep your peer's comments and suggestions in mind as your rewrite. Then share your revised essay with the same classmate.

Editing Strategies

Learning New Vocabulary

classifying

One way to learn new vocabulary is to classify words, terminology, or concepts according to their meaning or attributes.

1. Make a list of all the words in the Park essay that are used to describe people (for example, *genius*).
2. Make a list of all the slang expressions used in this essay (for example, *kids*).
3. Make a list of words that you can use to substitute for these slang expressions (for example, *children*).
4. Make a list of all the words that refer to time (for example, *six years, next fall*).
5. Make a list of all the words that refer to school (for example, *junior, high school*).

Commonly Confused Words

to/two/too

People in the United States are *too* ready *to* tell other people in the world *to* learn English, although the majority of Americans can speak only one language. Throughout much of the world, being able *to* speak at least *two* languages, and sometimes three or four, is necessary *to* function in society.

Examine how *to, two,* and *too* are used in the preceding paragraph. Then review how the same words are used in the Park essay. On the basis of what you observe, complete the following definitions.

_____ refers to the number 2.

_____ means "also" or "overly."

_____ means "toward" or is part of the infinitive verb form.

Fill in the blanks in the following sentences with *to, two,* or *too.*

1. Knowledge of _____ or more languages makes travel _____

   different countries more interesting and rewarding _____.

2. Scientists are beginning _____ believe that people who know

   _____ or more languages make more use of their brains than monolinguals.

3. Therefore, when it comes _____ languages, there is no such thing

   as _____ much knowledge.

Now write your own sentences using *to, two,* and *too.*

Mechanics

Paper Format

When you hand in a paper to a teacher or to another student to read, make sure that your paper is neat and readable. To do this, you should follow these ten steps:

1. Use $8\frac{1}{2}$-by-11-inch paper whether you are printing from a computer word processor or writing by hand. Smaller pieces of paper

get lost and are harder to read. Tear off the holes on the sides of continuous computer paper before handing it in.

2. Use dark blue or black ink if you write by hand. Pencil smudges easily, and other colors can distract your readers.

3. If you use a word processor, double-space. If you write by hand and have large handwriting or if your paper has narrow spaces, write on every other line.

4. Use 1-inch margins on all sides of your paper—top, bottom, left, and right. This is easy to do when you are writing by hand; margins are also easy to set on most word processing systems.

5. Put your name, date, and course number on the top of the page unless your instructor requires that they be somewhere else on the page.

6. Use a title, and center the title above the rest of the writing. Capitalize the first word and all major words in your title. Skip a line between the title and the first line of your writing.

7. Indent each paragraph about 1 inch, or five spaces on a word processor.

8. Make sure that your capital letters are distinct from your lowercase letters. Also make sure your *e*'s and *i*'s are distinguishable.

9. Make all your punctuation marks clear and distinct. Leave a space after each period. If you are using a word processor, leave two spaces between the period and the capital letter of the next sentence.

10. If you break a word at the end of the line, break it between syllables. Use the dictionary if you do not know where a syllable ends.

Editing Practice

After revising their writing for content (see page 13), writers often edit their writing for errors. The following is a draft of a response to the Park essay. Some of the errors the author has made are one formatting error, one paragraphing error, and four *to/too/two* errors. Find as many errors as you can and correct them. Answers are on page 320.

Having a little brother

I have lived in the United States for six years and my brother has lived here for too years. He came here last because my parents thought he was to young to travel. When we left my country, he was a baby. I studied hard, but it has taken me a long time too learn English. For my brother, it has been different. He speaks English so well already. He talks to all his friends in English, and he is an *A* student in the second grade. I believe I can learn a lot from watching and talking to him. I hope there are things he can learn from me, to.

Grammar Strategies

The Simple Present Tense

The simple present tense is used for several purposes:

1. *To describe habitual or routine activities.* Adverbs of frequency such as *usually, each day,* and *always* (see page 19 for a more complete list) sometimes are used with the simple present tense.

   Sometimes I *stay* up as late as 2 A.M. doing homework.
   I usually *do* my homework before I *watch* television.

2. *To describe states of being.* Verbs that refer to sensory perceptions, emotional states, conditions, judgments, and states of being are called *stative* verbs and are almost always in the simple present tense unless they are describing the past.

   They *want* me to be No. 1.
   I *love* my parents very much.
   I just *feel* like taking a break.

3. *To describe future actions.* Verbs that are used this way usually describe acts of arriving and leaving, and beginning and ending.

   My English class *begins* at eight o'clock.
   The bus *leaves* at ten minutes past each hour.

4. *To describe what is going on* in scientific experiments and other types of research, on television or radio, and in newspaper headlines.

   She *puts* the chemical in the tube and *heats* it slowly.
   The pitcher *throws* a curve ball at the batter.
   "Fires *rage* in California, *threaten* many homes"

□ □ □

EXERCISES   1. With a partner or in a small group, reread the Park essay, underlining each use of the simple present tense. Then together decide for each example you find which of the listed uses it illustrates.

2. Many people have problems with the subject-verb agreement involved in the simple present tense. Reread paragraph 3 on pages 3–4. List the subjects and verbs in each sentence in separate columns. Write the pronoun (*he, she, it, they*) that can be used to replace the various subjects:

Subject	*Verb*
The problem (*it*)	isn't
My mother and father (*they*)	expect

Circle a final *s* when it occurs in the verb form.

Notice that when using the irregular verb *be*, the following pattern applies:

I	am
you	are
he, she, it	is
we, you, they	are

Also notice the simple present tense for other verbs:

I, you, we, they	expect
he, she, it	expects

Decide whether to use the final *s* on the verbs in the following sentences:

a. Many ambitious parents _____ their children to
(want/wants)

succeed in school.

b. One of the smartest children in our class _____ as
(yawn/yawns)

she _____ that she _____ till after mid-
(explain/explains)   (study/studies)

night every night.

c. Her classmates _____ her that she _____
(tell/tells)   (study/studies)

too much and _____ too little.
(sleep/sleeps)

d. This student _____ that she _____ to do
   (feel/feels)   (need/needs)

as well in school as her twin brother, who always _____
                                                  (receive/receives)

straight A's in his classes.

e. The problem faced by this student _____ to be related
                                     (seem/seems)

to family expectations.

3. Review the sentences in Exercise 2 and decide which of the uses of the simple present tense they illustrate.
4. On your own or with a partner, reread the essay that you have written for this chapter or any other essay that you have written this semester, focusing on the simple present tense. Notice when and why you use the simple present tense in your writing, and make sure that you have used the correct verb endings.

Adverbs of Frequency

Adverbs of frequency are used to tell how often something happens or someone does something. On a continuum from the most often to the least, adverbs might be arranged this way:

always→generally→usually→frequently→often→
occasionally→sometimes→seldom→rarely→never

Another adverb of frequency, *ever*, which means "at any time," is often used in questions.

□ □ □

EXERCISES

1. Interview a member of your class, asking the following questions. Write down the answers so that you will be able to use them later.

   a. What subjects do your teachers generally ask you to write about in your classes?
   b. What subjects do you usually prefer to write about in your classes?
   c. Do your teachers generally give you a choice of several subjects to write about or only one?
   d. Do you ever find it difficult to get ideas when you start to write? If you do, what do you usually do to help you get going?
   e. Do you ever talk to your classmates before you start to write?
   f. When you write, what do you usually concentrate on?
   g. Outside of school, when do you usually write in English?

    h. Do you usually do your homework at home or in school?

    i. Do you ever do your homework on the way to school?

    j. Do you sometimes find it difficult to understand your teachers in your classes? If you do, what do you generally do to help you understand what is going on in class?

2. Reread your answers to the questions in Exercise 1 and discuss with the student you have interviewed any areas about which you are confused. Then write a paragraph describing the student you interviewed, using his or her answers from Exercise 1.

CHAPTER TWO

Observing the Family

PREREADING ACTIVITIES

1. In a small group, discuss the differences that you have observed in family life in your country and in the United States.
2. Think about the ways in which your own family has changed or responded to living in a different country; then discuss them with your group.
3. Will you raise your children differently from the way your parents raised you? In what ways? Why will you make those changes?

The Extended and Conjugal Nuclear Family

Peter L. Berger teaches sociology at Rutgers University, and Brigitte Berger teaches the same subject at Long Island University. They collaborated on Sociology: A Biographical Approach, *an introductory textbook that analyzes large-scale institutions in relation to the everyday experience of individuals in society. This excerpt is about the institutions of family and marriage.*

°based on marriage
°unit of parents and children living together

°family, relatives

Sociologists use the term *conjugal° nuclear family°* to refer to the type of family that now prevails in Western societies. What is meant by the term is quite simple, namely, a family which, in effect, consists only of a married couple and its children. This family type represents a considerable shrinkage both in the scope and the functioning of the 5 institution of family. In terms of scope, it has reduced the participant members to what could well be described as an irreducible minimum. Grandparents, aunts, uncles, cousins and their children—not to speak of remoter kin°—have virtually disappeared from the scene, at least as far as the household is concerned. What is more, the children 10 themselves normally leave the household once they themselves are grown up.

The modern family is built around the relationship between the two marriage partners. A contrasting type is the *extended family*, which is based on a much larger and more complex set of relationships. The 15 modern family, both as a social type and as a collection of values, has been one of the most successful exports of the Western world. It

°completely, fundamentally

°basic, essential

has rapidly advanced in Asia and Africa and is today well on its way to becoming a universal phenomenon. The conjugal nuclear family, both in fact and in principle, is radically° destructive of older family 20 traditions in almost every human society. Its values emphasize the worth of the individual as against those of his groups. Each individual is to be evaluated in his own terms, not through those of his groups. And it is as an individual that he, or she, has intrinsic° rights.

One of the most important consequences of these values, of course, 25 has been the assertion (an increasingly successful assertion) of the right of everyone, man or woman, to choose his or her marriage partner. The basis upon which this choice is to be made is supposed to be love, understood as an emotional thunderstorm, both unpredict- able and democratic, cutting across all traditional lines separating 30 people from each other. This is not exactly what happens in practice. On the contrary, it has been exhaustively shown that people marry by and large within certain social lines. In American society this is mainly in terms of class lines, although racial, ethnic, religious and geo- graphic lines are also very important. Love, then, may be a thun- 35 derstorm, but it seems to be rather careful where it hits at any given moment. Nevertheless, the *ideal* of the conjugal nuclear family entails a revolution in values. People rarely live up to their ideals in history, but the very fact that these ideals exist makes a profound difference for what in fact is happening. 40

Reading and Thinking Strategies

Discussion Activities

Analysis and Conclusions

1. Why do you think the family unit has changed from the large extended family to the smaller nuclear family? Think about social, economic, and employment factors. Do you have any evidence that the family is changing again? What factors might influence such a change?

2. Do you agree with the Bergers that the Western-style nuclear family has been adopted by many Asian and African societies that for- merly had traditional extended family patterns? Think about your own family and about the families you have observed. Describe the ways, if any, in which family structure has changed in the past few generations of your own family.

3. How do you think family problems are dealt with in a nuclear family and in an extended family? Who makes the decisions?

Writing and Point of View

1. Reread the excerpt and notice the way in which the Bergers use definitions (see page 27 for more information on using definitions) to help their readers understand unfamiliar terms. What words do they define? How do they define these words?

2. What is the Bergers' point of view on the emphasis on the individual in Western society? What is their point of view on the conjugal nuclear family? What specific words and phrases helped you determine their point of view?

3. Do the authors emphasize the extended or conjugal nuclear family in this excerpt? Why do you think they emphasize one concept more than the other?

Personal Response and Evaluation

1. Some sociologists think that family structures are too complicated for researchers to be able to classify families as simply extended or nuclear. Do you think the Bergers would classify a family comprised of a mother, her two children, and their grandmother as extended or nuclear? Using your observations and experiences, describe other types of nontraditional families you have seen. Would you classify them as nuclear or extended? How do you think decisions are made in families such as these?

2. "People marry by and large within certain social lines. In American society this is mainly in terms of class lines, although racial, ethnic, religious and geographic lines are also very important." According to what you have observed, what happens when people fall in love outside the lines mentioned by the Bergers? Which books, movies, or plays can you name that are about people who fall in love outside the lines? What happens to those people?

3. "People rarely live up to their ideals in history, but the very fact that these ideals exist makes a profound difference for what in fact is happening." What does this statement mean to you? Make a list of examples of specific ideals. Reread the Park essay on pages 3–4, thinking about her ideals—how would she define the ideal student, daughter, sister, and other people. How do her ideas correspond to your own?

Interview

Write down questions about your family or that of a friend that you would like to find out more about. Then interview a member of the family—an older relative if possible, a grandfather, grandmother, aunt, or uncle—asking your questions and any others that occur to you as you conduct the interview. Tape your interview or take careful notes. Some of the questions should be these: Where did the person grow up? What was the person's school life like? Did he or she have brothers and sisters? Did they get along? Did the extended family live together? What are the biggest changes in life that the person recalls? Write out your interview, both questions and answers. Then write an essay describing the person you have interviewed, which you will share with your class.

Journal Writing

In the past, a large family consisting of parents, children, grand-parents, aunts, uncles, cousins, and even more distant relatives often lived together or very near each other. In today's world, this is chang-ing. In your journal, write about your ideal family, the family you imagine for yourself in the future. You may prefer to describe your own family of today and your feelings about that family.

Writing Strategies

Essay Strategies

The Formal Essay

Although you will learn about many types of essays and styles of writing as you write in your college classes, it is important to know what is meant by the traditional or formal essay. Readers have particu-lar expectations when they read an essay. To meet these expectations, writers begin by learning the structure of the traditional essay.

Simply put, an essay is a series of paragraphs written on one theme. Traditionally, the main idea for the essay is found in the first para-graph, which is called the introduction. The main idea for an essay is called the thesis statement. The supporting points and details of the essay are found in the body paragraphs that follow the introduction.

Each of the developmental or body paragraphs contains a topic sentence that tells the main idea for that paragraph. The rest of the paragraph is made up of ideas or details that tell more about the main idea. These paragraphs may have different purposes, depending on the topic of the essay. A particular paragraph may describe, define, tell a relevant story, provide evidence to argue a point, compare and contrast, or analyze an issue. A writer often begins a new paragraph with a transition that connects the paragraph to the one that preceded it in order to help the reader follow the writer's train of thought.

The traditional essay ends with a concluding paragraph. In this paragraph, the writer ties together the important points that have been made in the essay. The conclusion lets the reader know that the writer has thought the topic through and believes that the ideas presented in the essay are complete.

Conclusions are usually short and may include a brief summary of the main points of the essay. Most writers agree that new ideas should not be presented in the conclusion, although a related story or idea might pull the theme of the essay together effectively.

Keep this standard structure in mind when you write your next essay.

In the preceding paragraphs, circle the words *introduction, main idea, thesis statement, body paragraphs, topic sentence,* and *conclusion.* Then answer the following questions on the basis of the information in those paragraphs.

1. What is the first paragraph of an essay called? _Introduction_

_____

2. What is the main idea for the whole essay called? _the_

thesis statement.

3. What do the body paragraphs contain? _topic sentence_

that tells the main idea for the paragraph.

4. What is the main idea for each body paragraph called? _____

_____

5. What is the final paragraph in the essay called? _Conclusion._

_____

6. What is the purpose of the final paragraph? _is the_

Summary of the main points of the essay.

■ ■ ■

A diagram of a formal essay follows. (Remember that this is a sample essay form; not all formal essays contain five paragraphs.)

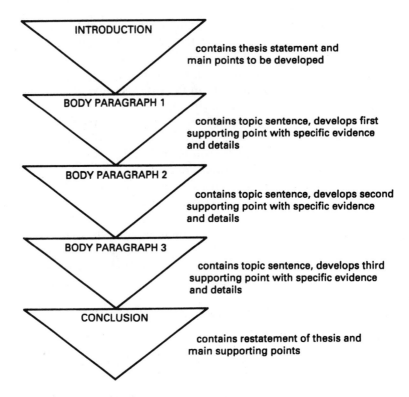

INTRODUCTION
contains thesis statement and main points to be developed

BODY PARAGRAPH 1
contains topic sentence, develops first supporting point with specific evidence and details

BODY PARAGRAPH 2
contains topic sentence, develops second supporting point with specific evidence and details

BODY PARAGRAPH 3
contains topic sentence, develops third supporting point with specific evidence and details

CONCLUSION
contains restatement of thesis and main supporting points

Although this approach to writing is quite formal and traditional, it is the type of writing required in many college first-year writing courses. It is useful to know these terms, and it is also good discipline for the writer to organize his or her ideas to fit this model. However, remember that this is just one model of writing.

☐ ☐ ☐

EXERCISES

1. Reread the Berger article with a classmate. With that classmate or in a small group, underline the main idea or thesis statement for the entire selection. Next underline the topic sentence or main idea for each paragraph. Then decide together which are the supporting details and what their purposes are (to describe, define, tell a story, and so on). Discuss your choices with your partner or group.

2. Reread one of your own essays with a classmate. Underline the main idea or thesis statement for the entire paper. Then underline the topic sentence or main idea for each paragraph. Discuss the supporting details and decide the purpose for each. After discussing your writing, you may decide to rewrite parts of your essay to clarify your main idea or supporting details.

Essay Form

The Introduction

A formal essay usually begins with an introductory paragraph. Generally, the introduction serves several purposes:

1. To capture the reader's interest
2. To state the thesis of the essay
3. To introduce the major ideas that will be developed in the body of the essay (Review the diagram on page 26.)

The introduction is useful to the writer as well as to the reader. It helps the writer plan the rest of the essay. If the introduction is well structured, the writer knows what the rest of the essay will contain. There are several ways to write an introduction to a formal essay.

1. **General statement.** One type of introduction starts with a general statement: "In recent years a new family structure is occurring in the United States." The essay then becomes more specific. "In 1984 the Census Bureau revealed that 25 percent of the families in the United States were single parent families." In this type of introduction, the writer takes the reader from the general (family structure) to the specific (single-parent family).

2. **Anecdote.** Another way to begin an essay is with an anecdote or a brief story. This is a very good way to capture readers' interest. It is a technique that is often used by newspaper and magazine writers.

3. **Question.** The introduction might ask a question that will be answered in the body of the essay. "If children believe they are already doing well—and if their parents agree with them—what is the purpose of studying harder?" writes Stevenson on page 6. This is another technique that creates a great deal of reader interest.

4. **Quotation.** An introduction can contain a quotation. Be sure to use quotation marks if you are using the exact words spoken or written by someone. "'Love, then, may be a thunderstorm, but it seems to be rather careful where it hits at any given moment,' write Peter and Brigitte Berger."

5. **Definition.** Some writers define a word or a phrase in their introduction that they will use throughout their writing to help readers grasp their ideas. (See, for example, the Berger selection on pages 21–22.) If you were rewriting Park's essay (see pages 3–4), what word would you define in her introduction that would make her essay clearer to you? Write the definition and add it in the appropriate

place in her essay. What word would you define in Stevenson's introduction (see page 6) that would make his writing clearer to you? Write the definition and add it in the appropriate place in his writing.

When you write, you can use one of these types of introductions or a combination of several of them. You may create your own method of introduction, but your overall goal is to engage your reader, to make your reader want to continue reading what you have written.

□   □   □

EXERCISES

1. What are five ways of writing an introduction? What is the overall goal of the introduction?
2. Read introductions from other selections in this book. What kinds of introductions have the various writers used? Is textbook material introduced differently from journalistic writing?
3. Independently or in a small group, look at the latest issue of a newsmagazine. What types of introductions do you find? Why? Discuss this with your group.
4. Using one of the techniques described in this chapter, rewrite the introduction to an essay you have written. Then read the original and the rewritten essay. Which do you prefer? Why?

Suggestions for Writing

Give yourself some time to think before you begin to write. Some people close their eyes when they think, and some stare at the wall or at the person in front of them. Do whatever feels right for you. Then choose one of the following topics to write about. If you have difficulty beginning to write, try the "Getting Started" suggestion on page 29.

You may find it useful to look at your journal or at the Berger selection before you begin to write. As you write this essay, try using the structure of the traditional essay. Think about the ways in which this structure is helpful in organizing your ideas and the ways in which this structure causes specific problems for you as a writer.

1. With the help of family members, construct a family tree in which you trace your great-grandparents, grandparents, aunts, uncles, cousins, and other relatives as far back as you are able. After studying your family tree, write an essay describing your family through the generations. As part of your essay, explain how the concepts of the conjugal nuclear family and extended family relate to your family.

2. Learning to live in a new society and culture can create problems in the relationships between parents and children. Do you agree or disagree? Write an essay in which you support your point of view with your observations and experiences.

3. Some people believe that teenagers have too much freedom in the United States. They think that if teenagers were required to have more responsibilities in their family, they would grow up to be better adults. Do you agree or disagree? Write an essay in which you support your point of view with your observations and experiences.

4. In your essay, define and contrast the extended family and the nuclear family. Using your observations and experiences, explain how these two family structures might deal with child rearing, school problems, and social problems such as drugs or premarital sex.

5. Write an essay in which you compare your life at your present age with that of one of your parents at the same age. In what ways are your lives different? In what ways are they similar? Explain the differences and similarities. As part of your conclusion, include what you have learned from writing about this.

Getting Started

Freewriting

It is like fishing. But I do not wait very long, for there is always a nibble—and this is where receptivity comes in. To get started, I will accept anything that occurs to me. Something always occurs, of course, to any of us. We can't keep from thinking.

WILLIAM STAFFORD, *A Way of Writing*

This will be one of the simplest yet probably most productive exercises in this book. Freewriting is a way of getting yourself to write. The technique is easy. Take out a pen or pencil and a blank piece of paper. Note the time and start writing. Write for ten minutes. Do not think about spelling, grammar, punctuation, or organization. Just keep writing. Do not stop even if the only thing you can write is "I have nothing to write about." You will not have to hand this paper in. Freewriting is simply for you; it is a way for you to loosen up your hand and your mind.

Many people say that freewriting helps them get over writing blocks, times when they feel they just cannot write. It is a technique that you can use at any time. All you need is paper, pen, and ten minutes. So anytime you want to practice your writing, freewrite.

Eventually, you may find that freewriting will help you produce ideas that you can use in your formal writing.

□ □ □

EXERCISES

1. Before you begin to freewrite, reread some of your earlier journal entries. These may give you ideas. You may also find it enjoyable to see how much progress you are making in your writing.
2. Choose a reading selection from this book and then freewrite. The reading may stimulate your thinking and give you some interesting ideas.

Revising

As practice in learning to revise an essay, it may be helpful to work with someone else's writing first. Working with a classmate, read the student essay that follows.

A Student Essay

Today, many teenagers enjoy their teenage years very much because they have a lot of wonderful times for themselves. They have more of the freedom and power to do whatever they want than teenagers of the past. Many of these teenagers do not have to carry the responsibility of supporting their families or of thinking seriously about making a   5
living.

In today's world, many young teenagers still depend on their parents. Their parents support them in everything such as their schooling and housing. For example, when I was a teenager my parents earned money to raise me. They provided for me to go to school and they paid   10
for my food. My parents also gave money to me to buy books, records, and movies. Thus I didn't have to worry about financial problems.

Many teenagers also have a lot of opportunities for themselves. They can find jobs and make money to spend on themselves. Some teenagers work in the supermarkets as cashiers for a few hours to earn   15
some money. Others work in stores as helpers to get a small amount of money for themselves. If these teenagers have money, they can use it for themselves to buy such luxuries as new clothes, albums, and trips. This money helps take away some of the pressure from the teenager's families.   20

Also, teenagers enjoy many types of entertainment during these years. Many young teenagers spend their time going to parties, movies, and other activities. They can also spend some times gathering with their friends. For example, many teenagers enjoy their time with their friends in the parks playing various kinds of sports like basketball and football. These are all advantages that the teenagers can have during their teenage years.

Lastly, as a teenager, many young people don't have the responsibility of supporting their own families yet because they still depend on their parents. Some of the teenagers are not ready to have their own families. They need more time to explore more about themselves. They want to go out to learn and to participate more in the outside world. So this is the time for the teenagers to enjoy themselves more than when they are older and have to work and have family responsibilities.

Therefore, we can see that many teenagers have a lot of fun in their teenage years. They have more of the freedom and power to enjoy themselves. I think that many teenagers should enjoy themselves more before they become adults because the teenage years can be the happiest time of a person's life.

Ping Ruan, People's Republic of China

With your partner, answer the following questions about this student's writing. (It is useful to write out your answers.)

1. What is this student trying to say—that is, what is her main idea?
2. What details did she include to support her point of view? Did she use a sufficient number of details to convince you?
3. What did you like best about the essay?
4. What part of the essay confused you?
5. If you could make two suggestions to help this student revise her essays, what would they be?

Next exchange a draft of an essay you are working on with that of a partner. After reading your classmate's essay, write the answers to the same five questions, and discuss them with your classmate.

Keeping your classmate's comments in mind, revise your own essay. Then share your revised essay with the same classmate.

Editing Strategies

Learning New Vocabulary

key words and concepts

One way to develop new vocabulary is to focus on the key words and concepts used by the author in the selection you have read.

□ □ □

EXERCISES

1. List six key vocabulary words that a student needs to know to understand the meaning of the Berger selection (pages 21–22).

_____   _____

_____   _____

_____   _____

How did you choose these words?

2. List four major concepts that a student has to understand to comprehend the meaning of the Berger selection. The first one is done for you.

conjugal nuclear family   _____

_____   _____

How did you choose these concepts? _____

_____

What is the difference between a word and a concept? _____

_____

3. Draw a line from each word in column A to the word or words in column B that are opposite in meaning. The first one has been done for you.

A	B
1. nuclear family	a. strangers
2. intrinsic	b. simple
3. reduce	c. extended family
4. kin	d. group
5. complex	e. extrinsic
6. minimum	f. increase
7. individual	g. constructive
8. destructive	h. maximum

With a classmate, write a paragraph using as many of these words as possible.

Commonly Confused Words

than/then

Helene called Thomas when she saw that the movie star he liked better than any other was starring in a new movie in their neighborhood. Then they went to see it together. When it ended, they talked in front of the movie theater more than usual. They thought the movie was better than the star's last one. Then they went to get something to drink and then they continued talking. Then it was almost midnight and they both had to rush home.

Examining the use of *than* and *then* in this paragraph should help you complete the following definitions.

_____ means "at that time."

_____ is used to show comparisons.

Fill in the blanks in the following sentences with *than* and *then*.

She lived in Ecuador until she was 5; _____ she moved to the

United States. _____ she started school, where she found it was

easier for her to understand English _____ to speak it. Her teachers

thought she knew less _____ she really did because they did not

know how to communicate with her _____.

Reread the last essay you wrote, and notice how you use these two words in your writing. Correct any errors you made.

Mechanics

Final Sentence Punctuation

Every sentence ending is signaled with a mark. A *period* is the most common indicator to the reader that a sentence has ended. A period is used to end a sentence that makes a statement or gives a command.

When is a *question mark* used? It is used at the end of a direct question. It is not used after an indirect question.

An *exclamation point* is used to express strong feeling. It can be placed after a word or a phrase or at the end of a sentence. However, writers should be careful not to overuse the exclamation point and not to use more than one at a time!

The word that follows the period, question mark, or exclamation point begins with a capital letter. Make sure that your reader always knows where your sentences begin and end.

Editing Practice

After revising their writing for content, writers often edit their writing for errors. The following paragraph is a draft of a summary of the Berger article that has not been edited. Some of the errors that the author has made are two punctuation errors, five tense choice errors, one pronoun error, two *than/then* errors, and two *to/too/two* errors. Find as many errors as you can and correct them. Answers are on page 320.

The Bergers are writing about the family from a sociological point of view! They are defining the too major types of family structures in most of the world: the nuclear family and the extended family. In the extended family, the larger family are living together, and they are helping each other to. The nuclear family, however, is consisting of the parent(s) and the children. They usually are having to handle difficulties on their own. When there are problems in the nuclear family, than they can ask for help from schools and religious institutions, but this is not always easy. Some of these families would rather solve its own problems then ask outsiders for advice. However, small families of parents and children alone often do not have the family support they are needing.

Grammar Strategies

The Present Continuous Tense

Draw rectangles around the subjects in the following sentences. Then draw circles around the verbs. The first one has been done for you.

1. People are living in a changing world right now.
2. Many families are experiencing changes in their relationships.
3. Like the extended family, the conjugal nuclear family is becoming less common in today's world.
4. Divorce and remarriages are creating new and different kinds of family structures.
5. At present, more children are growing up in single-parent families than in traditional two-parent families.
6. Many children are living with stepparents, grandparents, and aunts and uncles for some time in their lives.

Let's use these sentences to examine the present continuous tense.

In this tense, the verb *be* (*am*, _____, or *are*) is followed by the

_____ form of the verb. Some expressions that are used with the present continuous tense are *now, right now, at this moment*, and *at present*.

As a class or in small groups, answer the following questions using the present continuous tense.

The present continuous tense is used to describe actions that are happening right now or at the moment of speaking.

1. What are you doing right now?
2. What are two things that you are not doing right now that you would like to be doing?

The present continuous tense is used to describe things that are happening around us or in the world right now.

3. What do you think is the most interesting thing that is happening in the world right now?
4. Is your family changing in relation to the things we have read about in this chapter?

The present continuous tense is used to describe things that are happening in the near future.

5. When you watch the news, what are you waiting to find out about?

6. Are you doing anything special this weekend?

Certain verbs are not usually used in the continuous tenses (present continuous, past continuous, future continuous, present perfect continuous, and so on). Here is a list of these verbs:

appear	have	own	smell
appreciate	hear	possess	sound
be	know	prefer	taste
believe	like	recognize	understand
cost	love	remember	want
dislike	mean	see	
hate	need	seem	

These verbs can be divided into three basic categories:

1. *Words that relate to feelings.* For example, "I hate you" or "I love you" is treated as a permanent state of being, not just a present-moment feeling, whereas "I am feeling sick today" is correct because the verb is expressing a temporary state of being.

2. *Words that relate to ownership or possession.* For example, "I own a green convertible" or "I have a house in the country" is regarded as permanent, whereas "I am having some people over to dinner tonight" is correct because the verb does not express a permanent state of being.

3. *Words that relate to perception.* For example, "I see the blue sky above me" or "I smell the potatoes burning" is not treated as a continuous action, whereas "I am hearing Bach for the first time" is correct, since it expresses a perception that takes place at the moment the sentence is spoken and refers to an event that takes place over a period of time.

□ □ □

EXERCISES

1. In the following paragraph, choose the simple present or the present progressive tense. If either tense is possible, discuss the difference in meaning created by the tense you choose.

Some verbs you might use are *study, try, rely, find, want, depend, support, change,* and *receive.* You may also choose other verbs; there are many correct possibilities. Experiment and see how changing the verb or its tense can change the meaning of a sentence.

Sociologists such as the Bergers _____ the family all the time. They _____ to find out about the family structure in different parts of the world and during different periods of history. Family structure _____ all over the world. In many places, families _____ help outside of the nuclear family. This help _____ from the extended family, the community, or the tribe but not usually from outside institutions. However, in the United States, families _____ on institutions such as schools and religious groups to help them while they _____ their children. In the United States, the society _____ individual rights more than concern for others and cooperation. At present, the United States society _____ with serious problems such as crime, drugs, and alcoholism. Newcomers from other societies _____ for ways to prevent their family members from getting into trouble. At the same time, they _____ their children to be successful in their new society. The attempt to hold on to traditional values and to find success in the new culture _____ stress for many.

2. The writing in Exercise 1 would be easier to read if it were divided into paragraphs. Read it with a classmate and decide where new paragraphs should begin. Mark each new paragraph with the symbol ¶. Most writers agree that there should be three paragraphs. If you have any difficulty with this, review "The Paragraph" on pages 7–8.

Transitions and Tenses

The following paragraph is adapted from a *Newsweek* article titled "Playing Both Mother and Father." For easy reference, the sentences have been numbered. Underline all the transitions used in the paragraph. In the spaces provided after the excerpt, give the transition words in each sentence, the verb, and its tense. Then answer the questions. The first one has been done for you.

[1]<u>In recent years</u> a new family structure has been appearing in the United States: the single-parent family. [2]In the 1970s, nearly one out of every two marriages ended in divorce. [3]In the 1980s, this number was leveling off, and some sociologists were predicting that a trend toward stability was developing. [4]In the 1990s, the country is dealing with the problems left from the divorces and remarriages of the 1970s and 1980s. [5]According to Census Bureau statistics for 1984, single parents headed 25 percent of the families with children under 18 in the United States. [6]In the 1990 reports, single parents headed more than one-third of the families. [7]The Census Bureau estimates that one-quarter of now-married mothers and fathers with children will be single parents sometime in the next ten years. [8]Furthermore, about half the children born in the 1980s will spend part of their childhood living with only one parent.

Sentence 1

Transition: *In recent years*

Verb: *has been appearing*

Tense: *past continuous*

Why did the author use this tense in this sentence?

This tense describes actions that began in the past and are still happening right now.

Sentence 2

Transition: _____

Verb: _____

Tense: _____

Why did the author use this tense in this sentence?

_____

_____

Sentence 3

Transition: _____

Verbs: _____, _____, _____

Tense: _____

Why did the author use this tense in this sentence?

_____

_____

Sentence 4

Transition: _____

Verb: _____

Tense: _____

Why did the author use this tense in this sentence?

_____

_____

Sentence 5

Transition: _____

Verb: _____

Tense: _____

Why did the author use this tense in this sentence?

_____

_____

Sentence 6

Transition: _____

Verb: _____

Tense: _____

Why did the author use this tense in this sentence?

_____

_____

Sentence 7

Verbs: _____, _____

Tenses: _____, _____

Why did the author use different tenses in this sentence?

_____

_____

Sentence 8

Transition: _____

Verb: _____

Tense: _____

Why did the author use this tense in this sentence?

_____

_____

We have analyzed the structure of this paragraph so that you as writers can understand how and why writers change tense within a paragraph. What are some of the reasons?

_____

_____

As readers, we are also interested in the content of the paragraph.

1. What is the main idea of this paragraph?
2. How did the writer develop the paragraph?
3. Would you be interested in reading more about this subject? In other words, did the introduction engage you? .
4. Were you able to understand the main idea of the paragraph even if you did not know every word? Did you use context clues to help you with unfamiliar words, instead of interrupting your reading to look up each unfamiliar word in the dictionary?

The technique that we used with this paragraph is one that you can use with other reading materials—newspapers, newsmagazines, textbooks, and so on. It can help you to understand how a piece was written and why the author made certain decisions. Moreover, it can help you with your own writing.

CHAPTER THREE

Growing Apart

PREREADING ACTIVITIES

1. "The Last Word Was Love," written in 1974, is about children's expectations for their parents and the disappointments they sometimes feel about their parents. With other students in your class, make a list of the qualities you think make for a good family life.
2. After reviewing your list of positive family qualities, discuss the expectations that children have for their parents.
3. Discuss in what ways parents may disappoint their children. What do you think children can or should do about these disappointments? Is there anything that children can do to improve the quality of their family life?

The Last Word Was Love

William Saroyan (1908–1981) was born in Fresno, California, the son of Armenian immigrants. He wrote short stories, novels, and plays. He often wrote about the ways in which new immigrants adjust to life in the United States. This story is from Madness in the Family, *a book of short stories about family relationships.*

A long time ago when I was eleven my mother and my father had a prolonged quarrel.

The quarrel picked up the minute my father got home from work at Graff's, where he was a forty-seven-year-old assistant—to everybody. Graff's sold everything from food to ready-made clothing, animal 5 traps, and farm implements. My father had taken the job only for the daily wage of three dollars, which he received in coin at the end of every twelve-hour day. He didn't mind the nature of the work, even though his profession was teaching, and he didn't care that it might end at any moment, without notice. 10

He'd already had the job six months, from late summer to early spring, when the quarrel began to get on my brother's nerves. I didn't even begin to *notice* the quarrel until Ralph pointed it out to me. I admired him so much that I joined him in finding fault with my mother and father. 15

First, though, I'd better describe the quarrel, if that's possible.

To begin with, there was my mother running the house, and there was my father working at Graff's. There was my brother, Ralph, at the top of his class at high school. There I was near the bottom of my class at junior high. And there was our nine-year-old sister, Rose, just enjoy- 20 ing life without any fuss.

All I can say about my mother is that she was a woman—to me a very beautiful one. She had a way of moving very quickly from a singing- and-laughing gladness to a silent-and-dark discontent that bothered my father. I remember hearing him say to her again and again, "Ann, 25 what *is* it?"

Alas, the question was always useless, making my mother cry and my father leave the house.

During the long quarrel my father seemed hopelessly perplexed and outwitted by something unexpected and unwelcome, which he 30 was determined nevertheless to control and banish.

My brother, Ralph, graduated from high school and took a summer- time job in a vineyard. He rode eleven miles to the vineyard on his bicycle every morning soon after daybreak and back again a little before dark every evening. His wages were twenty-five cents an hour, 35 and he put in at least ten hours a day. Early in September he had saved a little more than a hundred dollars.

Early one morning he woke me up.

"I want to say good-bye now," he said. "I'm going to San Francisco."

"What for?" 40

"I can't stay here any more."

Except for the tears in his eyes, I believe I would have said, "Well, good luck, Ralph," but the tears made that impossible. He was as big as my father. The suit he was wearing was my father's, which my mother had altered for him. *What were the tears for?* Would I have them in my 45 own eyes in a moment, too, after all the years of imitating him to never have them, and having succeeded except for the two or three times I had let them go when I had been alone, and nobody knew? And if the tears came into my eyes, too, what would they be *for?* Everything I knew I'd learned from my brother, not from school, and everything he 50 knew he'd learned from my father. So now what did we know? What did my father know? What did my brother? What did I?

I got out of bed and jumped into my clothes and went outside to the backyard. Under the old sycamore tree was the almost completed raft my brother and I had been making in our spare time, to launch one 55 day soon on Kings River.

"I'll finish it alone," I thought. "I'll float down Kings River alone."

My brother came out of the house quietly, holding an old straw suitcase.

"I'll finish the raft," I said. I believed my brother would say some- 60 thing in the same casual tone of voice, and then turn and walk away, and that would be that.

Instead, though, he set the suitcase down and came to the raft. He stepped onto it and sat down, as if we'd just launched the raft and were sailing down Kings River. He put his hand over the side, as if into the 65 cold water of Kings River, and he looked around, as if the raft were passing between vineyards and orchards. After a moment he got up, stepped out of the raft, and picked up the suitcase. There were no tears in his eyes now, but he just couldn't say good-bye. For a moment I thought he was going to give up the idea of leaving home and go back 70 to bed.

Instead, he said, "I'll never go into that house again."

"Do you hate them? Is that why?"

"No," he said, but now he began to cry, as if he were eight or nine years old, not almost seventeen. 75

I picked up the raft, tipped it over, and jumped on it until some of the boards we had so carefully nailed together broke. Then I began to run. I didn't turn around to look at him again.

I ran and walked all the way to where we had planned to launch the raft, about six miles. I sat on the riverbank and tried to think. 80

It didn't do any good, though. I just didn't understand, that's all.

When I got home it was after eleven in the morning, I was very hungry, and I wanted to sit down and eat. My father was at his job at Graff's. My sister was out of the house, and my mother didn't seem to want to look at me. She put food on the table—more than usual, so I 85 was pretty sure she knew something, or at any rate suspected.

At last she said, "Who smashed the raft?"

"I did."

"Why?"

"I got mad at my brother." 90

"Why?"

"I just got mad."

"Eat your food."

She went into the living room, and I ate my food. When I went into the living room she was working at the sewing machine with another of 95 my father's suits.

"This one's for you," she said.

"When can I wear it?"

"Next Sunday. It's one of your father's oldest, when he was slimmer. It'll be a good fit. Do you like it?" 100

"Yes."

She put the work aside and tried to smile, and then *did*, a little.

"She doesn't know what's happened," I thought. And then I thought, "Maybe she *does*, and this is the way she is."

"Your brother's bike is in the garage," she said. "Where's *he?*"   105
"On his way to San Francisco."
"Where have you been?"
"I took a walk."
"A *long* walk?"
"Yes."   110
"Why?"
"I wanted to be alone."
My mother waited a moment and then she said, "Why is your brother on his way to San Francisco?"
"Because—" But I just couldn't tell her.   115
"It's all right," she said. "Tell me."
"Because you and Pop fight so much."
"*Fight?*"
"Yes."
"*Do we?*" my mother said.   120
"I don't know. Are you going to make him come home? Is Pop going to go and get him?"
"No."
"Does he *know?*"
"Yes. He told me."   125
"When?"
"Right after you ran off, and your brother began to walk to the depot. Your father saw the whole thing."
"Didn't he want to stop him?"
"No. Now, go out and repair the raft."   130
I worked hard every day and finished the raft in two weeks. One evening my father helped me get it onto a truck he'd hired. We drove to Kings River, launched it, and sailed down the river about twelve miles. My father brought a letter out of his pocket and read it out loud. It was addressed to Dear Mother and Father. All it said was Ralph had   135
found a job he liked, and was going to go to college when the fall semester began, and was well and happy. The last word of the letter was love.
My father handed me the letter and I read the word for myself.
That Christmas my father sent me to San Francisco to spend a few   140
days with my brother. It was a great adventure for me, because my brother was so different now—almost like my father, except that he lived in a furnished room, not in a house full of people. He wanted to know about the raft, so I told him I'd sailed it and had put it away for the winter.   145
"You come down next summer and we'll sail it together, the way we'd planned," I said.
"No," he said, "We've *already* sailed it together. It's all yours now."

My own son is sixteen years old now, and has made me aware lately 150
that his mother and I have been quarreling for some time. Nothing
new, of course—the same general quarrel—but neither his mother nor
I had ever before noticed that it annoyed him. Later on this year, or
perhaps next year, I know he's going to have a talk with *his* younger
brother, and then take off. I want to be ready when that happens, so I 155
can keep his mother from trying to stop him. He's a good boy, and I
don't mind at all that he thinks I've made a mess of my life, which is
one thing he is *not* going to do.

Of course he isn't.

Reading and Thinking Strategies

Discussion Activities

Analysis and Conclusions

1. What do you think the "quarrel" was about? Why did it bother
   Ralph so much that he wanted to leave home?

2. Why was the father working as an assistant at Graff's at the age of
   forty-seven? Why wasn't the father working as a teacher, the profession for which he had been trained?

3. Why don't the parents stop Ralph from leaving home?

Writing and Point of View

1. Saroyan shifts time periods in this story. What words does he use to
   let his reader know to which time period he is referring? What
   changes does Saroyan make in verb tenses that are used in the
   different parts of the story?

2. After reading "The Last Word Was Love," did you get a sense of the
   writer as a person? Describe the writer of this story based on what
   he has written. What makes you think that Saroyan himself is or is
   not the narrator of the story?

3. Fiction creates a mood or a feeling. What is the mood of this story?
   What elements or parts of the story create this mood? Here are
   some things to think about: In what part of the United States does
   the story take place? Does it take place in the city or in the country?
   On what project have the two brothers been working? What differences do you notice in the way the narrator (the person telling
   the story) communicates with his brother, father, mother, and sister?
   Does the story include any characters outside the family?

Personal Response and Evaluation

1. Do both parents feel the same way about Ralph's decision to leave home? Who do you think makes the decisions in this family? What in the story helps you answer these questions?

2. What does the title "The Last Word Was Love" mean? Why is it significant in this story?

3. Why does Saroyan end the story by referring to the narrator's own son? What does the last line, "Of course he isn't," mean to you as a reader?

Role Playing

1. Act out the short story with one student playing the narrator and other students playing the characters. One more student can read the background information. You might want to record this and play it back for the class, or individual students may want to listen to review the story.

2. Act out the following situation in your class. One of the children in a family wants to move away from home, but the parents do not think that the child is ready to live alone. Role-play this situation using members of the class to play the mother, father, children, and any other family members who might be involved in the discussion.

Journal Writing

Nothing is real, nothing is true, nothing happens, until it has been observed and noted and put down in words like bells, ringing the changes of love and hate, beauty and happiness, and misery. Without words, how much of us really does exist?

HAN SUYIN, *The Mountain Is Young*

Writing in a journal, whether it is shared or kept for yourself, is powerful. It is a means of touching on feelings and experiences hidden inside ourselves. Allowing your journal to express your deepest self will have a positive effect on all your writing.

"The Last Word Was Love" is about growing up and leaving home. It is about family expectations and family love. Have you ever thought about moving away from home and living on your own? Do you think that young people should remain at home with their families until they marry, or do you think that there is a proper time for them to move out on their own? Write your thoughts about these issues in your journal.

Writing Strategies

Essay Strategies

Writing Dialogue

When you read or write stories, plays, or film scripts, you should be aware of the way people talk to each other. Writers try to make the conversation or spoken interchanges between people as realistic as possible for their particular characters.

Look at the following interchanges from various pieces of writing and notice the differences in the ways in which the characters communicate. What do these interchanges tell you about the characters and about their relationships?

> At last she said, "Who smashed the raft?"
> "I did."
> "Why?"
> "I got mad at my brother."
> "Why?"
> "I just got mad."
> "Eat your food."

After reading this excerpt from "The Last Word Was Love" by William Saroyan, discuss the following questions.

1. Who is talking, and how do you, as a reader, know this?
2. How would you describe the relationship of these people?
3. What pictures of these people did you form as you read this? What do they look like and sound like to you as a reader?

> "What's the matter, Schatz?"
> "I've got a headache."
> "You better go back to bed."
> "No. I'm all right."
> "You go to bed. I'll see you when I'm dressed."

After reading this excerpt from "A Day's Wait" by Ernest Hemingway, discuss the following questions.

1. Who is talking, and how do you, as a reader, know this?
2. How would you describe the relationship of these people?
3. What pictures of these people did you form as you read this? What do they look like and sound like to you as a reader?

"You must not walk in any direction but to school and back home," warned my mother when she decided I was old enough to walk by myself.

"Why?" I asked.

"You can't understand these things," she said.

"Why not?"

"Because I haven't put it in your mind yet."

"Why not?"

"Aii-ya! Such questions! Because it is too terrible to consider. A man can grab you off the streets, sell you to someone else, make you have a baby. Then you'll kill the baby. And when they find this baby in a garbage can, then what can be done? You'll go jail, die there."

After reading this excerpt from "The Twenty-six Malignant Gates" by Amy Tan, which appears in her book *The Joy Luck Club*, discuss the following questions.

1. Who is talking, and how do you, as a reader, know this?

2. How would you describe the relationship of these people?

3. What pictures of these people did you form as you read this? What do they look like and sound like to you as a reader?

4. What differences do you find in the ways in which people talk in the excerpts from all three short stories? What does the dialogue tell you about the people?

5. Why do you think that writers use dialogue rather than just describing characters and discussing what they have said?

Essay Form

Narration: Telling a Story

Every day in our lives all of us tell stories. For example, we come home from school and tell our families what happened in class. We might discuss a bus trip and describe one of the people on the bus. We fill our stories with details that will capture the imagination of the listener. We tell stories to give ourselves pleasure and to give our listeners pleasure. Writer Joan Didion said, "We tell ourselves stories in order to live." Stories are a way of making sense of the world.

When we tell stories, we are aware of beginnings and endings. We usually tell a story in the order in which it happened; when we listen to stories, we also like to hear them in the correct order. Have you ever been telling a child an old, familiar story and, in trying to rush through it, left out a part? The child will usually stop you and beg you to tell the story "right," with all its parts in the right order. The rules we follow when we tell stories to friends and family are similar to the rules we follow when we write stories that will be shared with teachers and classmates.

"The Last Word Was Love" is an example of narration that uses *chronological order*, which means that events are told in the order in which they occurred. The Saroyan story begins, "A long time ago when I was eleven," and ends, "My own son is sixteen years old now . . ." Reread the story, noticing each time that Saroyan uses time phrases as transitions throughout the story. How do these help you follow the story?

In addition, Saroyan includes many details that describe his family and their life. When you write a narration, you can make your writing more interesting and richer by adding details that help the reader feel and almost see the experience. Writers do this by adding *sensory details*, details that help a reader to see, hear, smell, feel, and taste the experiences that are being described. Reread the Saroyan story, noticing the specific details he provides. Decide whether the details help the reader to see, hear, smell, feel, or taste the particular experiences he is describing.

When you do your own writing of a narrative or a story, keep in mind chronological order and the inclusion of sensory details to help your reader understand and enjoy your story.

□ □ □

EXERCISES

1. Compare the writing in the selection in Chapter 1 with the writing in the selection in this chapter. Which selection do you prefer and why? Is the vocabulary similar? Which selection did you find easier to read?

2. What kinds of reading do you do just for your own enjoyment? Share with a classmate the best article, book, or story that you have read in the past few months. What makes a piece of writing appeal to you?

Suggestions for Writing

You may want to look at your journal or try brainstorming or freewriting before you begin to write on these topics. Always spend some time thinking before you begin to write. Try the suggestion in "Getting Started" on page 51 if you need help in beginning your writing.

The first four suggestions are narratives or stories. When you write a narrative, keep in mind the three topics focused on in this chapter: chronological order, sensory details, and the use of dialogue.

1. Write a narrative about an experience between a child and a parent. Use dialogue. Refer to page 47 to see how your journal can help you with this writing.

2. Have you ever had an experience like the young brother's in which you were upset or confused? Write about your experience and tell what you learned from it.

3. Imagine that Ralph is telling the story "The Last Word Was Love." Rewrite the story from his point of view.

4. Imagine that Rose is telling the story. Rewrite the story and make whatever changes you think should occur if it was told from the point of view of a little girl.

5. In a small group, write a play based on this story. Use some of the dialogue from the story and some of your own. Use the following format.

   RALPH: I want to say good-bye now. I'm going to San Francisco.
   WILLIAM: What for?

   In your group, read your dialogue aloud to see if it sounds like people talking. You may decide to act out your play for the entire class.

6. Parents are often not sensitive enough in dealing with their children's problems. Do you agree or disagree? Write an essay in which you support your point of view with your experiences or observations.

7. Reread Sun Park's essay on pages 3–4. Write an essay in which you compare Park's parents and the parents described in "The Last Word Was Love" in relation to their expectations for their children. In your essay, state which parental style you prefer and explain why.

Getting Started

Brainstorming

Whenever possible, you should write about something that interests you. You will then have ideas on the subject and will probably be able to come up with something to say. Even if you are writing about a topic that interests you, however, you may have problems writing an essay. Brainstorming is a good technique to use to help you come up with ideas that will develop into your essay.

When you brainstorm, you develop ideas and supporting details by asking questions. The basic questions are Who? What? Where? When? How? and Why? The questions vary, based on the topic. For example, the following sample questions were used to brainstorm for an essay about a special relationship. Remember, brainstorming is used to help you get started writing. Don't worry about writing complete sentences. Just write down your ideas.

Who has the relationship?	My parents, who have been married for 35 years, have a special relationship.
What makes them special?	They are best friends. Even in difficult situations.
Where do they live?	In an old house that they have rebuilt themselves.
When did you realize that their relationship was special?	I came to visit them as they were refinishing a floor. They were working on the same area. They bumped heads and kissed. They were in their sixties.
How do they make you feel?	They have always made me feel like they loved me. Made me believe that I could succeed. Made me believe that relationships can last and grow.
Why do you want to write about them?	I want to show that people can be married for a long time and still be best friends, still be in love.

The next step is reading through the questions and answers and deciding what to emphasize in the writing. As you read through what you have written, this may become obvious. Although brainstorming is a good technique for getting started, you can use it at any time during the writing process. If you are stuck in the middle and need more support or more details, brainstorming can be helpful. It is a useful tool to help a writer create a rich, fully developed essay.

□ □ □

EXERCISES

1. Brainstorm about one or more of the following: a special relationship, teenage marriages, the high divorce rate, living together before marriage. Write down your questions and answers. They will be helpful when you begin writing.

2. Brainstorm with a classmate. One of you will ask the questions; the other will write down the answers. Then repeat the activity but reverse roles. At the end of the two sessions, you should have material for two essays.

Revising

Many writers are not quite sure what to do when they are told to revise their writing. They simply look for misspellings, grammar errors, and other surface problems, then copy the essay over and hand it in. This is not really revising, however; this is editing. Revising means rethinking and restructuring your writing.

One way to become more comfortable with revising is just to go ahead and do it. Here we suggest a simple and concrete method for getting the feel of revising. Although it is not something you would do all the time, it will give you some experience in making decisions about your writing. Use it first on the following student essay. Follow the steps in the order in which they are listed.

1. Choose an essay that you would like to revise.
2. Reread the essay slowly and carefully. Make a copy of the essay. (Save the original essay.)
3. Cross out and remove one sentence from any part of the essay.
4. Move one sentence from one place in a paragraph to a new place.
5. Add one new sentence to any paragraph in your essay.
6. Change one word in the essay to a synonym for that word.
7. Add one transition word or phrase (*therefore, however, but, moreover,* etc.) somewhere in your essay.
8. Rewrite the essay with all the changes you have made.

A Student Essay

I remember when my mother used to tell me that she would not die until she made of us independent young people. My brothers and sisters, all of us, grew up with that thought in mind. To me, that was a good statement from my mother which I will follow for my future children. I am an independent person and I feel I am the most free 5 man to make decisions in my life without being afraid of them. And I feel free to take action on my decisions. Because of being free to decide for myself and being self-sufficient in my entire life, I am very proud of my mother. She helped me become an independent person.

I know a lot of people that at my age are afraid of what to do in their 10 future lives. These people that I am talking about are people who are living with their parents. It has nothing to do with whether it is good or bad to live with their parents. The point is that these people are often handicapped in making decisions. I remember that one of these people that I am talking about asked me if I was afraid to live by myself or 15 if I feel like a woman because I have to cook my own dinner when I get home.

I could not answer these silly questions because I saw that this man's hands were tied about what to do with his future life. I believe that these dependent people will not have any choice when their parents 20 pass away. They are going to feel that it will be impossible for them to do anything without their parents to help them. They will regret the fact that they did not become independent before their parents passed away. Unfortunately, they are left handicapped to take action on their own decisions. 25

In conclusion, I think that all young people must become independent and not let their parents decide their lives for them. When people are no longer teenagers, they should leave their parents' homes and start their own homes. At this time, they should start their own independent lives. 30

Reynaldo Rivera, Puerto Rico

Look at Rivera's original essay and at your revised version of his essay. Which do you prefer? Which of the suggested changes was most difficult to make? Which of the suggested changes improved the essay the most? After you have discussed this essay, do the same revising exercise with your own writing. You may work alone or with a partner. Work through the exercise step by step.

After you have completed all the work involved, compare your original essay with the revised version. Which do you prefer? Why? Was it difficult to make the suggested changes? Think about how you decided which sentence to remove. Think about how you made the other decisions as well. These are the types of decisions that all writers make when revising their writing.

Editing Strategies

Vocabulary Development

idiomatic expressions using *at*

Each of the paragraphs that follow contains a context clue that will help you understand some of the idiomatic expressions used in the Saroyan story. Underline these context clues (the first one has been done for you). Then use the expressions when you answer the questions at the end of each paragraph.

1. **at any moment** (line 10)

Because the father in the story has no security in his job, he could lose his job at any time.

What could explain why the father could lose his job at any time, without being warned? How do you think this affects the rest of the family?

2. **at least** (line 36)

The family problems are made worse by the fact that the father works no less than 12 hours a day.

Ralph wants to go off on his own to see if he can make a better life for himself than his father has made for his family. Do you think it is the right time for Ralph at least to try to make a better life for himself?

3. **at any rate** (line 86)

The mother may not have known what was going on, but in any event, she knew something was different. The boy knew this because she gave him more food than usual.

Even if they are happy at home, some people think that children should move out on their own at any rate to find independence. Do you agree with this idea?

4. **at last** (line 87)

The room was quiet until finally she spoke to the boy.

She did not ask him about his brother at first. Why do you think she waits so long until at last she asks him why his brother has left home?

5. **at all** (line 157)

The narrator states that he does not mind in the least that his son is beginning to complain about his parents' arguing.

Do you think that most children are bothered at all by their parents' arguing, or is this just a normal part of family life?

prepositions

Many students of English have difficulty learning how to use prepositions correctly. One problem is that English has more prepositions than many other languages. In Spanish, for example, the preposition *en* is equivalent to three prepositions in English: *in*, *on*, and *at*. When you study prepositions, think about how they are used in your first language. Some students find it useful to create a personal association with what they already know about their own language and the new information they are learning about English.

The eight most frequently used prepositions in English (in alphabetical order) are *at, by, for, from, in, on, to,* and *with.*

In this chapter, we will look at some of the most common uses for the preposition *at* by comparing this preposition with *in* and *on. At* is used in the following ways.

1. To locate something in a specific location:

   I live *in* Fresno, California, *at* the corner of Hoyt and Blair streets.
   I live *in* Washington, D.C., *at* 3426 S.E. Columbia Avenue.
   My father worked *in* a store and usually got home from his job *at* Graff's after 8 at night.
   My mother was working *in* the house *at* the sewing machine.
   She was *at* home when I called her.

2. To locate something in a specific time:

   I was born *in* March *on* Monday *at* 3:46 A.M.
   He said he would meet me *on* Saturday at the library *at* noon.
   Father got paid *at* the end of every 12-hour day except *on* the weekend.
   She met him *at* the reopening of Ellis Island *in* 1990.

3. To indicate a state, condition, or involvement in a particular activity:

   I felt *at* a loss when my brother told me he was leaving home. Soon after he told me, I was *in* tears.
   The girl was *at* ease with her hands *in* her lap until the music started playing.
   His father was *in* the store *at* work when Ralph left home.
   Ralph was *at* the top of his high school class because he got A's *in* all his subjects.

4. To indicate direction toward a goal or an objective:

   I tried to look *at* him again, but it made me feel sad to look him *in* the eye.
   When he looked *at* me, I began to cry.
   He stared *at* the raft still floating *in* the river before he left home.

□ □ □

EXERCISE   In the following paragraph, fill in the blanks with *at* or *in*, using the examples as a guide.

Saroyan writes about a family that lives __*in*__ California. The older son, Ralph, is __*at*__ the top of his high school class, but he is not happy living __*at*__ home anymore. The father has a job __*at*__ Graff's, a local department store. They sell almost everything __*in*__ this store. Ralph seems disappointed _____ his father. He notices that he cannot look __*at*__ his father or look __*at*__ the man's eyes anymore. __*At*__ any rate, he knows that he is annoyed __*on*__ the way his father and mother talk to each other. He cannot live __*in*__ the same house with them anymore. He wants __*at*__ least to try to live on his own __*in*__ San Francisco.

Commonly Confused Words

live/leave

Ralph tells his brother that he cannot *live* at home anymore; he wants to *leave* his family and *live* on his own.

Notice how the verb forms of *live* and *leave* are used in the preceding sentence. Now complete the following definitions:

__*live*__ is a verb that means "to reside in a particular place."

__*leave*__ is a verb that means "to go away from a particular place, job, or situation."

Fill in the blanks in the following paragraph with the correct form of *live* or *leave*.

Ralph does not want to __*live*__ at home with his family anymore. He wants to __*leave*__ and move to San Francisco. There he will __*live*__ on his own. His brother does not want him to __*leave*__ the family because the brother knows that he will miss Ralph. The younger brother thinks that when Ralph _____, the family will never _____

together again.

Mechanics

Quotation Marks

Read the following excerpt from "The Last Word Was Love," and underline all the words that are enclosed by quotation marks, including words in this sentence.

"I want to say good-bye now," he said. "I'm going to San Francisco."

"What for?"

"I can't stay here any more."

Except for the tears in his eyes, I believe I would have said, "Well, good luck, Ralph," but the tears made that impossible.

Look closely at what you have underlined; then answer the following questions.

1. Do periods belong inside or outside quotation marks?

    _____

2. If you end a quotation and then identify who said it, does the quotation end with a period or with a comma? _____

3. In what tense are the quotations in the excerpt written?

    _____

4. In what tense is the story written? _____

5. Why are the story and the quotations written in different tenses?

    _____

6. In the directions, there are quotation marks around "The Last Word Was Love." What do those quotation marks indicate to the reader?

    Why do the words begin with capital letters? _____

    _____

7. One use for quotation marks is for the names of short stories. What is another use for quotation marks? _____

□ □ □

EXERCISES

1. Imagine that a new student in your college is lost. Write a dialogue in which the student asks you for directions to the bursar's office. Write your response using quotation marks and expressions such as *I said, she said,* and *he said.*

2. Imagine that you have just received a letter telling you that there is a problem with your school registration. Write a dialogue in which you go to the registrar's office to try to solve your problem. You may want to write this dialogue with a classmate and act it out for the class.

Editing Practice

The following paragraph is a first draft that contains many surface errors: one formatting error, one quotation mark error, two *live/leave* errors, three end punctuation errors, three *to/too/two* errors, and three present tense errors. Find and correct all the errors. Check your answers on page 320.

The Last Word Was Love is describing a family at a critical point in time. The oldest brother in the family decides to live the family and move too San Francisco! He is feeling disappointment with the way his parents leave. The younger brother is wanting to know why his brother wants to move away from home? Their mother seems too understand, but she is quiet and does not discuss the problem with her younger son. Although the members of the family seem two love each other, they do not communicate well!

Grammar Strategies

Forms of the Past Tense

"The Last Word Was Love" is written in the past tense, which is the tense most commonly used to tell a story. The various forms of the past tense are shown below.

Simple Past Tense

A paragraph from the story is reproduced here. Underline all the past tense verbs. The first one has been done for you.

When I <u>got</u> home it was after eleven in the morning, I was very hungry, and I wanted to sit down and eat. My father was at his job at Graff's. My sister was out of the house, and my mother didn't seem to want to look at me. She put food on the table—more than usual, so I was pretty sure she knew something, or at any rate suspected.

Now change all the verbs to the present tense and rewrite the paragraph in the lines below.

_____

_____

_____

_____

_____

_____

Read both paragraphs. Does the meaning seem changed? Which paragraph do you prefer? Which would you use to tell a story? Why?

Past Continuous Tense

The past continuous or progressive tense is formed with *was* or *were* and the *-ing* form of the verb. It is used to convey continuous action that took place in the past.

When I went into the living room, she *was working* at the sewing machine.
She *was talking* to me as I ate my food.
The raft *was sailing* down Kings River.
My brother *was crying*, and I started to cry, too.

In the following paragraph, choose the simple past tense or the past progressive tense of the indicated verbs.

My mother _____ in the kitchen when I _____
               (work)   (ask)

her about my brother. She _____ to be upset, too. She
                             (seem)

_____ me a knife and soon I _____ vege-
(hand)   (cut)

tables with her. She _____ the oil in the fry pan as I
(pour)

_____. I _____ that I _____ him to stay.
(talk)   (say)   (want)

She _____ at me and _____ her arms around me.
(look)   (put)

We _____ when my sister _____ in from school.
(hug)   (come)

Past Perfect Tense

The past perfect tense is used to express something that occurred in the past, before something else that happened in the past. If we are writing about two things that happened in the past and we want to show that one came before the other, we use the past perfect tense for the thing that happened first.

The past perfect tense is formed with *had* plus the past participle of the verb. (See Appendix A for a list of irregular past participles.)

> The suit he was wearing was my father's, which my mother *had altered* for him.
> Everything I knew, I *had learned* from my brother, not from school, and everything he knew, he *had learned* from my father.
> I ran and walked all the way to where we *had planned* to launch the raft, about six miles.

In each of these examples, which action came first?

The past perfect progressive tense is formed with *had* plus *been* and the *-ing* form of the verb.

> The mother and father *had been quarreling* for a long time before it began to bother Ralph.
> Under the old sycamore tree was the almost completed raft my brother and I *had been making* in our spare time, to launch one day soon on Kings River.

□ □ □

EXERCISES

1. In the following paragraph, choose the simple past, the past progressive, or the past perfect tense of the indicated verbs.

After my brother, Ralph, _____ from high school,
(graduate)

he _____ to look for a job near home. He
(begin)

_____ a job 11 miles away in the vineyards. To get there,
(find)

he _____ every morning soon after daybreak. Before
     (bicycle)

he _____ there for a long time, he _____ to
   (work)   (start)

complain that he _____ tired all the time. He finally
             (feel)

_____ my father that he _____ to move to
   (tell)   (decide)

the city where he _____ to find more job opportunities.
            (hope)

2. The following paragraph is taken from "The Last Word Was Love."
   Fill in the past tense verbs as you remember them from the story.
   Decide whether you need the simple past, the past progressive, or
   the past perfect tense. Then go back to the story and compare your
   answers with the original. Decide which you prefer and why.

   I _____ hard every day and _____ the

   raft in two weeks. One evening my father _____ me get

   it onto a truck he _____. We _____ to

   Kings River, _____ it, and _____ down the

   river about twelve miles. My father _____ a letter out

   of his pocket and _____ it out loud. It was addressed

   to Dear Mother and Father. All it _____ was

   Ralph _____ a job he liked, and _____

   to go to college when the fall semester _____, and

   _____ well and happy. The last word of the letter

   _____ love.

Sentence Variety

Writers use a variety of sentences to keep their writing interesting
and lively. Too many short sentences can sound choppy and immature,
just as too many long sentences can be dull and difficult to read.
Writers maintain a balance of different length and different types of
sentences.

Sentences are made up of different types and numbers of clauses. A
clause is the part of the sentence that contains the subject and the
predicate.

An independent clause can stand alone as a sentence.

A dependent clause cannot stand alone. It needs an independent clause to make it a complete sentence.

When students do their homework, they should focus on their work.

DEPENDENT CLAUSE   INDEPENDENT CLAUSE

Clauses determine four major sentence types:

1. The *simple sentence* has one independent clause:

   She studied hard for all of her classes.

2. The *compound sentence* has two or more independent clauses:

   I tried to speak Vietnamese, and my friend tried to speak English.

3. The *complex sentence* has one independent clause joined to one or more dependent clauses. A complex sentence contains either a subordinating word such as *although, when,* or *because* or a relative pronoun such as *that, who,* or *which*:

   When she handed in her homework, she forgot to give the teacher the last page.
   I admired him so much that I wanted to run away with him.

4. The *compound-complex sentence* has two or more independent clauses and one or more dependent clauses.

   Although she always did her homework, she often handed it in late because she copied it over until it was perfect.

□   □   □

EXERCISES

1. With a partner, reread the Saroyan story to find examples of each of the four sentence types.
2. Reread the Park essay to find examples of each of the four sentence types.
3. Reread the Berger selection to find examples of the four sentence types.
4. What differences did you find in the types of sentences used in these pieces of writing? What was the predominant type in each story? How does the use of a sentence type affect you as a reader? Is one type of sentence easier to read than another for you?

5. Working with a partner, read one essay each of you has written to find examples of each of the four sentence types.

■ ■ ■

The Compound Sentence

To form compound sentences, join two related independent clauses with a semicolon (;) or use a coordinating word. Some commonly used coordinators are *and, but, or, yet, for, so,* and *nor*. Use a comma before the coordinator.

> Graff's sold food and clothes, and it sold farm implements as well.
> The boys built the raft, but they did not sail it together.

Each of the following sentences uses some type of coordination. Analyze these sentences very carefully by performing three operations on each one. (The first sentence has been done for you.)

Put a rectangle around each subject.

Put a circle around each verb.

Put a triangle around each coordinator and the comma that precedes it.

1. My mother ran the house, and my father worked at Graff's.

2. My brother was my best friend, for we shared many things.

3. He left home, so I had to learn to do without him.

4. There were no tears in his eyes, but he just couldn't say good-bye.

5. I will move to San Francisco, or I will lose my mind.

6. My mother seemed to want him to stay, yet she said nothing.

7. My mother didn't talk to my father about it, nor did I talk to anyone for a while.

Complex Sentences

Commas with Subordinate Clauses

There are several types of sentences that we can use when we write. Most writers vary sentence types to make their writing more interesting to the reader. If you examine professional writing, you will usually find a combination of short sentences and long sentences. In this chapter, we will examine the use of subordination to create longer sentences.

In each of the following sentences, draw a rectangle around the subject and a circle around the verb. The first one has been done for you.

1. ☐I☐ ⬭came⬭ to the United States with my parents.

2. I was almost 14 years old.

3. I have lived in the United States for six years.

4. I am still unable to think about my home country with detachment.

Notice in each sentence there is one subject and one verb. If you were to read an entire essay made up of sentences such as these, you might find it choppy and immature. To vary the sentences, it is possible to combine some of these sentences using subordinators. Subordinators are special words that are used to make connections. Some commonly used subordinators are *after, as, because, before, if, since, until, when, where*, and *while*.

Each of the following sentences uses some type of subordination. Analyze these sentences very carefully by performing four operations on each one. (The first sentence has been done for you.)

Put a rectangle around each subject.

Put a circle around each verb.

Put a triangle around each subordinator.

If there is a comma in the sentence, underline it.

1. ☐I☐ ⬭came⬭ to the United States with my parents △when☐ I☐ ⬭was⬭ almost 14 years old.

2. Although I have lived in the United States for six years, I am still unable to think about my home country with detachment.

3. As I practiced more, my English began to improve.

4. I have to return to my home country one day because I want to know myself better.

5. When I try to review my life, I feel both happy and sad.

On the basis of what you have observed in this exercise, complete the following sentences.

When two complete sentences are connected by a subordinator and the subordinating word is the first word in the sentence, a comma _____ needed. If the subordinating word occurs in the
(is/is not)

middle of the sentence, a comma _____ needed.
(is/is not)

☐   ☐   ☐

PAIRED EXERCISE

With a classmate, reread the Berger article on pages 21–22 and decide together what types of sentences the authors used. Do this activity with your own writing. Do you need to improve your sentence variety?

Language and Communicating

CHAPTER FOUR

Learning a Language

PREREADING ACTIVITIES

1. As a class, discuss Vietnam. Where is it, and what do you know about its history?
2. If there are Vietnamese students in your class, they can become the experts about their country. If not, the class should decide what resources to use to find out information about the weather, food, religion, clothing, and family relationships of Vietnam. Groups of students can gather information in the various areas and then report to the class.
3. In small groups, students can discuss specific methods that have helped them learn English and other methods that have not worked for them. Each group should prepare and present a short (three- to five-minute) presentation of its findings to the class.

Language Barrier Is Thwarting Young Vietnamese Immigrants in Elmhurst

The New York Times in 1982 published a series on the lives of immigrants in New York. This article, by Dena Kleiman, deals with some of the difficulties faced by a young Vietnamese family trying to adjust to a new language, a new culture, and a new way of life.

She stays up half the night copying over the notes she took in class, hoping the repetition alone will help her absorb the English. She keeps long lists of vocabulary words and has not missed a day of school since she began. She gets all of her assignments done early—including the report on *Death of a Salesman*, but after reading the play at least four times, she is still not sure who the salesman is. 5

And Khan Duong, who is 20 years old, is failing at Newtown High School.

There are few at Newtown, in Elmhurst, Queens, who know about Miss Duong—how she is already in charge of a household of five, that 10 in addition to school she works stuffing Chinese-style steam buns in a factory and practices the piano two hours a day instead of eating lunch.

Few know about her arrival here—how she and her cousins set off in a small boat three years ago from Vietnam, leaving their parents 15 behind—and that today they live on their own. Most at school only know that Miss Duong, who gave herself the name "Matina" because she thought it sounded American, is having trouble with English.

Yet even those who have been in her class 40 minutes a day, five days a week, do not understand the scope of the problems linked to 20 her troubles learning English—her fear of getting lost on the subway, the loneliness of being unable to make friends, the frustration of missing jokes.

°varied

Hers is not a unique story for Newtown High School, or for anywhere else in Elmhurst, the city's most ethnically diverse° neighbor- 25 hood, where the struggle to understand English is often among the most baffling challenges to newcomers to this country. What makes her story and that of her cousins different, however, is that they are so young and are facing this challenge entirely on their own.

"Nobody teach you," said Miss Duong. "Find out by yourself." 30

°crowded

Miss Duong and her cousins live in a cramped° but tidy two-bedroom apartment. Three of the cousins sleep on mattresses on the floor. The living room serves as entertainment center, dining room and study hall, organized so that each of the cousins has a desk facing away from the television set. 35

It is quite different from the homes they lived in north of Saigon, children of well-to-do parents with businesses and live-in help.

There was little in their childhood to prepare them for their journey to America, which included 45 days on a ship without a chair or a bed and often no water. There was little, too, in their past to prepare 40 them for their lives here.

"I die already," Miss Duong said. "Now I am reborn again."

The five cousins, who range in age from 12 to 22, spend much of their time together. Since they are afraid to go outside at night, they remain indoors even on weekends. Because money is tight, they rarely 45 get to Manhattan and have been to a movie only once in three years. Ashamed of their English, they do not talk to their neighbors.

°contradiction

"We don't know anyone," said Miss Duong, who believes she and her cousins are among the few foreigners around. The irony° is that almost everyone else in the building and many in her school are new- 50 comers to this country, too.

Lac Hua, 22, the eldest of the cousins, earns the money to pay the bulk of the family's expenses—including the $453 a month they pay for rent—by driving a truck. All five contribute for food, including Vinh Hua, 12, and his sister, Thuong Hua, 19, who receive public assistance. 55

Since Vinh, who came here at the age of 9, is the only one who does not hold even a part-time job, he is also responsible for dusting the floor, changing the water in the fish tank and doing the wash.

°complexly

°impossible to see

°qualified

Spend an evening with this young family, and one is moved by their energy and sense of structure. Miss Duong and Miss Hua do the cooking. Vinh washes the dishes. Ky Trung, 17, the fifth cousin, scrubs the pots. They sit in a circle and have dinner together as a family—American or Vietnamese specialties ranging from spaghetti to intricately° spiced rice, but always with chopsticks, even when the menu features "Shake and Bake" chicken.

Then at about 9 o'clock, the activity comes to a halt and it is time for study until 1 in the morning.

"'Invisible.'° I don't know what that means," Miss Duong said the other night, picking up her assignment: the prologue to *Invisible Man* by Ralph Ellison. She reached for a dictionary, but found no help. She asked Miss Hua, who is also a senior at Newtown and is doing better than Miss Duong. But Miss Hua shrugged her shoulders.

Miss Duong, who has already been at the high school three years, is afraid that unless her English improves soon she may be denied a diploma. Under New York state law, students are entitled to a free public education until the age of 21. While she would be eligible° for alternative academic programs, this may be the last year she can graduate from a regular high school.

"If I miss now, then what?" said Miss Duong, adding that in Vietnam she received high marks.

Reading and Thinking Strategies

Discussion Activities

Analysis and Conclusions

1. According to Kleiman's article, Khan Duong studies very hard. Despite all her hard work, she is not doing well in school. Do you think there is anything wrong with the way she is studying English? Can you suggest any ways in which she might improve her study techniques?

2. How has Khan Duong changed as a person since she moved to the United States? In what ways is she more independent and self-sufficient than before?

3. Do you think Khan Duong speaks English outside the classroom? Use examples from the article to support your point of view.

Writing and Point of View

1. Dena Kleiman reports about Khan Duong and her family. She does not give her opinions or make suggestions. Why not? For whom was this article originally written?

2. Why is the second paragraph of the article (lines 7–8) only one sentence long? How does this make you as the reader feel? What in the article makes you think it was written for a certain audience?

3. Are there any words or details that make you feel that the author is sympathetic to Khan Duong and her family? What are they?

Personal Response and Evaluation

1. Do you know any people like Khan Duong who completely changed their lifestyles when they moved to the United States? How has the change affected them?

2. What should Khan Duong do to create a better life for herself and her family in the United States?

3. Dena Kleiman wrote the story of Khan Duong and her family. Why do you think she chose to write about this group? What do you think she hoped would happen after people read her story?

Response Paragraph

After you have read the article about Khan Duong, write a paragraph telling how the article made you feel. Think about the ways in which your experiences are similar to or different from Khan Duong's. What particular ideas from this article will you remember?

Share your paragraph with your classmates. As a group, what do you think you can learn from Khan Duong's experiences?

Journal Writing

After reading about Khan Duong and her family, think about your own experiences learning English. Close your eyes and think about the word *English*. What thoughts come to your mind? Think about the word *future*. When you are ready, write down your thoughts. Do not worry about writing complete, grammatically correct sentences. Write, and the writing itself will help you become a better writer.

Writing Strategies

Essay Strategies

The Journalistic Approach to Writing

Dena Kleiman wrote the article about Khan Duong for a newspaper. She uses techniques that have been used by journalists for many years to get information about their subject and to write effective, communicative stories. Most journalists use the *who, what, where, when, why, how* method. They ask themselves these questions:

Who is involved?

What is happening or has happened?

Where is the event occurring?

When did it happen?

Why did it happen?

How will it affect the people or things involved?

Some journalists try to answer in short form as many of these questions as possible in their first paragraph, which they call the *lead paragraph*. The next paragraphs add details and support for the lead. Other journalists answer in the lead paragraph only as many questions as they think will make the reader interested in reading further. They answer the rest of the questions during the course of the article. Of course, journalists cannot always find all the answers, but they give as much support and detail as possible to keep their writing interesting, lively, and informative.

□ □ □

EXERCISES

1. Reread the Kleiman article to find the answers to Who? What? Where? When? Why? and How? How many of these did she answer in her lead paragraph? How did she add details and support throughout the article?

2. Reread the Park essay on pages 3–4 to find the answers to the same questions. How many of these did she answer in her lead paragraph? How did she add details and support throughout the article?

3. Reread one of your own essays, noticing which of these questions you answered and which you did not. Try adding answers to some of the questions you did not write about in your earlier draft. Decide whether answering these questions improves your essay or makes it less effective.

Essay Form

Understanding the Essay Question

When you read an essay question, first ask yourself: *What is the subject of the question?* Then reread the question several times, thinking about what the question is asking. Make sure you understand all the vocabulary. Focus on the subject, and decide if you have enough ideas about it to write an essay.

What is the essay asking you to do? Usually the essay question itself suggests a particular way for you to develop your ideas. The words in the essay questions may ask you to *narrate, describe, compare* or *contrast, analyze, explain, argue,* or *classify.* Each of these is a slightly different job or method of development for you as a writer.

To *narrate* is to tell a story, to re-create or create a story with characters, setting or place, and plot. Narration usually includes some description and some dialogue or conversation between people.

To *describe* means to tell in a word picture how something or someone appeared. As a writer, you should keep in mind all the senses in your description—sight, sound, smell, touch, and taste.

To *compare* means to look at two or more ideas, things, or events to point out what is similar and what is different about them. To *contrast* means to look only for the differences.

To *analyze* means to break down an idea, a thing, or an event into its separate parts.

To *explain* means to discuss and analyze the step-by-step sequence in which something occurred. This sequence is also called a cause-and-effect relationship because it traces a succession of events (the cause) that led to a particular situation (the effect).

To *argue* means to use reasons to support or prove that something is true or false, has value or not, or ought to be done or not. As part of your argument, you may include comparison, description, narration, and analysis.

To *classify* means to divide a large set of items into smaller groups and to identify the qualities of each group. For example, you can divide the large set of *trees* into smaller groups: *deciduous* (trees that lose their leaves) and *evergreen* (trees that are green throughout the year).

□ □ □

EXERCISES

1. Look at the "Suggestions for Writing" that follow. With a partner, discuss what the subject of each question is and what the essay question is asking you to do. For extra practice, you can do this exercise with other "Suggestions for Writing" in other chapters in the book.

2. Share an essay that you have written this semester with a partner. Together, discuss the subject of the essay and the way you have chosen to write about it.

3. As a group, reread the Kleiman selection and other selections in the book. Keep in mind that many writers use a combination of methods of development in their writing. Decide which method or combination of methods the authors used.

Suggestions for Writing

One of the most important parts of writing comes before you ever put your pen to paper. It occurs when you are thinking about what you are going to write. Be sure to allow yourself some time to think before you write. Try "Brainstorming with a Partner" below to help you get started.

Choose one of the following topics to write about. You may find it useful to look at your journal or to brainstorm before you start writing.

1. Tell a story about someone who has had problems learning English or getting used to living in a new country. What has this person learned from facing these problems?

2. Compare your experience living in a new country and learning a new language with Khan Duong's experience. Use the article for information.

3. Many people say that learning a new language is easier for children than it is for adults. Do you agree or disagree? Explain your point of view, telling about yourself and people you have known or read about. Try to convince your audience.

4. Write an essay in which you compare your first language with English. What are some of the similarities and differences? Be sure to mention word order, plurals, and questions.

5. Write an essay comparing Khan Duong's educational experiences with your own or with those of Sun Park (pages 3–4). In your essay, explain the reasons for the differences in educational success.

Getting Started

Brainstorming with a Partner

One technique that writers use to get started writing essays, stories, or papers is brainstorming, as described on pages 51–52. Another related technique is brainstorming with a partner. Discuss with a classmate some of the writing topics that you are considering. Once you have each decided on a topic, ask each other the questions listed on page 73 and any others that relate to your particular topics. Write down ideas together for either partner's topic. Jot down words, phrases, or whole ideas that occur to the two of you as you talk. Brainstorm until you have filled a page with ideas that you have developed together. At that point, you have enough to begin your writing. When you are finished, share what you have written with your partner.

re are many languages in the world. In the United States, there
any people who came from other countries, so many people
different languages here. Those are different from each other
much, but there are similarities, too. My first language is Korean.
really different from English. Of course, there are some sim- 5
ies between them, but they are mostly very different.

hen I came to the United States, I was afraid of people because I
i't know how to speak English. I couldn't read the signs around me
in English. It was hard to learn English in the beginning because it's
very different from Korean. For example, the subject comes first in 10
English and also in Korean but the verb comes at the end of the
sentence in Korean, not right after the subject like it does in English.

In Korean, there are not such things as articles. That is the reason I
often forget to put articles in sentences. In questions, Korean has more
ways to say than in English. When people ask questions as negatives in 15
English it is negative. No matter what people say, the answer has to be
"no," but in Korean it could be "yes" or "no." Making plurals of nouns
is very similar as English. In Korean we put one letter as "s" in English
but in Korean that's not really important. When people write, it
matters. But when people talk, they often don't use it. 20

Each language is unique, although there may be some similarities
between them. English and Korean are very important to me. There
are some differences and similarities between them but both are
important to communication and I am glad that I could learn English
and Korean. 25

Sohyung Kim, South Korea

Revising

With a partner, discuss Sohyung Kim's first draft, asking the following questions.

1. What specific words or ideas in the first paragraph make you want
   to read more?

2. What is the main idea that holds together the entire piece of
   writing?

3. What are the supporting details—facts, observations, and experiences that support the main points?

4. What in the final paragraph tells you as a reader that the piece of
   writing is complete?

5. What one idea will remain with you after reading this essay? Why
   did you choose this particular idea?

When you finish discussing Kim's essay, reread your own essay. Keep in mind that your writing is not in its final form. With your partner, discuss your writing using the same five questions you used when discussing Kim's. Then rewrite your essay, keeping your partner's suggestions in mind. Share your revision with your partner.

Editing Strategies

Vocabulary Development

in

Review the article about Khan Duong, noting how often the preposition *in* is used. This exercise will help you become familiar with the use of *in* in place expressions. Two examples have been chosen from the article. Find three more examples, and write them in the blanks.

in class

in Elmhurst

_____

_____

_____

These examples show that *in* is used to give the feeling of being inside or within something, whether it be a country, a city, an apartment, or a box. We use the following expressions:

in class	in the fish tank
in a factory	in the car
in a small boat	(*but not* in the floor)

What is the difference in meaning between "*in* the refrigerator" and "*on* the refrigerator"? Between "*in* the desk" and "*on* the desk"?

A few special expressions involving transportation use *on*:

on the train

on the bus

on the plane

on the ship

□ □ □

EXERCISE   Fill in the blanks in the following sentences with either *in* or *on*.

1. The cousins live _____ Elmhurst, _____ a two-bedroom apart-

   ment _____ the third floor.

2. Every afternoon Khan Duong gets _____ a bus to go to work

   _____ a factory where she puts filling _____ Chinese-style
   steam buns.

3. When Khan Duong puts her hands _____ the piano keyboard, she
   feels happy.

4. Thuong Hua used a pot holder to reach _____ the oven to check

   the chicken; then she looked at the soup pot _____ the stove.

5. The cousins stay _____ their apartment on the weekends because

   they are afraid to get _____ the train to go to Manhattan.

■ ■ ■

make and *do*

The words *make* and *do* have very special uses in English. As you read
the following paragraph, underline *make* and *do* each time they appear,
along with the words that directly follow them. The first three have
been done for you.

Every evening Khan Duong and Thuong Hua <u>do the cooking</u>. They
<u>make an effort</u> to <u>make a meal</u>* that everyone will enjoy. Usually it
takes a while to make dinner, but at other times they make do with
leftovers. After dinner, Vinh does the dishes. They do without television so that they can begin to do their homework early. The family
members try to make time to do the housework too, but they usually
have to wait for the weekend. Then they do the wash at the laun-
dromat. They do all the floors; they mop the kitchen and the bathroom

*In some parts of the United States, people say "fix a meal" or "fix dinner."

and vacuum the living room and the bedrooms. Soon it is Monday morning again. When the alarm rings, they get out of bed, do a few exercises, make their beds, and make breakfast. Then they rush off to school and, as usual, try to do their best in all their classes.

Make a list of the *make* and *do* phrases you underlined. The first three have been done for you.

Make	*Do*
make an effort	do the cooking
make a meal	_____
_____	_____
_____	_____
_____	_____
_____	_____
_____	_____
_____	_____

Write five sentences using *make* and *do* to describe things that you typically do at home.

Note: *Homework* and *housework* are always singular, without a final *s*:

I do my homework for all my classes after I finish dinner.
He does all his housework on Saturday.

Fill in the blanks in the following sentences with *homework* or *housework*.

_____ is schoolwork, assignments for classes.

_____ is cleaning work done in a person's home.

Now answer these questions, using *make* and *do*.

1. In your family, who usually makes dinner?
2. Who usually does the dishes?
3. What time of day is best for you to do your homework?
4. Do you prefer to do your homework in a quiet atmosphere or with the radio or television playing?
5. Before you leave the house for school, do you usually have enough time to make breakfast? To do the dishes? To make your bed? To do exercises? To do housework? To do homework?

Commonly Confused Words

they're/there/their

This exercise focuses on words that are often confused in writing because they are spelled differently but pronounced the same. These words are called *homonyms*. Looking at these words in context should help you understand how they are used.

There are many reasons why Khan Duong and her cousins find life in the United States difficult. *They're* afraid to talk to new people because of *their* English. They do not realize that *they're* not alone; many people in the United States are learning English as *their* second language.

Examining this paragraph should help you complete the following definitions.

_____ means "they are."

_____ means "belonging to them."

_____ means "in that place or at that point."

Fill in the blanks in the following sentence with *they're, there,* or *their*.

Khan Duong and her cousins would like to succeed in _____

education so _____ trying very hard, but _____

are many problems and responsibilities that are making it hard for

them.

Now write sentences of your own using each of these words.

Mechanics

Plurals

One common problem in editing writing and looking for surface errors is recognizing plural forms. Test your knowledge of plurals in the next paragraph by circling and correcting each singular noun that should really be a plural. There are 20 missing plurals. Can you find them all?

Thousands of man, woman, and child have left Vietnam to come to the United State. They have had to leave their parent, friend, and family behind. When these person arrived, they suffered many crisis; often they found their life were difficult. They had to attend class to learn the new language, and they usually had to move to overcrowded city in order to get job opportunity. Traditionally, person have come to the United State from country all over the world. Despite the many difficulty of adjusting, these immigrant give a vitality to the country, and the country offers many possibility to these newcomer.

Turn to page 320 to check your answers. If you made more than two mistakes, review the following rules.

regular plurals

The regular plural of a word is usually formed by adding an *-s* to the singular form. The article about Khan Duong and her family has many examples of regular plurals.

Singular	*Plural*
cousin	cousins
parent	parents
newcomer	newcomers

Can you find three more examples of regular plurals in the article? List them with the singular forms on the left.

_____　_____

_____　_____

_____　_____

special plurals

Many words follow special rules to form their plurals.

Words that end in a consonant (*b, c, d, f, g*, etc.) plus *y* form their plurals by changing the *y* to *i* and adding *-es*.

body	bodies
country	countries
baby	_____
library	_____
city	_____
family	_____

Words that end in a vowel (*a, e, i, o, u*) plus *y* form their plurals by adding *-s*.

journey	journeys
attorney	_____
ashtray	_____
boy	_____
highway	_____

Words that end in *s, sh, ch, ss, zz,* or *x* usually form their plurals by adding *-es*.

plus	pluses	mattress	_____
brush	brushes	wish	_____
patch	patches	watch	_____
class	classes	business	_____
fizz	fizzes	buzz	_____
wax	waxes	tax	_____

Words that end in one *z* usually double the *z* and add *-es*.

quiz   quizzes   whiz   _____

Words that end in *o* usually form their plurals by adding *-es.*

tomato   tomatoes   hero   _____

veto   vetoes   mosquito   _____

Many words that end in *f* or *fe* form their plurals by changing the *f* to *v* and adding *-es.*

life   lives   housewife   _____

knife   knives   yourself   _____

leaf   leaves   wolf   _____

calf   calves   half   _____

There are some exceptions to this rule, however.

roof   roofs
belief   beliefs

irregular plurals

Some words have irregular plurals. This means that the plurals have special forms and do not use the regular *-s* form we have already learned. Here are some examples of irregular plurals:

man   men   woman   women
child   children   foot   feet
tooth   teeth   goose   geese
mouse   mice   ox   oxen

Here are some other words with special plurals:

Singular	*Plural*
crisis	crises (crucial turning point in politics, story, play, or everyday life)
criterion	criteria (standard or rule to judge something by)
axis	axes (fixed or center line about which things are arranged, as in a graph or on a globe)
medium	media (means or agency; instrument of communication)

false plurals

Some words that end in *s* are not plural. These words are treated as singular in sentences. They are followed by the singular form of the verb, as you can see in the following examples.

news	No news is good news.
	The news is on television at 6 o'clock.
measles	Measles is a very contagious disease, and many children get sick from it.
mumps	Even though it is usually not a serious sickness for children, mumps is often dangerous for adult males.

uninflected plurals

There are also a few words, mostly the names of animals, for which the plural form is the same as the singular form.

sheep	One sheep always gets lost from the flock.
	There are thousands of sheep in New Zealand.
fish	The shiny silver fish is swimming downstream.
	They saw hundreds of fish in the aquarium.
deer	The deer is a very graceful animal.
	Many deer live in the woods.
moose	The moose is a large animal that looks like a deer.
	Moose have large antlers.

□ □ □

EXERCISE   In the following paragraph there are 20 missing plurals. Using what you have just practiced, make the corrections.

Khan Duong and her family are not all that unusual. There are many family of young man and woman and sometimes even child from many country all over the world who are living in and trying to adapt to the big city of the United State. At first, they get lost trying to find bus that will take them to job, library, movie, and school. They have many difficulty communicating with their new neighbor. Eventually, though, their life begin to make sense again. The successful one start their own business, make new friend, find new responsibility, and develop new strategy for living in their new country.

Editing Practice

The following piece of writing would be easier to read if it were divided into sentences and paragraphs. Read it with a classmate and mark where new sentences should begin and where it should be divided into a second paragraph. Check your answers on page 321. As a second step, create your own compound and complex sentences, as described on page 63, to help you practice sentence variety.

One part of learning a new language involves learning to use the language with others. Recently, a researcher in the way people learn languages wrote that if people want to learn how to talk in a second language, they should not be afraid to make mistakes, they should make contact with speakers of the new language, they should ask for corrections, and they should memorize dialogues, if students want to learn to read, they should read something every day, they should read things that are familiar, they should look for meaning from the context without always looking at the dictionary, to gain confidence, they should start by reading books at the beginner's level.

□ □ □

PAIRED EXERCISE

After reading and editing this paragraph about language learning, write an essay with a partner in which you describe which strategies mentioned in the paragraph would help Khan Duong to improve her understanding of English. Include in your essay why you think these strategies would be helpful for her and which of them have been useful to you in learning English.

Grammar Strategies

The Present Perfect Tense

Examine the following sample sentences. Then fill in the blanks in the paragraph and sentences that follow.

She has not missed a day of school since she began.
They rarely get to Manhattan and have gone to a movie only once in three years.

> Miss Duong has been at the school for three years.
>
> It has taken her several years to get accustomed to her new lifestyle.

In the present perfect tense, the word _____ follows the
                                              (has/have)
subject *she*. The word _____ follows the subject *it*. Since we
                              (has/have)
know that *it* is third person singular, we can assume that *he* is followed

by the word _____. The third person plural, *they*, is followed
                 (has/have)
by the word _____.
                 (has/have)

To make the present perfect tense negative, add *not* between *have* or
has and the past participle.

She has _____ missed a day of school.

You have _____ looked at the mail.

Adverbs such as *always, never,* or *rarely* belong between *have* or *has*

and the _____ _____.

> She has never missed a day of school.
> It has never snowed in New Jersey in July.

To form a question, place *have* or *has* in front of the _____.

> Has she missed any days of school?
> Have they been to Connecticut?

The present perfect tense has two uses. The first is to embrace the
past, the present, and the future all at once.

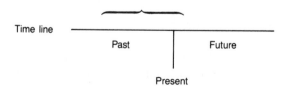

Time line

Past   Future

Present

I have started each day in the same manner for the past 80 years.

The second use is to indicate the indefinite past. The present perfect tense is used in this case when the specific time when something occurred is not important; what is important is that it ever occurred at all.

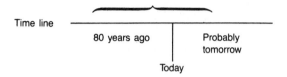

Time line

80 years ago Today Probably tomorrow

They have learned to speak three languages fluently.

It does not matter when we heard this. If when we heard it is important, we use the past tense:

She played the piano last week.

Read the following dialogue, observing how the present perfect tense is used.

AN INTERVIEW WITH A SUCCESSFUL STUDENT

TEACHER: I noticed that your grades have improved recently and that you have become a more successful student. What have you learned that you think would help other students?

STUDENT: You're right. I have changed. When I think about it, I guess I have changed in three main ways.

TEACHER: What are they?

STUDENT: When I first came here, I used to look up every word that I didn't know in the dictionary. Many times I didn't understand the dictionary meaning, and even if I did, I would forget the new words very fast. Now I have learned to read the next few words or sentences before I go to the dictionary. I have found that sometimes I can figure out the word from the context of the rest of what I am reading.

TEACHER: That's interesting. How else have you changed?

STUDENT: At first, I was afraid to talk to my teachers when I had a problem. I thought that it was my fault and that they would think that I wasn't intelligent.

TEACHER: Oh.

STUDENT: I have discovered that in college in the United States, teachers expect students to ask questions. In fact, I have learned a lot from asking questions. I also have gotten to know some of my professors too. I have also told a couple of professors that they were speaking a little fast for me to understand them. At first, I was nervous about this because I thought that they would get annoyed. But they didn't. One even thanked me for telling her, and she has begun to speak a little slower.

TEACHER: That sounds like good advice. What else have you learned that has helped you become more successful in college?

STUDENT: Well, I always used to study alone. Then one of my teachers suggested that a small group of us meet as a study group. At first, I didn't like it, and I didn't say much. But now I always try to say at least something each time we meet. Not only that, but I have discovered that I learn from listening and talking to other students.

TEACHER: Your advice sounds very important. I think that other students will learn from you.

STUDENT: I hope so. These things have made a big difference for me.

☐ ☐ ☐

EXERCISES

1. Reread this interview, underlining each use of the present perfect tense. Decide with a classmate why that tense was used in each instance.
2. Discuss the following questions.

   a. What changes has the student made that have affected his college success?
   b. How does this student's experience in college compare with your own?
   c. What changes have you made in your own learning strategies that have helped you achieve success?

Contrasting Tenses

The Simple Present and the Present Perfect

Decide which tense you prefer in each of the following sentences.

1. She _____ long lists of vocabulary words and _____ a
      (keep)   (not, miss)

   day of school since she began.

2. What _____ her story and that of her cousins different,
      (make)

   however, _____ that they _____ so young and that they
                (be)   (be)

   _____ this challenge entirely on their own ever since they
      (face)

   arrived in the United States.

3. Yet even those who _____ in her class 40 minutes a day, five
(be)

days a week, _____ understand the scope of the problems
(not, do)

linked to her troubles learning English.

4. Because money _____ tight, they rarely _____ to Manhat-
(be)   (get)

tan and _____ to a movie only once in three years.
(be)

5. Miss Duong, who already _____ at the high school three years,
(be)

_____ afraid that unless her English _____ soon, she
(be)   (improve)

may be denied a diploma.

The Present Continuous and the Present Perfect

Decide which tense you prefer in each of the following sentences.

1. Khan Duong _____ at Newtown High School although she
(fail)

_____ very hard to succeed ever since she arrived.
(try)

2. Miss Duong _____ at the high school for three years, and she
(be)

_____ trouble with several subjects.
(have)

3. Miss Hua _____ better than Miss Duong, even though they
(do)

_____ together.
(study, always)

4. Because they _____ life in New York to be expensive, every
(find)

member of the family except Vinh, who is only 9 years old,

_____ to earn some money.
(try)

5. They _____ their neighbors, many of whom _____
(meet, not)   (learn)

English as a second language too.

□ □ □

EXERCISE   Using the following sentence to begin your writing, write a paragraph
about your own experiences learning English.

I have studied English for _____ years, and I have found a few
strategies that have helped me to improve.

CHAPTER FIVE

Succeeding in School

PREREADING ACTIVITIES

1. Spend about five minutes writing the answer to the question "What is an American?" Discuss your answers in class.
2. As a class, talk about your experiences with teachers in the United States and in any other country in which you have attended school. Discuss some of the differences in teaching styles that you have observed.
3. In a group, make a list of the characteristics that teachers should have to help their students to learn. If there was disagreement in your group, explain how you resolved the disagreement.

Student-Teacher Relationships

Gary Althen has been the foreign-student adviser at the University of Iowa for many years. He has also lived and worked in Peru and Malaysia. This excerpt is from his book American Ways: A Guide for Foreigners in the United States. *In this book, Althen uses the term* American *to refer to a citizen of the United States. Although he is aware that there are differences among people, he tries to describe general patterns of behavior in his book.*

My adviser wants me to call him by his first name," many foreign graduate students in the U.S. have said. "I just can't do it! It doesn't seem right. I have to show my respect."

On the other hand, professors have said of foreign students, "They keep bowing and saying 'yes, sir, yes, sir.' I can hardly stand it! I wish 5 they'd stop being so polite and just say what they have on their minds."

Differing ideas about formality and respect frequently complicate relationships between American professors and students from abroad, especially Asian students (and most especially female Asian students). The professors generally prefer informal relationships (sometimes, 10 but not always, including use of first names rather than titles and family names) and minimal acknowledgment of status differences. Many foreign students are accustomed to more formal relationships and sometimes have difficulty bringing themselves to speak to their teachers at all, let alone address them by their given names. 15

The characteristics of student-teacher relationships on American campuses vary somewhat, depending on whether the students involved are undergraduate or graduate students, and depending on the size and nature of the school. Graduate students typically have more intense relationships with their professors than undergraduates do; at smaller schools student-teacher relationships are typically even less formal than they are at larger schools.

To say that student-teacher relationships are informal is not to say that there are no recognized status differences between the two groups. There are. But students may show their difference only in subtle ways, mainly in the vocabulary and tone of voice they use when speaking to teachers. Much of their behavior around teachers may seem to foreign students to be disrespectful. American students will eat in class, read newspapers, and assume quite informal postures. Teachers might not enjoy such behavior, but they tolerate it. Students, after all, are individuals who are entitled to decide for themselves how they are going to act.

American teachers generally expect students to ask them questions or even challenge what they say. Teachers do not generally assume they know all there is to know about a subject. Nor do they assume that they invariably explain things clearly. Students who want clarification or additional information are expected to ask for it during the class, just after class ends, or in the teacher's office at the times the teacher has announced as "office hours." Students who do not ask questions may be considered uninterested or uncommitted.

While most teachers welcome students' questions and comments about the material being covered in the course, they do not welcome student efforts to negotiate for higher grades. Teachers normally believe that they have an acceptable system for determining grades, and, unless it seems possible that a mistake has been made, teachers respond very negatively to students who try to talk them into raising a grade. Some foreign students, particularly ones from countries where negotiating is a habit, severely damage their reputation in teachers' eyes by trying to bargain for better grades.

Reading and Thinking Strategies

Discussion Activities

Analysis and Conclusions

1. What problem does Althen describe in paragraphs one and two? What effects could this problem have on the relationships between teachers and students?

2. From your own observation, what behaviors do teachers in the United States seem to value in students? What does this tell you about the culture in the United States? From your observation, what behaviors do teachers in other countries in which you have studied value in students? What does this tell you about the culture in that country?

3. In many classrooms in the United States today, the teacher is from one culture and the students are from many different cultures and countries. What effects might this have on the classroom? What suggestions do you have to help people in the classroom get to know each other better?

Writing and Point of View

1. Althen moves from the specific to the general in this selection. Where does this happen in the writing, and why do you think he does this?

2. What audience do you think Althen is writing this for? If you were writing this to help teachers in the United States understand students from different cultures, what changes would you make in the selection?

3. What is Althen's point of view about student-teacher relationships? Does he state his point of view? Why do you think this is so? What is the purpose of this piece of writing?

Personal Response and Evaluation

1. Althen states that American teachers often prefer informal relationships with their students. Have you found this to be true? If so, why do you think this is the case?

2. Althen states that students from some cultures have difficulty asking questions in class. Have you found this to be true? If so, what can these students do so that their teachers know that they are interested and involved in the class?

3. The words of a language are only part of what you learn when you live in a new country and learn a new language. What cultural differences have you observed?

Group Activity

After reading and discussing the Althen article, as a group project, make a list of suggestions that will help a student become successful in college in the United States. When you have completed this list, you may want to share it with other classes and compare your ideas with the students in those classes.

Journal Writing

> A primary reason for my success in the classroom was that I couldn't forget that schooling was changing me and separating me from the life I enjoyed before becoming a student.
>
> RICHARD RODRIGUEZ, *Hunger of Memory*

What you write in your journal should come from inside you, from your own experiences. Here are some suggestions that may help you decide what you want to write:

Think about your experiences learning English. Think about the Rodriguez quote. Has it been easy for you? What kinds of problems have you had? Have you discovered anything about yourself by learning a new language? Do you like English? Do you feel or act differently when you speak English? When you dream, what language do you dream in?

One student wrote in his journal, "It hurts my ears to listen to English for a long time. The sounds are sharp and come by so fast that I get a headache listening to it." Have you ever felt this way?

Writing Strategies

Essay Strategies

Specific Details

Writers use specific details to tell about experiences that they have had in their own lives, that other people they know have had, and that they have read about or seen in movies or on television. Writers often use direct quotations or detailed descriptions to make these specific details come alive to the reader.

☐ ☐ ☐

EXERCISES

1. Reread the article about Khan Duong on pages 69–71, looking for specific details about her life.
2. Reread Sun Park's essay on pages 3–4, looking for specific details about her life.
3. Reread the Althen selection on pages 90–91. Where does he use specific details? Why?

■ ■ ■

Generalizations

Writers sometimes use ideas or statements that emphasize the extensive or general qualities of a subject. These statements are broad and somewhat imprecise, so writers must be careful not to use *always* or *never* when they write such general statements. If they do, readers will think that the writers are exaggerating. When using generalizations, writers must support them with specific details to convince readers that their sweeping statements are logical and realistic.

☐ ☐ ☐

EXERCISES

1. Reread the Althen selection, looking for his use of the word *generally*. Every time you find this word, underline the entire sentence. Why did he use *generally* in these sentences?
2. Reread the Kleiman article on pages 69–71. What generalizations does Kleiman make about Khan Duong?
3. Reread the Berger selection on pages 21–22. What generalizations do the Bergers make about families?
4. Reread the Sun Park essay on pages 3–4. What generalizations does Park make in this essay?

Essay Form

Using Inductive Reasoning

When writers support their ideas, they often begin with specific details and then use these details to lead to a generalization about an idea or a problem. The type of logical thinking that moves from specific details to a broad idea or belief is referred to as *inductive reasoning*.

Althen uses specific examples of talk from students and teachers in the first two paragraphs to lead the reader to his generalization in paragraph 3.

Using Deductive Reasoning

Writers often vary their approach to ordering their ideas. They may begin with the general statement or assertion and then follow this with the specific details that support the main assertion. This type of logical thinking is referred to as *deductive reasoning*.

☐ ☐ ☐

EXERCISES

1. Reread the Althen article to find examples of inductive reasoning. Then find examples of deductive reasoning.

2. Review the article on Khan Duong on pages 69–70 to find the specific details that Kleiman used to support her generalizations. Did she rely on inductive or deductive reasoning in the examples you have identified?
3. Review the Sun Park essay on pages 3–4 to find the generalizations. Did Park rely on inductive or deductive reasoning in the examples you have identified?
4. With a classmate, look at one of each other's essays and together decide where and why you used inductive or deductive reasoning.

Suggestions for Writing

Before you begin to write, try brainstorming with a small group, as described below. You may also want to look in your journal for ideas. When you do begin to write, keep your audience in mind. Try to make your writing interesting to your readers as well as to yourself.

1. Write an essay titled "Student-Teacher Relationships," describing your observations attending school in a country other than the United States.
2. Write an essay comparing the schools in another country in which you were a student with the schools in the United States.
3. Write an essay in which you describe an effective teaching style and explain why you think that teaching style helps students.
4. Write an essay to other ESL students in your school who are trying to become successful in a U.S. college, advising them what they should do to improve their chance for success in college.
5. Over a billion people in the world speak more than one language fluently, yet many people in the United States are reluctant to learn a second language. Based on your experience, write an essay convincing students in your college born in the United States that it is important to learn a second language.

Getting Started

Small Group Brainstorming

Meet in a small group to discuss possible topics for writing. Each person should have a notebook open to an empty page. As you are talking together, every time you hear an idea or a word that makes you think about writing your essay, jot it down. After several minutes of talking, each of you should have a list of ideas and words.

As you brainstorm in the group, ask each other *who, what, where, when, why,* and *how* questions about schools, teachers, and students. When each of you has enough ideas, read through your list of ideas and words and add any details that you will develop later in your writing.

Revising

Writing is a personal experience, but it is also a communicative activity. One way to find out how your writing communicates your ideas is to share it with a peer. Practice doing the following revising activity using the two drafts of Mohibur Rob's essay on pages 96–98. When you finish discussing Rob's essay, reread your essay with a classmate. Keep in mind that your writing is not in its final form. As you read now, you may want to make changes. You may add or delete ideas. You may want to move or remove sentences or paragraphs. You may decide that other words express your meaning better.

Ask your partner the following questions about your writing, and write the replies on a piece of paper that you will refer to when you revise.

1. What in the first paragraph makes you want to read more?
2. What specific details does the writer use?
3. What generalizations does the writer include?
4. Does the writer use inductive or deductive reasoning?
5. Does the draft have a clear ending so that a reader knows the piece is completed?

Write your revision, and share it with your partner.

A Student Essay (First Draft)

Teaching is the basic way to educate the student. It differs from country to country. My native country is Bangladesh, and its teaching method and education system is much different from the United States of America. Here are a few comparisons between the two countries. 5

The basic teaching system of Bangladesh is very different from the United States of America. In Bangladesh, teachers lecture in the class and ask the students to follow the lecture and memorize the book. To get the good grade, students should write what the teacher lectures in class and whatever is written in the book. If some students have 10 different opinions than the teacher, they will not get good grades in the examination. But in America when teachers lecture in class, students take notes, study different books, and draw their own opinions. These opinions could differ from the teacher's opinion and conception. As long as the students can prove their logic, they will get good 15 grades. In this way, students in America develop their own opinion and ideas.

The examination system of both countries is also very different. In Bangladesh, most of the schools and colleges have two major examinations throughout the year. One is midterm and the other is final 20 examinations. The formats of the examinations are also different. Students have to write five or six essay questions in the examination. But in America, there is a semester system and there are many examinations throughout the year or semester. There are three formats of the examination. One is multiple-choice questions, another is true- 25 false questions, and the third one is essay type questions. These examinations are cumulative.

In Bangladesh, teachers are respected like parents. Students respect the teachers and obey their words. Students must pay attention when a teacher teaches the class. If teachers find someone who is not paying 30 attention, that student will be punished by standing on the chair, standing in front of the class, or the teacher can throw that student out from that class. In the elementary class, the teachers can beat the student. All students must be in the class as long as the teacher is present in the class. If someone wants to go out of the class, that 35 student needs permission from the teacher. In the United States of America, beating students or punishing in front of the class is not possible. Students can go out from the class whenever they want to, and they don't need permission from the teacher. Students treat the teacher like a friend, not a parent. They also respect the teachers. 40

As a matter of fact, there are many differences in the teaching systems between the two countries. Both countries have their own ways of teaching methods and educational systems, depending on economic, social, and cultural positions.

Mohibur Rob, Bangladesh

A Student Essay (Revised)

Although most educators agree that teaching is the basic way to educate a student, teaching itself differs from country to country. For instance, my native country is Bangladesh, and its teaching method and educational system are much different from those of the United States of America. In this essay, I will discuss a few differences between 5 the two countries.

The basic teaching system of Bangladesh is very different from that used in the United States of America. In Bangladesh, teachers lecture in the class and ask the students to follow their lectures and memorize the books. To get a good grade, students should be able to write exactly 10 what the teacher lectures in class and whatever is written in the book. If some students have different opinions from the teacher and they express these, they will not get good grades in their examinations. But in America it is different. When teachers lecture in class, students take notes, study different books, and draw their own opinions. These opinions could differ from the teacher's opinion and conception. As long as the students can prove their logic, they will still get good grades. In this way, students in America are encouraged to develop their own opinions and ideas.

The examination system of both countries is also very different. In Bangladesh, most of the schools and colleges have only two major examinations each year: midterms and final examinations. Not only is this different from America, but also the formats of the examinations are different. Students have to write five or six essay questions in the examination. However, in America, there is a semester system, and there are many examinations throughout the two semesters each year. There are three basic formats for examinations: multiple-choice questions, true-false questions, and essay questions. Some teachers create combinations of these three types of examinations, too. The examinations are cumulative, and a student's grade is based on an average of the various tests.

Classroom behavior is different in the two countries as well. In Bangladesh, teachers are respected like parents. Students respect the teachers and obey their words. Students must pay attention when a teacher teaches the class. If teachers find someone who is not paying attention, that student will be punished by being made to stand on a chair or stand in front of the class, or the teacher can throw that student out of the class. In the elementary classes, teachers can beat students. All students must be in the class as long as the teacher is present. If someone wants to go out of the class, that student needs permission from the teacher. In the United States of America, beating students or punishing them in front of the class is not possible. Students can leave the class whenever they want to, and they don't need permission from the teacher. Students treat the teacher like a friend, not a parent. They also respect the teachers, but in a different way, not through fear.

As a matter of fact, there are many differences in the teaching systems of the two countries. I have focused on only a few of these. Both countries have their own teaching methods and educational systems. Each country's system seems to work for its particular population.

Mohibur Rob, Bangladesh

□ □ □

EXERCISES

1. Read the first and second drafts of Rob's essay. With a partner, discuss the specific changes he has made in his writing.

2. Decide with a classmate which draft of the essay you prefer and why. Would you recommend that he make any other changes to improve the essay?

Editing Strategies

Use of the Definite Article

the

Read the following paragraphs from *Language Two* by Heidi Dulay, Marina Burt, and Stephen Krashen, noticing how the word *the* is used with country names.

Over a billion people in the world speak more than one language fluently. In the Philippines, for example, many people must speak three languages if they are to engage fully in their community's social affairs. They must speak the national language, Pilipino; one of the eighty-seven local vernaculars; and English or Spanish. In small countries, such as the Netherlands or Israel, most children are required to study at least one foreign language in school, and sometimes several. Most adults in the Netherlands speak German, French, and English in addition to Dutch. Even in the United States, whose inhabitants are notoriously unconcerned about languages other than English, about 10% of the residents usually speak at least one language in addition to English in the course of their daily lives. Throughout much of the world, being able to speak at least two languages, and sometimes three or four, is necessary to function in society.

Find four country names in the excerpt you just read. Copy them in the spaces provided below. If *the* comes before the country name, copy it too. The first one has been done for you.

the Philippines   *the Netherlands*

the United States   *Israel*

Notice that some place names occur with *the* and some do not. *The* does not occur with names of continents:

Australia   Africa

South America   Europe

In general, *the* does not occur with country names:

France   Turkey
Japan   Chile

unless the name of the country refers to a political union or association:

the United Arab Republic   the British Commonwealth

or unless it uses common nouns plus a proper noun with an *of* phrase:

the Dominion of Canada   the Kingdom of Thailand

or unless it is plural:

the West Indies   the United States

In general, *the* does not occur with names of cities:

New York   Paris
Bangkok   Caracas

The is used for names of mountain ranges:

the Himalayas   the Alps

but it is not used with the name of a single mountain:

Bear Mountain   Mount Everest

The is used with most bodies of water:

the Pacific Ocean   the Red Sea
the Mississippi River

but it is not used with lakes and bays:

Lake Erie   Hudson Bay

unless they are plural:

the Great Lakes   the Finger Lakes

The is used with deserts, forests, and peninsulas:

the Sahara   the Black Forest

the Gobi Desert   the Iberian Peninsula

The is used with the names of geographic areas and points on the globe:

the Northwest   the Midwest

the South Pole   the equator

The is not used with names of languages:

Mandarin   Arabic   Spanish   Korean

These are some of the rules for using *the* with place names and languages. Apply these rules to the following sentences. Write *the* in the space if it is needed; otherwise leave the space blank.

1. _____ English is the primary language spoken in _____ Australia, which is located between __*the*__ Indian Ocean and __*the*__ Pacific Ocean.

2. The enormous land mass extending from _____ Russia in __*the*__ north to _____ Iran in __*the*__ south and eastward via _____ Afghanistan and _____ Pakistan to __*the*__ northern India and _____ Bangladesh is predominantly Indo-European in speech.

3. The Malayo-Polynesian language family includes languages spoken in _____ Indonesia, _____ Madagascar, __*the*__ Philippines, and other islands as far east as _____ Hawaii.

4. The Sino-Tibetan group is the second largest language family in number of speakers; the major languages in this group are __*the*__ Burmese, dialects of _____ Chinese, _____ Thai, and _____

Tibetan. However, the majority of speakers in this group speak

_____ Mandarin and _____ Cantonese.

5. Some important language families are found on the continent of

_____ Africa and throughout __*the*__ Middle East.

□ □ □

OPTIONAL EXERCISE

Use the rules you have just learned to correct the six *the* errors in the following paragraph. In some cases you will need to delete *the*, and in others you must add *the*.

My best friend moved to the New Jersey from the Philippines three years ago. Now she lives in the Hoboken and she can see *the* Hudson River and the boat that travels up to the Bear Mountain each day. She has learned to speak the English and she plans to travel to the Canada next year as an exchange student.

Commonly Confused Words

advice/advise

"I would like to give you some *advice* about how to act in your college classes, if you don't mind," said my new friend.
"I would appreciate it if you would *advise* me as to the best way to succeed in this school," I reassured my friend.

Notice how *advice* and *advise* are used in the preceding sentences. Now complete the following definitions.

_____ is a noun that refers to an opinion given to help or counsel someone.

_____ is a verb that refers to the making of recommendations to help or counsel someone.

Fill in the blanks in the following sentences with *advice* or *advise*.

1. Some people do not like to receive _____ from strangers.

2. They believe that people who _____ others often do not have enough experience with the situation themselves.

3. My experience is to listen to _____ whenever it is sincerely offered, but I always maintain the right to reject the

   _____, too.

4. She always likes to _____ her friends, but she should

   listen to some _____ sometimes herself, too.

□ □ □

EXERCISE

Write about the best piece of advice you have ever received and the worst piece of advice you have ever received. Explain how you made your choices.

Mechanics

Capital Letters

When editing for surface errors, many writers have difficulty with capital letters. Test your knowledge of capital letters by trying to find the 30 missing capital letters in the following paragraph.

Sung Hee moved to massachusetts from korea. She attended boston university and lived in a dorm with her cousin. She began to work on saturday nights at filene's, a big department store, and she practiced english with her customers. on sundays Sung Hee usually rented a little chevrolet from avis. Carrying a tourist book called *inside massachusetts,* she visited such historic sites as plymouth rock and the old north church. She spent hours at the boston public library looking at the john singer sargent murals. She met tony at a midnight showing of *casablanca,* and last christmas they said "i do." Now she is teaching tony korean and planning to travel home to introduce him to her family.

Turn to page 321 to check your answers. If you had more than two mistakes, review the following rules.

Capital letters are used for the following terms:

1. The first word in a sentence, names of people, and the pronoun *I*:

   My friend thinks that I will be able to read Shakespeare soon.

2. Names of the months, days of the week, and holidays:

   Miguel was born in November, on the fourth Thursday, Thanksgiving Day.

3. Names of particular places, languages, and nationalities:

   The Brazilian girl in my class speaks French because she went to Le Havre High School in Montreal.

   Note: Do not use capital letters if the specific names are not used:

   He enjoys attending college and working in a store, but he likes to have time to visit museums and churches.

4. Titles of books, magazines, newspapers, stories, articles, films, television programs, songs, and poems:

   When I saw Aida she was carrying *The Silent Language*, *Omni*, and the *Washington Post*.
   She was going to see the movie *Hamlet* with her class.

5. The first word in a direct quotation:

   Tony said, "You can really do a lot if you try."

6. Brand names of products:

   The man bought Pampers and Pepsi-Cola at the A&P.

7. Names of religious and political groups, companies, corporations, and clubs:

   Françoise joined the Republican party when she was in college, but she became less active when she started to work for General Motors because she was very busy with her job, her commitment to Catholicism, and to Literacy Volunteers of America.

□ □ □

OPTIONAL EXERCISE

The following paragraph has 35 missing capital letters. Can you find them all?

when mikhail and fatima volunteered to work one afternoon in the western college post office, they were in for a surprise. in one corner, there were many boxes piled high. they found three heavy cartons of french language tapes addressed to professor maude cousteau, now of the ford foundation. she had left the school back in february and had moved to new mexico. fatima accidentally opened a box filled with the lotus 1-2-3 programs needed for the college ibm computers. "mr. smith, this post office is a mess," mikhail told the postmaster. "i know it, son. we just have to get a little more organized. the u.s. mail has to go through, and we will do it. soon." mikhail and fatima left there wondering if the college mail would ever get through.

The answers are on page 321.

Editing Practice

All writers make surface errors in their first drafts. Sometimes it is difficult to find your own errors, but practice will help you improve your editing skills. Here we present a first draft that contains four subject-verb agreement errors, three preposition errors, four *the* errors, three plural errors, thirteen capital letter errors, and three inconsistencies in person. Find and correct these errors. Answers are on page 321.

Marie learn languages very easily. She was born on haiti and has spoken the french and the creole all her lives. Now marie also know the english, spanish, and italian. She has a special technique that always work for her. At night you go to sleep by hypnotizing yourself as you stare at a poster of the stained-glasses window of notre dame cathedral on the paris. Her sony walkman tape deck is in her head, and she listen to a different language tapes each night.

Grammar Strategies

Point of View/Voice

Everything that is written is written from someone's point of view or perspective. When we write, we must decide who will narrate or be the voice for what we write. We have several voices to choose from; we refer to these as "persons."

There are first person singular and plural, second person singular and plural, and third person singular and plural. First person singular is *I*. First person plural is *we*. Second person singular is *you*. Second person plural is *you*. Third person singular is *she, he, it, one,* or a singular subject. Third person plural is *they* or a plural subject.

In general, first person is more personal and third person is more formal. We rarely use second person for essay writing. Whatever person is used, it is important to maintain a consistent point of view. If a writer moves from person to person in a single piece of writing, it can be confusing to the reader. In the following paragraph, the writer did not maintain a consistent person. Change the paragraph to make it consistent.

We can learn about language learning by observing yourselves. The problems that they have can probably be generalized to other language learners. Although they may think that English is more difficult to learn than another language, David Crystal, a noted linguist, tells us in his book *Linguistics* that there is no such thing as a most complex language. "A thing is more difficult to do depending on how much practice we have had at doing it and how used we are to doing similar things." Based on that statement, you can learn that if we really want to learn a new language, we must practice.

The Future Tense

will

One of the most common ways of expressing the future and making predictions is to use *will* followed by the simple form of the verb.

	Singular	*Plural*
First Person	I will study	we will study
Second Person	you will study	you will study
Third Person	he will study she will study it will ring*	they will study

*What is wrong with using *it will study*?

Here are some sample sentences using the future tense:

The teacher *will* expect you to ask questions in class.
Students *will* dress casually in most classes.

The Althen article at the start of this chapter discusses some of the expectations that teachers in colleges in the United States have for their students. For the most part, the article is written in the present tense.

□ □ □

EXERCISES

1. As a group, change paragraphs 6 and 7 to the future tense. What changes did you have to make?
2. Use the information from Exercise 1 and your own experiences to write a letter of advice to a friend or relative who is about to enter school in the United States. Tell that person what to expect in classes in the United States.
3. Use your own experiences to write a letter of advice to an American friend who is about to travel to your home country and attend school there. Tell that person about the school and about teachers' expectations.
4. In the following paragraph, notice the patterns for creating negatives and questions with *will*.

   Lecture classes will seem difficult to some students who are learning English. Often teachers will talk fast unless you ask them to slow down. Many teachers will not explain difficult words and ideas. You will have to raise your hand or go to see them after class. During office hours, you will ask your teacher politely, "Will you explain Picasso's cubism again? I am a little confused about some of his paintings that you showed in class today. I will be glad to come back to see you if this is a busy time for you."

   a. When you create a negative with *will*, where does *not* belong?

Note: The contraction *won't* is often used in writing and conversation instead of the full form *will not*.

    b. When you ask a question with *will*, where does the subject belong?

_____

    5. Write two questions using *will* that you will ask of a classmate—for example, "What will you do this weekend?" Ask your questions of the person sitting to your right. (If there is no one to your right, ask the questions of anyone you choose.)

■ ■ ■

be going to

    When we speak about the future, we often use *be going to*. This form is sometimes used in writing, but it is more common in speech. When you hear it spoken, *going to* may sound like "gonna" or "gunna." However, it means the same thing as *will* and can often be used interchangeably. However, there are some special uses for each. *Going to* is often used to express specific future plans or intentions, whereas *will* is almost always used to express promises, requests, offers, and predictions. *Will* is more often used in formal writing than *be going to*.

    I *am going to* go to the movies tomorrow night.
    They *are going to* get married next month.
    He promises that he *will* (*is going to*) return the car tonight.
    Will you lend me $5?
    Will anyone trade a ticket to the football game for $50?
    It *will* (*is going to*) snow tomorrow.

☐ ☐ ☐

EXERCISES

    1. Write a paragraph telling what you are going to do next weekend. (If you do not have any plans, you may want to write about what you are going to do next month or next summer.)
    2. Imagine that you are a fortune teller who can make predictions about the future. Write a paragraph telling what you believe will happen in your family, your city, or your country in the next year. Or write a paragraph telling what will happen to some of the characters in a television program you have seen or a book or story you have read.

Pronouns

    The pronouns have been left out of the following sentences. On the basis of what you know about sentence structure, fill in the appropriate pronouns.

1. Many foreign graduate students in the U.S. have said, "_____

   adviser wants _____ to call _____ by _____ first name.

   _____ just can't do _____."

2. On the other hand, some professors have said of foreign students,

   "_____ keep bowing and saying 'yes, sir, yes, sir.' _____ can

   hardly stand _____. _____ wish _____ would stop being so

   polite and just say what _____ have on _____ minds."

3. Graduate students typically have more intense relationships with

   _____ professors than undergraduates do; at smaller schools
   student-teacher relationships are typically even less formal than

   _____ are at larger schools.

4. American teachers generally expect students to ask _____ ques-

   tions or even challenge what _____ say.

   Refer to the Althen selection on pages 90–91 to check your answers.
   If you had difficulty, refer to the pronoun chart that follows and do
   the Optional Exercise on page 111.
   In general, a pronoun takes the place of a noun. To determine
   which pronoun to use, you need to know its referent, the noun to
   which it refers. For example, in the sentence before this one, to what
   noun does *it* refer? _____

Pronoun Chart

Subject	Object	Possessive		Reflexive
I	me	my*	mine	myself
you	you	your*	yours	yourself
she	her	her*	hers	herself
he	him	his*	his	himself
it	it	its*	—	itself
we	us	our*	ours	ourselves
you	you	your*	yours	yourselves
they	them	their*	theirs	themselves

*These words are not used alone. They are followed by nouns or subject words.

Pronoun Rules

1. **Pronouns take the place of nouns. Pronouns must refer clearly to the nouns they replace.**

   When she graduated from high school, they wanted her to go to college, but she thought she should get a job.

   Who is "she"? Who are "they"? You should make clear all the characters or topics in your story or essay before you use a pronoun.

2. **Pronouns should not shift point of view unnecessarily.**

   On the other hand, you know how important it is to get an education.

   Who is "you"? The reader, the writer, a friend of the reader's? Unless there is a clear reason to use *you*, it can be confusing to the reader.

   Rewrite the sentence to make it clearer.

   _____

   She listened to it, and in the end I applied to college and got a job at night.

   Who is "I"? The paragraph is written in the third person. Why does the writer suddenly shift the point of view?

   Rewrite the sentence to make it clearer.

   _____

3. **Pronouns must agree in number with the word or words they replace.**

   We want you to get that degree and have an easier life than we've had. She listened to it, and in the end I applied to college and got a job at night.

   What is "it"? Her parents are two people, and they said several things.

   Rewrite the sentence to make it clearer.

   _____

□　□　□

OPTIONAL EXERCISE

A fable is a fictitious story that is meant to teach a lesson called the *moral*.

The following is a famous fable told by Akiba Ben Joseph, a great scholar and head of the school for rabbis in Palestine in the first century. Fill in the appropriate pronouns. Answers are on page 322.

Once upon a time there was a smart young man who decided to trick a wise old man. _____ caught a little bird and held _____ in one hand behind _____ back. The boy approached the wise man and said, "Sir, _____ have a question for _____. _____ want to see how very wise _____ are. _____ am holding a bird in _____ hand. Is _____ alive, or is _____ dead?"

The boy thought that if the man said the bird was dead, _____ would open _____ hand to reveal the live bird, but if the man said the bird was alive, _____ would crush the bird, killing _____. The old man stared into the boy's eyes for a long time. Then _____ said, "The answer, my friend, is in _____ hands."

What is the moral of this fable?

Additional Writing Practice

Writing a Fable

Every country in the world has fables or stories that are told to and read to children to help them learn the moral lessons of life. In some of these fables, the main characters are animals; in others, they are humans.

□ □ □

EXERCISES

1. Write a fable that you remember from your childhood to share with the other members of your class. You may write the moral at the end of the fable, or you may ask members of your class to decide the moral.

2. Create your own fable to share with the members of your class. You may write the moral at the end of the fable, or you may ask members of your class to decide the moral.
3. Read the following fable, written by Jennifer Pram-On Korakot, a student from Thailand.

Berry Stupid

Strolling along by a tranquil river one morning, Billy Bob saw some berries on the water. He hadn't had breakfast that morning, so he was very hungry. Looking at the berries resting so peacefully on the water, his stomach started growling for food. Without hesitation, Billy Bob dived into the water to get the berries. Little did he realize that the water was shallow. As he crawled out of the water, the only berry Billy Bob had was a berry-sized bump on his head. As he sat by the riverbank rubbing his head, he looked up and realized the berries in the water were a reflection of the berries hanging from the tall berry tree above him.

Moral: Look before you leap.

CHAPTER SIX

Communicating and Caring

PREREADING ACTIVITIES

1. The story you will read in this chapter is by Ernest Hemingway. Based on what you know about him or his writing, what do you expect to find in the story?
2. Discuss some of the differences you have noticed in living in two different cultures.
3. If you or anyone you know has been sick in the United States, did you have any problems in getting help, getting medicine, or communicating to someone what was wrong?

A Day's Wait

Ernest Hemingway (1899–1961) was an American writer who often wrote about relationships. The story "A Day's Wait" is about one day in the life of a father and his young son who is suffering from the flu and a mysterious fear.

*H*e came into the room to shut the windows while we were still in bed and I saw he looked ill. He was shivering, his face was white, and he walked slowly as though it ached to move.

"What's the matter, Schatz?"

"I've got a headache." 5

"You better go back to bed."

"No. I'm all right."

"You go to bed. I'll see you when I'm dressed."

But when I came downstairs he was dressed, sitting by the fire, looking a very sick and miserable boy of nine years. When I put my 10 hand on his forehead I knew he had a fever.

"You go up to bed," I said, "you're sick."

"I'm all right," he said.

When the doctor came he took the boy's temperature.

"What is it?" I asked him. 15

"One hundred and two."

Downstairs, the doctor left three different medicines in different colored capsules with instructions for giving them. One was to bring

°laxative, cleanser of the bowels

down the fever, another a purgative,° the third to overcome an acid condition. The germs of influenza can only exist in an acid condition, 20 he explained. He seemed to know all about influenza and said there was nothing to worry about if the fever did not go above one hundred and four degrees. This was a light epidemic of flu and there was no danger if you avoided pneumonia.

Back in the room I wrote the boy's temperature down and made a 25 note of the time to give the various capsules.

"Do you want me to read to you?"

"All right. If you want to," said the boy. His face was very white and there were dark areas under his eyes. He lay still in the bed and seemed very detached from what was going on. 30

I read aloud from Howard Pyle's *Book of Pirates;* but I could see he was not following what I was reading.

"How do you feel, Schatz?" I asked him.

"Just the same, so far," he said.

I sat at the foot of the bed and read to myself while I waited for it to 35 be time to give another capsule. It would have been natural for him to go to sleep, but when I looked up he was looking at the foot of the bed, looking very strangely.

"Why don't you try to go to sleep? I'll wake you up for the medicine." 40

"I'd rather stay awake."

After a while he said to me, "You don't have to stay in here with me, Papa, if it bothers you."

"It doesn't bother me."

"No, I mean you don't have to stay if it's going to bother you." 45

I thought perhaps he was a little lightheaded and after giving him the prescribed capsules at eleven o'clock I went out for a while.

°partly frozen rain

It was a bright, cold day, the ground covered with a sleet° that had frozen so that it seemed as if all the bare trees, the bushes, the cut brush and all the grass and the bare ground had been varnished with 50

°dog often used for hunting

ice. I took the young Irish setter° for a little walk up the road and along a frozen creek, but it was difficult to stand or walk on the glassy

°slid

surface and the red dog slipped and slithered° and I fell twice, hard, once dropping my gun and having it slide away over the ice.

°drove out of hiding
°flock or group
°a type of wild birds

We flushed° a covey° of quail° under a high clay bank with over- 55 hanging brush and I killed two as they went out of sight over the top of the bank. Some of the covey lit in trees, but most of them scattered into brush piles and it was necessary to jump on the ice-coated mounds of brush several times before they would flush. Coming out while you were poised unsteadily on the icy, springy brush they made difficult 60 shooting and I killed two, missed five, and started back pleased to have found a covey close to the house and happy there were so many left to find on another day.

At the house they said the boy had refused to let any one come into the room. 65

"You can't come in," he said. "You mustn't get what I have."

I went up to him and found him in exactly the position I had left him, white-faced, but with the tops of his cheeks flushed by the fever, staring still, as he had stared, at the foot of the bed.

I took his temperature. 70

"What is it?"

"Something like a hundred," I said. It was one hundred and two and four tenths.

"It was a hundred and two," he said.

"Who said so?" 75

"The doctor."

"Your temperature is all right," I said. "It's nothing to worry about."

"I don't worry," he said, "but I can't keep from thinking."

"Don't think," I said. "Just take it easy."

"I'm taking it easy," he said and looked straight ahead. He was 80 evidently holding tight onto himself about something.

"Take this with water."

"Do you think it will do any good?"

"Of course it will."

I sat down and opened the Pirate book and commenced to read, but 85 I could see he was not following, so I stopped.

"About what time do you think I'm going to die?" he asked.

"What?"

"About how long will it be before I die?"

"You aren't going to die. What's the matter with you?" 90

"Oh, yes, I am. I heard him say a hundred and two."

"People don't die with a fever of one hundred and two. That's a silly way to talk."

"I know they do. At school in France the boys told me you can't live with forty-four degrees. I've got a hundred and two." 95

He had been waiting to die all day, ever since nine o'clock in the morning.

"You poor Schatz," I said. "Poor old Schatz. It's like miles and kilometers. You aren't going to die. That's a different thermometer. On that thermometer thirty-seven is normal. On this kind it's ninety- 100 eight."

"Are you sure?"

"Absolutely," I said. "It's like miles and kilometers. You know, like how many kilometers we make when we do seventy miles in the car?"

"Oh," he said. 105

But his gaze at the foot of the bed relaxed slowly. The hold over himself relaxed too, finally, and the next day it was very slack° and he cried very easily at little things that were of no importance.

°limp

Reading and Thinking Strategies

Discussion Activities

Analysis and Conclusions

1. What is the relationship between the boy and his father? Did you think it was odd that the boy's mother did not figure in the story?

2. Why do you think Schatz didn't just tell his father what he was afraid of? Why wouldn't he want his father to know that he was afraid? What does this say about the father? About the son?

3. Does Hemingway help you to picture the boy and the father? How did you see them? Describe what the father looks like. Describe what the boy looks like. When you read, do you usually picture the characters inside your head? Does it help you if the author describes the characters carefully, or do you prefer to use your imagination?

Writing and Point of View

1. For the first half of the story, we do not know who the narrator (teller of the story) is; in other words, we do not know from whose point of view the story is being told. When you began reading the story, who did you think "I" was? What clues did you have?

2. When Schatz asks his father if "it" will bother him, what is "it"?

3. Fiction creates a mood or a feeling. What is the mood of this story? What elements or parts of the story create this mood? Some things to think about are these: In what season does the story take place? Where does it take place—the city or the country? What does the father leave the house to do? Are the boy and the father alone in the house? Do we meet any other characters?

Personal Response and Evaluation

1. If you were Schatz's father or mother, how would you have handled the situation?

2. Have you had any similar experience with a child?

3. If Schatz were a girl, how would the story change? Why?

Response Paragraph

1. As soon as you finish reading "A Day's Wait," write a paragraph describing how the story made you feel and what personal memo-

ries it brought to your mind. Share your paragraph with a class-mate.

2. Write a paragraph explaining how Schatz's confusion about the temperature corresponds to some of the confusion felt by Khan Duong and her family (see page 69). Have you ever felt confused by cultural differences? Share your paragraph with others in a small group.

Journal Writing

First, I do not sit down at my desk to put into verse something that is already clear in my mind. If it were clear in my mind, I should have no incentive or need to write about it. . . . We do not write to be understood; we write in order to understand.

C. Day Lewis, *The Poetic Image*

Writing in a journal, whether it is shared or kept for yourself, is powerful. It is a means of touching on feelings and experiences hidden inside yourself. Allowing the journal to express your deepest self will have a positive effect on all your writing.

"A Day's Wait" is about a fundamental fear in life, the fear of dying. It is about a boy's unexpressed fear and in some ways his unexpressed love as well. Have you ever felt afraid? Have you ever thought about dying? Did this story make you think about your parents and your relationship with them when you were a child?

Writing Strategies

Essay Strategies

Developing Your Writing Using Sensory Details

In Chapter Five, we discussed the use of details to support the main idea or to help form generalizations. Details are also used to make writing vivid and exciting, to help the reader fully experience what is being described.

Sensory details come to us through our senses—sight, smell, hear-ing, touch, and taste. When we write, we carefully choose words that describe our sensory experiences. Look at the differences in these two pairs of descriptions:

My bedroom is pretty, and it is my favorite room.
My bedroom is painted lavender, except for the windows, which

are white. There is a big, fluffy rug on the floor where I usually lie down to do my reading and homework.

My sister's baby is cute and cuddly.
My sister's baby has big, brown eyes and soft, dark hair. His skin is as soft as a pile of cotton balls. His fingers are so strong that when he holds on to my hair, I have to pull with all my strength to get it away from him.

As a reader, which of each pair of descriptions is easier to picture? As a writer, when would you use the shorter description and when would you use the more detailed description?

□ □ □

EXERCISES

1. Write two descriptions of a room that you know well—your living room, kitchen, or bedroom, for example. Write a short description and then a detailed description. Share both with a classmate. Discuss the differences and how you decide how much detail to include in your writing.
2. Write two descriptions of a room from your past—your fifth grade classroom or your old bedroom, for example. Follow the same steps as in Exercise 1.
3. Write two descriptions of scenes from nature—a sunset, a day at the beach, or a snowy day, for example. Follow the same steps as in Exercise 1.
4. Discuss what you have learned about your own writing from doing the practice writing in Exercises 1–3.

Essay Form

Describing a Place

When writers use description, they paint a picture with words. They try to present a clear and vivid picture of what they have experienced.
In "A Day's Wait," Ernest Hemingway writes:

It was a bright, cold day, the ground covered with a sleet that had frozen so that it seemed as if all the bare trees, the bushes, the cut brush and all the grass and the bare ground had been varnished with ice. I took the young Irish setter for a little walk up the road and along a frozen creek, but it was difficult to stand or walk on the glassy surface and the red dog slipped and slithered and I fell twice, hard, once dropping my gun and having it slide away over the ice.

1. What picture forms in your mind as you read this paragraph?
2. If you have never seen ice, what does Hemingway compare it to that will help you picture this wintry day?

In Mike Rose's book *Lives on the Boundary*, he writes:

Let me tell you about our house. If you entered the front door and turned right you'd see a small living room with a couch along the east wall and one along the west wall—one couch was purple, the other tan, both bought used and both well worn. A television set was placed at the end of the purple couch, right at arm level. An old Philco radio sat next to the TV, its speaker covered with gold lamé. There was a small coffee table in the center of the room on which sat a murky fishbowl occupied by two listless guppies. If, on entering, you turned left you would see a green Formica dinner table with four chairs, a cedar chest given as a wedding present to my mother by her mother, a painted statue of the Blessed Virgin Mary, and a black trunk. I also had a plastic chaise lounge between the door and the table. I would lie on this and watch television.

1. What picture forms in your mind as you read this paragraph?
2. What do you know about Mike Rose's family from reading about their living room?

A student from Afghanistan, Zelimin Sarwary, writes about a visit to the home of a family friend, Nasema:

The dining room was in a square shape about 18 feet wide. Nasema, as was customary, had no dining table or cabinet in her dining room. Instead of a cabinet for china wares, the dining room had four shelves which Nasema decorated with antique things such as ancient spoons, plates, glasses, teapots, cups, china, and so on. The decoration of the dining room made my mother enjoy Nasema's delicious home-cooked meals even more. Because Nasema had no dining table, she had to use a cloth on the floor and place the food on it.

There were three bedrooms of equal size, one white, one pink, and one light green. Nasema and her children slept on the soft comfortable cotton mats, the "toshaks," that the Afghan people sleep on. The colors are sometimes coordinated with the walls. The bathroom was large and was without a shower. Seldom did Nasema wash herself and her children at home. Regularly they went to a "hammom" or sauna because it was warm and more comfortable than home where there were not so many people.

The simple hammom Nasema used held about four hundred people. It had five different rooms for different purposes. The very first room was used by those who paid money to the cashier and their clothes were kept there. The second was used for changing clothes. It had about twenty benches. Each bench seated about ten people. In the third room, people washed their bodies. It had two white and black stone "Dake Done" or communal bath tubs, one for hot water and the other for cold water. Against the wall, there were two cubicles. For some reason, the people called those two cubicles the "Bride's House." They had only cold water. People usually went there at the very end and took a cold shower. After that, they went to the dressing room to get dressed. There were a few masseuses for the customers. The women's hammom was separated from the men's but up to five-year-old boys were allowed to go with their mothers. People in Afghanistan believe that up to five-year-old boys are not mature enough to think about sex.

After the hammom, Nasema and my mother stayed up half the night talking about the Soviet invasion of Afghanistan. They both cried. Night passed and the following morning came.

1. What picture forms in your mind as you read this descriptive essay?

2. What do you know about Nasema and Afghanistan from reading this essay?

Suggestions for Writing

Before you begin to write, you may want to review your journal or any other writing you have done for this chapter. Try clustering to help you get ideas, as described in the "Getting Started" section on page 121. Always spend some time thinking before you begin to write.

1. Imagine that Schatz is a girl. Rewrite the story, making whatever changes you think should occur.

2. Have you ever had an experience like Schatz's in which you were afraid to reveal your true feelings to an adult? Tell the story of this experience, and tell what you learned from it.

3. Learning to communicate in a new language or culture can create confusing situations such as Schatz's or Khan Duong's. Reread those two selections, and think about the experiences and problems presented. Then write an essay about a similar situation and your solution to the problem. What have you learned from your experience?

4. Reread Zelimin Sarwary's essay about Afghanistan (pages 119–20). Write an essay describing a familiar place that you know well from your past. Use many sensory details so that your reader can experience the place as fully as possible.

5. Write a story that teaches other students in your class something about your culture or background that they do not know. In the story, carefully describe the setting or place where the story occurs.

Getting Started

Clustering

Sometimes even though we have ideas about a subject, we cannot seem to write them down. The blank page fills us with fear. One technique that may help you overcome this problem is clustering. It is a simple but effective method to get started writing.

First, begin with a blank notebook page. In the middle of the page, write your nucleus word (the key concept you will be writing about) and circle it. (In our example, the nucleus word is *father*.) Then write down any other words that occur to you; circle these words and draw arrows connecting your original word to them.

Write the words down quickly, just as they occur to you. Connect words where you think they belong together. When something new occurs to you, go back to the nucleus and draw a new arrow and circle. You can have as many circles as you have ideas. Don't try to make sense, and don't worry if the clustering doesn't seem to be going anywhere. If you temporarily run out of ideas, doodle a little bit by drawing your circles or arrows darker. Keep clustering until you get a sense of what you are going to write. Then stop clustering, read the ideas in the circles, and start to write.

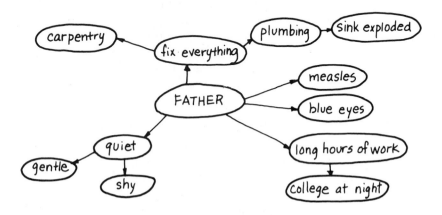

There is no right or wrong way to form clusters. When you start to write, the words will come and begin to take over; the writing will come easily. Don't stop yourself. Let it happen and see what occurs in your writing.

☐ ☐ ☐

EXERCISES

1. Begin with a clean page. Write the word *fear* in the middle of the page and circle it. Let your mind begin to make connections. You may want to close your eyes. When a word comes to you, write it on the page, circle it, and draw an arrow to it from your nucleus or from its connecting word. Let yourself go, and do not judge or even really think about what you are writing. You will know when to stop when you feel a strong urge to write, when you suddenly know what you want to say. Then glance at your word clusters and begin writing on a new page. Write until you feel that you have written out all your ideas. You may want to look at your clustering again to see if you had any ideas that you did not develop. Then read what you have written, and spend a few minutes making any changes that you think will improve the piece of writing.

2. Do the same with the word *father* or *mother*.

Revising

When you have finished writing your essay, separate yourself from your writing by reading the following student essay. Then practice by revising this essay.

A Student Essay

Nine years ago, I used to play with my friends in the playground in front of my school. We were sitting down in the grass. Where I was sitting, I didn't see a big green insect near my hands. Suddenly, the insect bit me in my right palm. Since I was with my friends, I didn't cry because they might think I am a "cry baby." 5

I ignored the pain. When I got home, I acted like nothing happened to me, but I was hiding my hand because it was swollen. My big brother came home from school, and he started to play a joke on me. He grabbed my right hand and said, "You're getting fat," and then I told him an insect had bitten me. I asked him not to tell my mother, but he 10 took my other hand and compared the two. He said that my right hand was swollen and I would have to go to see a doctor. He ran into the kitchen and told my mother. My mother called me and looked at my hands. The color of my hand had changed to yellowish because of the pus and probably the poison from the insect. 15

My mother took me to a doctor. The doctor gave me a big, long needle and then stuck another needle in my hand to suck out all the pus and poison. My mother was watching, and then she fainted be-cause she has high blood pressure. After a few minutes she got up, and I was sitting next to her. When she asked me if I was all right, I said, 20 "I'm fine."

On our way home, I was thinking that maybe it would be better not to tell her something like this if it happened again. I realized that some people who have illnesses get sicker when they panic. So either I will tell her, but she will not go to the hospital with me, or I will not tell her 25 at all. What do you think?

Marina Ibea, The Philippines

Write the following questions on a separate piece of paper and answer them first about either Marina Ibea's or Zelimin Sarwary's writing. When you have finished thinking about either of these student essays, you will have given yourself time to separate from your own writing so that you can look at it now from a fresh perspective. Copy the questions again, and write the answers to them after reviewing your own essay.

1. What is the main point of the draft?
2. What is the best sentence in the entire piece of writing?
3. What is the weakest sentence in the entire piece of writing?
4. Are the same words used over and over? How can some variety be added to this writing?
5. Is there any place in the writing where the ideas do not connect? If so, how can this be improved?
6. Does the conclusion work; does it tie the ideas together?

Editing Strategies

Idiomatic Expressions

Each of the following paragraphs contains a context clue that will help you understand some of the idiomatic expressions used in the short story. Underline these context clues; the first one has been done for you. Then use the expressions when you answer the questions that follow each paragraph.

1. *take it easy* (line 79)

Schatz cannot take it easy; he cannot <u>relax</u>. All he can do is worry about dying.

Sometimes when we have a problem, we cannot take it easy. Some people have special exercises such as yoga or meditation that help them to take it easy. What techniques help you to take it easy when you are nervous?

2. *after a while* (line 42)

At first Schatz is very afraid. Then he finds out about the different kinds of thermometers; after a while, he feels a little better. After some time has passed, he knows that he will recover.

After a while, did you begin to feel more comfortable speaking English? How long did it take?

3. *for a while* (line 47)

Papa goes out for a while. He leaves the house for a short amount of time.

Sometimes before we fall asleep, we may read for a while to help us relax. What do you do to help you relax for a while before you fall asleep at night?

4. *out of sight* (line 56)

When Papa is hunting, he tries to shoot the quail, but some of them fly out of sight so that he can no longer see them. When we say good-bye to someone at an airport, we may wait at the window and watch until the plane is too far away for us to see it.

What other experiences have you had of watching something until it was out of sight?

Now write sentences of your own using these idiomatic expressions.

Commonly Confused Words

your/you're

"You go up to bed," I said, "*you're* sick."
"*Your* temperature is all right," I said. "It's nothing to worry about."

Notice how *your* and *you're* are used in the preceding sentences. Now complete the following definitions.

_____ is a contraction of the words *you are*.

_____ means "belonging to you."

Fill in the blanks in the following sentences with *your* or *you're*.

1. "Did you lose _____ wallet?" the waitress asked, holding it in her hand.

2. "_____ going to have to practice every day if you want to compete in the Olympics," the coach announced.

3. "_____ visiting the Sears Building on _____ trip to Chicago, aren't you?" Willie asked.

Mechanics

The Apostrophe

The apostrophe creates an editing problem for many writers. In the following sentences, underline the words that have an apostrophe ('). Then examine the sentences to decide how it is used.

1. "What's the matter, Schatz?"
2. "I've got a headache."
3. When the doctor came, he took the boy's temperature.
4. I read aloud from Howard Pyle's *Book of Pirates*.

An apostrophe can be used in two ways:

1. It can be used in contractions to show that part of a word is missing.
2. It can be used to show possession, that something belongs to someone.

The apostrophe in sentences 1 and 2 is used to show _____.

The apostrophe in sentences 3 and 4 is used to show _____.

Note: Contractions are found mostly in dialogue and informal writing. The uncontracted forms are usually used in formal writing and speech. In the Hemingway story, contractions are used in the dialogue, but uncontracted forms are used in the narration and description.

☐ ☐ ☐

EXERCISES

1. In each of the following sentences, the apostrophe is used to indicate that part of a word is missing. In the blank, fill in the complete word. The first has been done for you.

_is___ a. "What's the matter, Schatz?"

_____ b. "I've got a headache."

_____ c. "No. I'm all right."

_____ d. "I'd rather stay awake."

_____ e. He'd better not get out of bed today.

_____ f. He's got a high temperature because of the flu.

2. The second use for the apostrophe is to show possession, that something belongs to someone. Fill in the blanks showing the possessive form.

   a. the bag that belongs to the doctor   *the doctor's bag*

   b. the father of Schatz   *Schatz's father*

   c. the dog that belongs to Papa   _____

   d. the car that belongs to Robert   _____

3. In the following paragraph, fill in the nine missing apostrophes and 12 quotation marks. Answers are on page 322.

   Ernest Hemingways story A Days Wait tells about a young boy who is afraid of dying. He hears the doctor say, His temperature is one hundred and two degrees. He remembers his friends at school in France saying, Schatz, you cant live with a temperature over forty-four degrees. The boys temperature is very high. You dont have to stay in here with me, he tells his father, if it bothers you. His father doesnt know whats really bothering the boy. When he finds out, he says, Schatz, its like miles and kilometers. Schatz believes his father, but still he doesnt relax for several days.

Editing Practice

The following paragraph is a first draft that has not yet been edited for surface errors. Correct the 11 capital letters errors, one missing set of quotation marks, four preposition errors, four *the* errors, and one *they're/their/there* error. Answers are on page 322.

My sister, hilda, lives on an apartment in the top of a high hill in the san francisco. She works as a computer operator on a big bank their, and when she looks out her window, she sees the golden gate bridge. She loves heights. She even flew on a private airplane over rocky mountains. Once she said to me, I saw both pacific and atlantic oceans in one day. She would like to travel around the world someday.

Grammar Strategies

Adjective Word Order

When we describe, we use adjectives—sometimes series of adjectives. In English, there is a required order for these adjectives. Below is a chart illustrating adjective word order. After studying the chart, read the sentences that follow it, using the words provided to fill in the blanks in the proper order. The first one has been done for you. Check your answers by referring to the chart. This chart is meant to help you when you write, but you do not have to memorize it. The more you

Articles and Possessives	*Numbers: Ordinal and Cardinal*	*General Descriptive Adjectives and Some Adjectives Ending in -ed, -ing, -y, -ful, -ous**	*Size**	*Shape*	*Age*	*Color*	*Adjectives of Nationality and Religion and Some Adjectives Ending in -ic, -al, -ed, -y*	*Noun Adjuncts*	*Nouns*
the	two		big	angular	old	green	air-conditioned	convertible	cars
her	three	lovely	little	slender	newborn	gray	Burmese		cats
Louise's		famous		long		blue	lacy	evening	gown
a		chipped	huge	square		blue and white	English	soup	bowl
a		weeping	tiny	round	old	gray-haired	French		lady
a	first	quick					comic		scream

*These positions are sometimes interchangeable.

write, the more familiar you will become with word order, and it will eventually become natural to you.

1. There stood, facing the open window, *a comfortable,*
   (roomy, comfortable, a, armchair)

   roomy armchair   .

2. The doctor examined the boy and then left the prescriptions for

   _____.
                          (medicines, three, different, the)

3. It was _____, the
                          (cold, a, day, bright)

   ground covered with sleet.

4. Papa took _____ for a
                          (two, the, setters, young, Irish)

   walk on the road.

5. Papa saw _____ staring
                          (face, tiny, Schatz's, angular)

   at him.

     The following sentences are not from the story. Fill in the adjectives in the order required. Refer to the chart if you have difficulty.

6. Papa climbed _____ to
                          (winding, the, staircase, long, dark)

   his room.

7. He sat at _____ and
                          (desk, old, wooden, carved, his)

   began to write.

8. Staring at his son's picture, he held _____
                          (old, his, pen, green, fountain)

   _____ in his hand.

9. He wanted to write, but suddenly he felt very tired; he sat on
   _____ and fell asleep.
         (plaid, the soft, old, brown)

□ □ □

EXERCISE   Describe a person you saw on the street today, using long strings of descriptive words. After you have finished, refer to the chart to check the order of your adjectives.

Society and Playing Roles

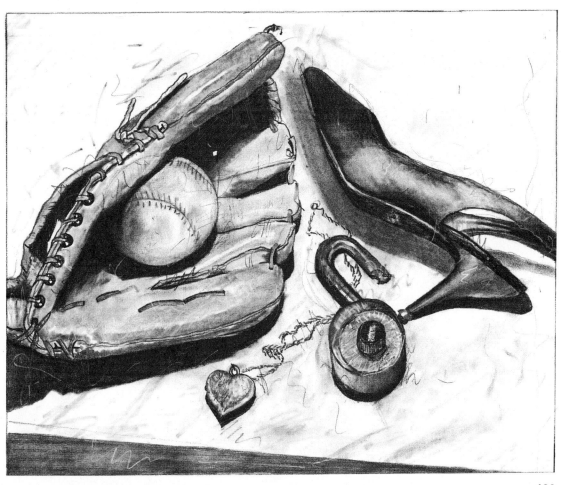

CHAPTER SEVEN

Dating Practices

PREREADING ACTIVITIES

1. In a group, discuss your observations about dating in the United States. Think about what you have seen on your college campus, on the streets, and at parties. What patterns have you observed in relation to who asks for the date, who pays, and how people act on dates?
2. In a group, discuss the way dating is portrayed on television, in books, and in the movies. What patterns have you observed in relation to who asks for the date, who pays, and how people act on dates?
3. Compare your personal observations with what is presented in the media. What differences do you find? How do you explain these differences?

Will You Go Out with Me?

The following article from Newsweek *was written by Laura Ullman when she was a student. Today she is a free-lance writer living in Los Angeles with her husband and daughter. Ullman enjoyed writing this article about the dilemma of whether or not a woman should ask a man out on a date, and she continues to write humorous articles about everyday life.*

°not patient; desirous to do something right away

°sport of jumping from an airplane, opening a parachute, and floating to the ground

Every day I anxiously wait for you to get to class. I can't wait for us to smile at each other and say good morning. Some days, when you arrive only seconds before the lecture begins, I'm incredibly impatient.° Instead of reading the *Daily Cal*, I anticipate your footsteps from behind and listen for your voice. Today is one of your late days. But I 5 don't mind, because after a month of desperately desiring to ask you out, today I'm going to. Encourage me, because letting you know I like you seems as risky to me as skydiving° into the sea.

I know that dating has changed dramatically in the past few years, and for many women, asking men out is not at all daring. But I was 10 raised in a traditional European household where simply the thought of my asking you out spells "naughty." Growing up, I learned that men call, ask and pay for the date. During my three years at Berkeley, I have learned otherwise. Many Berkeley women have brightened their social lives by taking the initiative with men. My girlfriends insist that it's 15 essential for women to participate more in the dating process. "I can't

131

°spoke out suddenly

°gather

°conventional or typical; characteristic

°worrying or bothering about

°kindly or politely

°opened the zipper

°refusal to accept a person or thing

sit around and wait anymore," my former roommate once blurted° out. "Hard as it is, I have to ask guys out—if I want to date at all!" Wonderful. More women are inviting men out, and men say they are delighted, often relieved, that dating no longer depends solely on their 20 willingness and courage to take the first step. Then why am I digging my nails into my hand trying to muster° up courage?

I keep telling myself to relax since dating is less stereotypical° and more casual today. A college date means anything from studying together to sex. Most of my peers prefer casual dating anyway because 25 it's cheaper and more comfortable. Students have fewer anxiety attacks when they ask somebody to play tennis than when they plan a formal dinner date. They enjoy last-minute "let's make dinner together" dates because they not only avoid hassling° with attire and transportation but also don't have time to agonize. 30

Casual dating also encourages people to form healthy friendships prior to starting relationships. My roommate and her boyfriend were friends for four months before their chemistries clicked. They went to movies and meals and often got together with mutual friends. They alternated paying the dinner check. "He was like a girlfriend," my 35 roommate once laughed—blushing. Men and women relax and get to know each other more easily through such friendships. Another friend of mine believes that casual dating is improving people's social lives. When she wants to let a guy know she is interested, she'll say, "Hey, let's go get a yogurt." 40

Who pays for it? My past dates have taught me some things: you don't know if I'll get the wrong idea if you treat me for dinner, and I don't know if I'll deny you pleasure or offend you by insisting on paying for myself. John whipped out his wallet on our first date before I could suggest we go Dutch. During our after-dinner stroll, he told me 45 he was interested in dating me on a steady basis. After I explained I was more interested in a friendship, he told me he would have understood had I paid for my dinner. "I've practically stopped treating women on dates," he said defensively. "It's safer and more comfortable when we each pay for ourselves." John had assumed that because I 50 graciously° accepted his treat, I was in love. He was mad at himself for treating me, and I regretted allowing him to.

Larry, on the other hand, blushed when I offered to pay for my meal on our first date. I unzipped° my purse and flung out my wallet, and he looked at me as if I had addressed him in a foreign language. 55 Hesitant, I asked politely, "How much do I owe you?" Larry muttered, "Uh, uh, you really don't owe me anything, but if you insist . . ." Insist, I thought, I only offered. To Larry, my gesture was a suggestion of rejection.°

Men and women alike are confused about who should ask whom out 60 and who should pay. While I treasure my femininity, adore gentlemen and delight in a traditional formal date, I also believe in equality. I am grateful for casual dating because it has improved my social life immensely by making me an active participant in the process. Now I can not only receive roses but can also give them. Casual dating is a 65 worthwhile adventure because it works. No magic formula guarantees "he" will say yes. I just have to relax, be Laura and ask him out in an unthreatening manner. If my friends are right, he'll be flattered.

Sliding into his desk, he taps my shoulder and says, "Hi, Laura, what's up?" 70

"Good morning," I answer with nervous chills. "Hey, how would you like to have lunch after class on Friday?"

"You mean after the midterm?" he says encouragingly. "I'd love to go to lunch with you."

"We have a date," I smile. 75

Reading and Thinking Strategies

Discussion Activities

Analysis and Conclusions

1. Why does Ullman think that men are pleased that women are asking them out?

2. In lines 51–52, why was John "mad at himself for treating" Ullman to dinner? In lines 55–59, why was Larry upset? Explain Larry's attitude about paying for a date.

3. According to Ullman, how has casual dating changed the dating situation in her college? How has it changed her social life?

Writing and Point of View

1. To whom is the first paragraph of the article addressed? Who is "you"?

2. The final paragraph is only one sentence long. Is this an effective conclusion to the article? Would you change it in any way?

3. What is Ullman's main idea? Did she convince you? What examples did she use to support her ideas?

Personal Response and Evaluation

1. Do you think it is easier for a woman to ask a man for a casual date or a formal date? Explain, using your observations or experiences.

2. Should women ask men out on dates? Explain, using your observations or experiences.

3. Who should pay for a date? Why? Would you ever "go Dutch" on a date?

Small Group Discussion

In a small group, discuss the best way to deal with one or more of the following situations.

1. Someone asks you on a date and you do not want to go, but you want to be polite to the other person.
2. Someone asks you on a date and your parents do not allow you to date yet.
3. Many of your college friends are dating, and one of them wants to set up a date for you. However, in your culture, people do not date casually.
4. You ask someone on a date. The person refuses and tells you that you two should just be friends.

As a class, discuss the results of your discussions. Some groups may role-play some of these situations for the entire class.

Journal Writing

It is well to understand as early as possible in one's writing life that there is just one contribution which every one of us can make: we can give into the common pool of experience some comprehension of the world as it looks to each of us.

DOROTHEA BRANDE, *Becoming a Writer*

Each of us has a unique vision of the world. We have all dreamed a personal dream of the person we will love. In addition to that dream, we have had real experiences. In your journal, write about the characteristics that you value in a friend or a date. Are these characteristics different from what you would value in a husband or a wife? Can men and women be just friends? Should men and women be friends before they get married? Do people who have arranged marriages fall in love? Is love necessary in order for a marriage to survive and be successful? Write about as many of these ideas as you choose.

Writing Strategies

Essay Strategies

Use of the Anecdote

Reread the first paragraph and the four final paragraphs of Ull-man's essay. Her essay begins and ends with an anecdote or short, amusing story taken from her own experience. Many writers use anec-dotes from their personal experience to enrich and personalize their writing. Using anecdotes is also an effective way to engage the reader, that is, to get the reader interested in reading what you have written. Audience engagement is an important aspect of successful writing. If the reader is interested in your writing, then communication is going on between writer and reader. This is the real purpose of writing.

Any anecdote you use should relate to the topic of your essay. Be sure you make a smooth transition from the anecdote to the body of your essay.

EXERCISES

1. Reread the first paragraph of the Kleiman article on page 69. The writer tells a short story about Khan Duong's daily life. In what tense is it written? Why? The second paragraph seems ironic at first. We ask ourselves how this hardworking student could possibly be failing. We are engaged; we want to read more.
2. Reread the Park essay on pages 3–4. What anecdotes or short stories does she tell that relate to her main idea? How do these anecdotes affect you as a reader?
3. Choose one of the student essays that have appeared so far in this book. Read it with a partner. Does the writer use anecdotes? If so, what is the purpose of the anecdotes? If not, what kind of anecdotes would you suggest that the writer add to make the piece more effective?

Essay Form

Writing an Explanation

In the Ullman essay, the author is explaining the dating patterns on her campus so that you will understand why she is going to ask out a male student. When you explain something in writing, you are making it clearer to a reader. Some of the steps that are useful in helping a writer to explain or teach something to a reader include these:

1. *Look around you* as you did in the "Prereading Activities" on page 131. Observe patterns in the way people act and think in relation to the subject you are going to explain. Or carefully observe the process you are going to explain in your writing. What in the Ullman essay tells you that she looked around her before she began writing?

2. *Define* your subject. Some writers use the dictionary or another source book to help them define the process or pattern about which they are writing. What does Ullman define in this essay?

3. *Describe* in detail the steps that are needed to understand the process or pattern. Readers see the picture through your words, so make them clear and direct. What specific descriptions did you find in the Ullman essay? How do they add to the overall effectiveness of the essay?

4. *Compare* your subject to others. What two types of dating does Ullman compare in this essay? Why does she make this comparison?

5. *Analyze* the parts or steps of the pattern or process you are explaining. Then tell how these steps work together. Tell the reader about the history and the future of your subject. What does Ullman include about her personal history in relation to dating? What does she tell the reader about the history of dating on her campus? What predictions does she make about the future of dating?

6. *Evaluate* the reasons why the pattern or process you are explaining is important for the reader to think about and know. What does Ullman write to convince you that the issue she is explaining is important to you as a reader?

You will not need to use all six of these steps in every essay that you write, but keeping them in mind can help you write clear and effective essays. Reread other essays in this book to evaluate which of these steps the writers used and how effectively they used them.

Suggestions for Writing

Choose one of the following topics to write about. Before you start writing, you may want to try the paired clustering activity in "Getting Started" on page 137.

1. Describe a first date, real or imagined. Use lots of detail to make the experience come alive for the readers. What made this date unique? Why did you choose to write about this particular date?

2. "There is no such thing as love at first sight. For love to be real, people must know each other for a long time and have many shared experiences." Do you agree or disagree? Support your point of view with your own experiences or observations.

3. Compare a casual date with a formal date. Consider such things as where people go, what they wear, and who pays for the date.

4. On the basis of your own observations, do you think that dating patterns have really changed in recent years? If you are a woman, would you ask a man out? If you are a man, would you go out with a woman who invited you? Would you go on a Dutch date? Should the man always treat?

5. "When a man wants to show a woman that he cares and respects her, he pays for their date." Do you agree or disagree with this statement? Support your point of view with your own experiences and observations.

6. Many people believe that men and women cannot really be friends. They feel that there is always an attraction between people of the opposite sex. Write an essay analyzing your feelings on this subject. Give examples from your experiences and observations.

Getting Started

Paired Clustering

In Chapter Six, you used clustering to help you think of ideas and get started writing. In this chapter, you will use a similar technique, except that you will work with a partner. One of you should write the word *dating* on a blank piece of paper. Draw a circle around the word and say all the words that come to your mind about dating. Each of you writes down words on the page as quickly as they occur to you. After about five minutes, stop and look at the cluster you have created.

Next each of you should choose as many of the words and ideas from the big cluster as you need to form your own personal cluster, which you will use when you begin to write.

A Student Essay

In recent years, dating patterns have changed. There are many things such as girls paying for the guys, girls asking guys out, and girls are not shy anymore.

In my family, my mom doesn't agree with girls paying for guys. However, it doesn't always go the old way anymore. When I go out with my girlfriend, she sometimes pays for the date. She doesn't believe that guys should pay all the time. She said that by letting guys pay, they tend to get the wrong ideas. By paying for the date, the guy would not have any wrong ideas.

When I was growing up, girls were not supposed to ask guys out. They would have to wait until guys asked them out. But now that has changed. My friend, Peter, was asked by a girl to go out on a date. He told me he was surprised to hear a girl ask him out, but he liked the idea of girls asking guys out.

Today's girls are not shy anymore. They see guys who are good-looking and they go to ask them out. In the old days, it was shameful to see girls asking guys out. Today it's not shameful, it's courageous.

I feel it is a good change for the girls because it gives them the right to choose anyone they want to go out with. There are many ways that dating has changed, some bad and some good, but I think girls asking out guys is good.

Koan Ung, Cambodia

Revising

With a partner, answer the following questions, looking at Koan Ung's essay on dating.

1. What in this essay tells you that the writer looked around and observed the way people act and think?

2. Did the writer define any terms or ideas?

3. What specific descriptions do you find in this essay? How do they add to the overall effectiveness of the essay?

4. What specific comparisons can you find in this essay?

5. Does the writer tell you about the history and the future of the subject of the essay? If not, would this add to your understanding of the subject?

6. Where in the essay does the writer evaluate the reasons why the subject is important for you to know about?

Next, with your partner, answer the same questions, looking at the draft of the essay that you have just written. Do the same with your partner's essay. Revise your draft, keeping in mind what you have discussed. Then share your revision with your partner.

Editing Strategies

Word Development

adverbs using -*ly*

One way to enhance your vocabulary is to learn new word forms based on words you already know. A common occurrence in English is for an adverb (a word that modifies a verb, an adjective, or another adverb) to be formed by adding -*ly* to an adjective. The following examples show how to combine sentences and change adjectives into adverbs.

She waits.

She is anxious

    She waits anxiously.

    Anxiously, she waits. (Notice the comma.)

She wants to ask him out.

She is desperate.

    She _____ wants to ask him out.

    _____, she wants to ask him out.

She accepted his treat.

She was gracious.

    _____

    _____

She asked a question.

She was polite.

    _____

    _____

He kissed her.
He was tender.

_____

_____

He spoke to her about where they would go.
He was quiet.

_____

_____

She flung her money on the table.
She was careless.

_____

_____

He told her he wished he hadn't paid for dinner.
He was angry.

_____

_____

_____

_____

Now use these adjectives and adverbs in sentences of your own.

Idiomatic Expressions

Each of the following paragraphs contains a context clue that will help you understand some of the idiomatic expressions used in Ullman's article. Underline these context clues; the first has been done for you. Then use the expressions when you answer the questions that follow each paragraph.

1. **go Dutch** (line 45)

   When friends go out together or when women ask men out on dates, they usually go Dutch. In this way, <u>each person pays for himself or herself.</u>

   Sometimes women prefer to go Dutch on dates. Why might a woman prefer to go Dutch? When would you choose to go Dutch on a date?

2. **chemistries clicked*** (line 33)

   Ullman describes a couple who at first were just friends. Then their chemistries clicked; they felt attracted to each other as lovers.

   When people's chemistries click, their relationship may become more serious. Have you heard of a friendship that changed when the couple's chemistries suddenly clicked?

3. **treat (someone) to (something)** (lines 48, 52)

   Ullman writes about a date with John during which he treated her to dinner. If someone pays for you to do something, that person treats you to it.

   On dates, the man often treats the woman to dinner. How would you let someone know that you want to treat him or her to something?

4. **take the initiative** (line 15)

   Women are beginning to take the initiative with men in relation to dating. In the past, the man was the one who made the first call and showed his interest in a woman.

   Men always took the initiative. Who do you believe should take the initiative in relation to dating?

**Chemistries clicked* is a colloquial expression that you would ordinarily not use in formal writing.

Commonly Confused Words

though/thought/through

Read the following paragraph; then complete the definitions that follow.

Even *though* Ullman's family *thought* it was not proper, she decided to try to ask a man out on a date. She *thought through* exactly what she would say. She asked him, *though* she felt sure he would say no. When she was *through*, he smiled and accepted. She *thought* she had succeeded.

_____ is the past tense of *think*.

_____ means "even if" or "and yet."

_____ means "in one side and out the other" or "from the first to the last of."

Fill in each of the following blanks with *though, thought,* or *through*.

1. She _____ he would say no, even _____ she hadn't even asked him yet.

2. As she watched him walk _____ the door into the

   classroom, she felt afraid, _____ her friends told her that everyone did it.

3. He helped her get _____ the ordeal by smiling at her.

Now write your own sentences using *though, thought,* and *through*.

☐ ☐ ☐

EXERCISE

Choose the present, past, or present perfect tense for each of the following sentences. Be prepared to explain your choice of tense.

1. Since I came to the United States, I _____ many
   (observed)

   different kinds of dating patterns.

2. Last week, a girl in my math class _____ me to meet
   (ask)

   her in the library to go over our homework.

3. She _____ the freedom of being able to ask a guy out.
   (enjoy)

4. We _____ to the cafeteria and _____
   (go)   (talk)

   about math for almost an hour.

5. I guess dating _____ in the past few years on many
   (change)

   college campuses.

6. Now almost everyone in my school _____ comfort-
   (feel)

   able about informal study dates.

7. However, when it _____ to formal parties and din-
   (come)

   ners, some of my classmates _____ of girls asking
   (not approve)

   guys out.

8. What do you think the students in your school _____
   (feel)

   about dating?

Mechanics

The Comma

All the commas have been left out of the following letter. Fill in the commas where you think they belong. Then check your answers on page 322.

March 14 1992

5516 Buena Vista Avenue
Miami Florida 33158

Dear Aunt Millie

I think you should sit down before you read this letter and I think you should have your handkerchief handy. I am sitting here in Santo Domingo with Luis your favorite nephew. He was happy to see me and he wants you to know how much he misses seeing you and the rest of the family. Luis said to give you 10000 kisses when I get home so I know I will be busy. I am sure you want to know how everyone else is but I have not traveled out to see the rest of the family yet. Well Luis says they are all fine. By the way he is married and he has a little girl. Just like that you are a great-aunt. Even though you have never seen her her name is Millie. Standing there with her short curly hair she looks just like you. Millie your new 4-year-old niece says "Hi!" I will bring you a picture of her some homemade candy and a crocheted scarf. I guess I will see you soon won't I?

Always

Carmen

Carmen

Commas are used in a great many ways.

1. Commas are used with dates:

    March 14, 1992

2. Commas are used with openings and closings of letters:

    Dear Aunt Millie,
    Always,

3. Commas are used with addresses:

    5516 Buena Vista Avenue, Miami, Florida 33158

4. Commas are used with numbers:

    10,000
    1,000,596

5. Commas are used between complete thoughts that are connected by coordinating words such as *for, or, and, yet, not, so,* and *but:*

    I think you should sit down before you read this letter, and I think you should have a handkerchief handy.
    He was happy to see me, and he wants you to know how much he misses seeing you and the rest of the family.

    Note: If the complete thoughts are very short, no comma is necessary:

    I arrived and he met me.

6. Commas are used to separate introductory material from the rest of the sentence:

   Well, Luis says they are all fine.
   Suddenly, the door opened.
   Just like that, you are a great-aunt.
   By the way, he is married, and he has a little girl.

7. Commas are used after introductory clauses beginning with *after, although, as, as if, because, before, even, even though, if, since, so that, though, unless, until, when, whenever, where, wherever, whichever, while,* and *whoever:*

   When she got the good news, Millie seemed happy.
   When she finally let me inside, she looked strange.
   Even though you have never seen her, her name is Millie.
   As she grabbed me around the waist, she looked deep into my eyes.

   Note: If these introductory clauses are short, the comma may occasionally be omitted:

   As she died she looked at us in amazement.

8. Commas are used after introductory *-ing* phrases:

   Standing there with her short curly hair, she looks just like you.

9. Commas are used to set off words that identify or repeat something in a sentence; these words could be omitted without changing the meaning of the sentence:

   Millie, your new 4-year-old niece, says . . .

10. Commas are used to set off quotations:

    Millie says, "Hi!"

11. Commas are used between items in a series:

    I will bring you a picture of her, some homemade candy, and a crocheted scarf.

12. Commas are used before tag questions (short questions added to a statement to seek confirmation):

I guess I will see you soon, won't I?

□ □ □

EXERCISE   Insert commas where they are necessary in the following paragraph.

Traveling to a different country whether it is returning home or going to a new destination is exciting. When the airplane arrives in the airport safely even people who travel often are glad. Suddenly they are in a new exciting world. Feeling tired they get off the plane and they head for their destination. They convert their money wait in line for taxis and spend too much money on foolish things. On the way home they feel mixed emotions but overall most of them are glad they took the chance and traveled.

Check your answers on page 323.

Editing Practice

The letter on pages 143–44 is all one paragraph. Decide where there should be paragraph breaks. Rewrite the letter, inserting the paragraph indentations and all necessary commas.

Grammar Strategies

Modal Auxiliaries

Modal auxiliaries are a special group of words including *can, could, have to, may, might, must, shall, will, would, should,* and *ought to.* These words are followed by the simple form of the verb ("I can *swim*," "He ought to *go*"). To make a modal negative, add *not* after the modal and before the verb ("I *will not* swim," "They *should not* eat that apple"). Modal auxiliaries are not usually indicators of time and tense, although most users of English agree that "I can swim" has a different time meaning than "I could swim."

Some of the uses for modals are as follows:

1. To make general requests (*can, could, will, would*) and to request permission (*may, might*):

   Can/Could/Will/Would you help me revise my essay?
   May/Might I borrow that book?

2. To show inference or prediction:

   Someone's ringing the doorbell.
   It *could/might* be Marie. (It's a possibility.)
   It *may* be Marie. (It's a strong possibility.)
   It *should* be Marie. (It probably is Marie.)
   It *will* be Marie. (It is definitely Marie.)

3. To show ability (*can, be able to*):

   I *can* swim.
   I *am able to* swim.

4. To offer advice (*might, could, should, had better, must, have to, will*):

   He *might/could* study English in school. (It's possible.)
   He *should* study English in school.
   He *had better* study English in school.
   He *must* study English in school.
   He *has to* study English in school.
   He *will* study English.

5. To show desire (*would like to*):

   She *would like to* learn English more quickly.

6. To present an offer (*would like*):

   Would you *like* something to eat?

7. To show preference (*would rather, would prefer to*):

   I *would rather* drink tea *than* coffee.
   I *would prefer to* drink tea instead of coffee.

□ □ □

EXERCISE   Read the following paragraph about the Ullman article, and underline the following modal auxiliaries: *can, can't, has/have to, had better, may, might, must, ought to, should, will, won't,* and *would rather.*

Ullman writes that at the University of California in Berkeley, women may ask men out on dates. They can feel comfortable because it is done all the time. Men ought to feel flattered, not threatened, when they are asked out by a woman. Some women would rather have men ask them out, but like Ullman, occasionally, they will ask men out on a casual date. The only problem is that women had better get ready to be rejected once in a while, too. Ullman thinks that dating in college should be casual and relaxed. Casual dating may help men and women feel at ease with each other, and, in the long run, that will help them when they have to make future partner choices.

Examine the use of the modal auxiliaries in the paragraph; then answer the following questions.

1. Is there any ending on the verb that follows the modal auxiliary?
2. In a group, reread each of the sentences and decide the meaning of each modal auxiliary as it is used.
3. In a group, rewrite this paragraph in the past tense. What changes would you have to make in the sentences and in the modal auxiliaries? Why would you make those changes?

Countables and Uncountables

Examine the following two sentences:

People have fewer anxiety attacks when they ask someone on a casual date than on a formal date.
People have less trouble when they ask someone on a casual date than on a formal date.

In the space provided, copy the words that are different in these two sentences.

_____

_____

One of these is countable and the other is uncountable.

Which is countable? _____

Which is uncountable? _____

If you had any difficulty, read the explanation that follows.

In English, certain nouns are uncountable. An article (*the, a, an*) is usually not used with an uncountable noun. Two basic types of uncountable nouns are *mass nouns* and *abstract nouns*. Mass nouns include liquids such as water, milk, soda, coffee, tea, rain; solids that are made up of many small particles such as sand, salt, pepper, snow; and gases such as air, hydrogen, oxygen, smoke. Abstract nouns include concepts such as love, hate, anger, fear, beauty, ugliness, intelligence, life, freedom, success, truth, and peace and categories such as money, furniture, merchandise, food, vocabulary, equipment, luggage, homework, advice, and information.

Uncountable nouns are treated as singular subjects and take singular verbs. They do not use an *-s* ending to show the plural.

> So much information is reported each day that no one can keep track of it all.
> Water is finite, and we must conserve it.
> Her vocabulary seems excellent.
> The new furniture looks beautiful in the living room.

Here are some uncountable and countable nouns.

Uncountable	*Countable*
water	five bottles of water
clothing	a coat, ten shirts, a pair of socks
furniture	a couch, two couches, four tables
information	a fact, two ideas, three opinions
homework	three pages of assignments
housework	washing dishes, mopping floors
laundry	two loads of laundry

Using the uncountable and countable nouns in the lists, fill in the blanks in the following sentences.

1. I did lots of _____ for my math class.

2. My husband washed two _____ of _____ in the machine when he came home from work.

3. The bride and groom bought new _____ for their apartment.

4. Watching the news on television provides most people with

   _____ about what is going on in the world.

5. The hall closet was filled with _____ and _____. It

   was so full that some of the _____ fell on the floor.

☐ ☐ ☐

EXERCISE

In the following paragraph, fill in each blank with a verb that makes sense to you as a reader. Think about countables and uncountables when you decide if verbs need an *-s* ending or not.

Life _____ confusing when students first _____ college. Although academic freedom _____ students to choose some of their own courses, placement tests _____ them from taking some of their favorite courses. Those first weeks, homework in each class _____ due every day. New students _____ lots of questions, but fear _____ them back from asking them the first few days. A tremendous amount of information _____ available if students _____ where to find it. Signs _____ all over the college walls. The best advice _____ not to give up. Success _____ with perseverance.

The Gerund (*-ing*) Verb Form

When we write, we decide which verb form (*-s, -ed, -ing*) to use on the basis of the tense of the verb. In addition, when we have two verbs together, we must decide which form to use for the second verb. Usually the preposition *to* is followed by the simple form of the verb;

for example, "I like to sing." There are special rules for the verb form that should follow some verbs. We see several examples of these in the article:

> I *keep telling* myself to relax since dating is less stereotypical and more casual today. (paragraph 3)
>
> They not only *avoid hassling* with attire and transportation but also don't have time to agonize. (paragraph 3)
>
> They *alternated paying* the dinner check. (paragraph 4)
>
> "I've practically *stopped treating* women on dates," he said defensively. (paragraph 5)
>
> He was mad at himself for treating me, and I *regretted allowing* him to. (paragraph 5)

Here is a list of some of the verbs that require the verb that follows to be in the *-ing* (gerund) form:

alternate	deny	miss	report
appreciate	dislike	postpone	resent
avoid	enjoy	practice	resume
consider	escape	quit	stop†
delay	finish	regret*	

The verb form that should follow most prepositions (*on, in, off, up, by, about, from, of*) is the *-ing* gerund form. Several examples of this from the Ullman article are reproduced next. Underline the preposition and the verb that follows it. The first one has been done for you.

1. Instead <u>of reading</u> the *Daily Cal*, I anticipate your footsteps from behind.
2. Many Berkeley women have brightened their social lives by taking the initiative with men.
3. A college date means anything from studying together to sex.
4. I don't know if I'll deny you pleasure or offend you by insisting on paying for myself. (There are two examples in this sentence.)
5. During our after-dinner stroll he told me he was interested in dating me on a steady basis.
6. He was mad at himself for treating me, and I regretted allowing him to.

---

*In a formal letter, regret is followed by the infinitive form of the verb (*to* plus the simple form of the verb): "I regret to tell you . . ."

†*Stop* can be followed by either the *-ing* form or the *to* form, but the meaning changes:
   I *stopped talking* to my best friend. (We no longer talk.)
   I *stopped to talk* to my best friend. (We spent some time talking.)

There is a special list of expressions after which *to* is followed by the *-ing* gerund form. This is very unusual. *To* is almost always followed by the simple form of the verb with no ending. However, the following expressions are followed by the *-ing* gerund form:

admit to

confess to

look forward to

be used to*

get used to*

Here are some examples of how these words are used in sentences:

The young man *admitted to asking* his brother's girlfriend out on a date.
She *confessed to flirting* with her math teacher.
Ullman *looks forward to having* lunch with the man in her class.
Ullman is not *used to asking* men out on dates.
She says that she will try to *get used to doing* this so she can improve her social life.

☐ ☐ ☐

EXERCISE

In the following sentences, fill in each blank with a verb that makes sense to you as a reader.

1. The teacher finished _____ and then asked for questions about the examination that Thursday.

2. The students appreciated _____ about what would be on the test.

3. One of the students asked the teacher to postpone _____ the test until Monday.

4. The teacher told the students that they had to get used to

_____ tests every week.

5. A few students considered _____ after class to study together in small groups.

---

*Notice that the meaning of *be used to* and *get used to* is different from *used to*, which we studied in Chapter 6. *Be used to* and *get used to* mean "to get accustomed to."

Combining Sentences

As discussed earlier, combining sentences is a way of making sentences longer and more interesting. Writers vary the length of their sentences by combining shorter sentences into a variety of longer sentences. Here we will practice writing sentences that begin with *-ing* phrases. For this to be effective, the subject in the two sentences must be exactly the same.

I grew up.
I learned that men call, ask, and pay for the date.
    Growing up, I learned that men call, ask, and pay for the date.

I wait for you to get to class.
I am incredibly impatient.

    Waiting for you to get to class, I am _____.

She treasures her femininity.
She also believes in equality.

    _____ing her femininity, she also _____.

He feels shy.
He hasn't asked her on a date yet.

    _____ing _____, he _____.

He slides into his desk.
He taps her shoulder and says, "Hi."

    _____, _____.

Now write a sentence of your own using this pattern. Notice where the comma goes in this type of sentence.

CHAPTER EIGHT

Comparing the Sexes

PREREADING ACTIVITIES

1. The title of the textbook excerpt you are about to read is "How Different Are the Sexes?" What do you expect will be some of the differences mentioned in the article?
2. In a small group, discuss whether you feel that males and females are treated differently in your home, in school, in your neighborhood, and in society in general. Each group should present its ideas to the class as a whole.
3. In a small group, discuss the advantages and disadvantages of being a male or being a female. Each group should present its ideas to the class as a whole.

How Different Are the Sexes?

The following excerpt is from Ian Robertson's 1989 textbook Society: A Brief Intro-duction. *The excerpt is about differences between males and females. Before you read this, discuss in what ways, if any, girls should be raised differently from boys and why.*

Throughout the world, the first question parents ask at the birth of a child is always the same: "Is it a boy or a girl?" The urgency of the question reveals the great importance that all human societies attach to the differences between men and women.

The division of the human species into two fundamental categories   5
is based on *sex*—the biological distinction between males and females. All societies, however, elaborate this biological fact into secondary, nonbiological notions of "masculinity" and "femininity." These con-cepts refer not to sex but to *gender*—the culturally learned differences between males and females. In other words, male or female is what, by   10
birth, you *are;* but masculine or feminine is what, with appropriate socialization, you may *become*. Gender thus refers to purely social characteristics, such as differences in hair styles, clothing patterns, occupational roles, and other culturally learned activities and traits.

Biological Evidence   15

Men and women are different in their *genes*, which provide the inherited blueprint for their physical development. Females have two

similar chromosomes (XX), while males have two dissimilar chromosomes (XY). Except in the area of short-term feats of physical strength,
the male's lack of a second X chromosome makes him in many respects 20
the weaker sex. Male infants are more likely than females to be still-
born or malformed. Throughout the life course, the death rate for
men is higher than it is for women. Women are more resistant than
men to most diseases and seem to have a greater tolerance for pain
and malnutrition.   25

   Men and women also have differences in their *hormones*, chemical
substances that are secreted by the body's various glands. The precise
effects of hormones have not been fully determined, but it is known
that they can influence both physical development and emotional
arousal. Both sexes have "male" as well as "female" hormones, but the 30
proportion of male hormones is greater in men and that of female
hormones is greater in women. The present consensus among researchers is that hormonal differences probably do have some influence on the behavior of men and women but that this influence varies
greatly—not only among individuals, but also within the same person 35
over time.

Psychological Evidence

   Although there are many differences among both individual men
and individual women, the typical personality patterns of adult men
and women are clearly dissimilar in many ways. For example, men 40
tend to be more aggressive and to have greater mathematical ability;
women tend to be more nurturant and more emotional. But are these
differences inborn or learned? In the case of adults, this question
cannot be answered, since it is impossible to untangle the effects of
biological and social influences on personality. Psychologists have 45
therefore focused much of their research on very young infants, reasoning that the earlier sex-linked differences in behavior appear, the
more likely they are to be the result of inborn factors.

   Many studies of young infants have found sex-linked personality
differences early in life. Even in the cradle, for example, male babies 50
are more active than females; female babies smile more readily and are
more sensitive to warmth and touch than males. But these are only
general tendencies. Many male babies show traits that are more typical
of female babies, and vice versa. These and other findings seem at first
sight to indicate some inborn personality differences between the 55
sexes, but it is possible that even these early variations are learned.
From the time children are born, parents and others treat them in
subtly different ways according to their sex. In fact, experiments have
shown that if adults are told that a girl infant is a boy, they will
respond to her as if she were a boy—for example, by commenting on 60
the infant's sturdiness and playing with her vigorously. But if they are

told the same child is a girl, they are likely to remark on her prettiness and to touch her more gently. Infants may therefore learn to behave differently even in the first few weeks of life.

Reading and Thinking Strategies

Discussion Activities

Analysis and Conclusions

1. What is the difference between sex and gender?
2. What evidence does Robertson provide to prove that males are the weaker sex?
3. Why is it difficult to answer whether differences between the sexes are inborn or learned?

Writing and Point of View

1. On pages 73–74, several essay types are defined. Which of these types best describes the Robertson article?
2. Robertson defines several words in this excerpt. What words does he define, and how does he let the reader know that these words are important?
3. Reread the textbook excerpts on pages 21 and 90. In what ways are these excerpts similar, and in what ways are they different? What characteristics do you notice that make textbook writing different from other writing?

Personal Response and Evaluation

1. In almost all societies, women live longer than men. Why do you think this is so?
2. Compare gender—the culturally learned differences between males and females—in the United States and in any other country you have lived in or visited.
3. Are boy babies treated differently from girl babies? Describe some differences in treatment that you have observed. Think of colors that babies are dressed in, the toys they are given, how much they are held, and the way people play with them.

Debate

While working on this chapter, it might be interesting to have several class debates. Divide the class into men and women, or use any other division that seems to work. Each group is given a point of view on a topic. Together the group members create an argument based on facts and observations. Then the actual debate can begin. It might be useful to audiotape or videotape the debate for later class discussions.

The following are some points of view that might be considered for debate.

Team A	*Team B*
Women are the weaker sex.	Men are really the weaker sex.
Children should be brought up as equals; there should be no differences in treatment.	Boys and girls should be brought up differently. This is necessary for their future roles in life.
Women are not psychologically equipped to hold positions of power.	Women can deal with positions of power as well as men can.
There can never be true equality between men and women.	Men and women must develop true equality for there to be peace in the world.

Note Taking

For practice in taking notes from a lecture class, your teacher will read several paragraphs from "How Different Are the Sexes?" aloud to the class. Take notes as if you were planning to study from them. Then meet in a small group to compare your notes. Discuss how you decided what to write down. What do you think are the most important ideas? Justify your choices.

Journal Writing

"Should I marry him?" I asked myself in English.
"Yes."
"Should I marry him?" I asked myself in Polish.
"No."

Eva Hoffman, *Lost in Translation*

When you write in your journal, think about what it means to be a male or female in our society today. Have your views about relationships between men and women changed since you learned English? Have your views changed since you started college? Write about what it means to be a man or a woman in today's society. Write about the ways in which your ideas have changed about male and female relationships.

Writing Strategies

Essay Strategies

Using Definitions in Your Writing

As part of writing this selection, Robertson defined several words or terms that he thought would not be familiar to his readers. Many writers use definitions as part of their writing no matter what type of writing they are doing. Whether they are creating an explanation, a comparison, an analysis, or a persuasive piece of writing, a definition may add substance and believability.

The purpose of defining a word or a term is to make it more understandable to the reader. There are a few steps that can assist you in defining terms in your writing. One way is to place the term to be defined in a broader context of related things. The next is to look for the special characteristics that make this term different from other related terms. For example, in paragraph 1 Robertson defines *sex* by broadening it into the class of "distinctions." He breaks this down into distinctions that are "biological" and finally into "male and female."

The division of human species into two fundamental categories is based on *sex*—the biological distinction between males and females.

When Robertson defines *gender*, he places this in the broad class of "differences." He breaks this down into differences that are "culturally learned" and finally into "male and female."

These concepts refer not to sex but to *gender*—the culturally learned differences between males and females.

Reread the Robertson article to find any other terms that he has defined. Notice how he indicates to his readers that he is about to define a term. Look carefully at how he breaks the term down into an explanation in simpler, more easily understandable words.

Essay Form

Comparison and Contrast

In "How Different Are the Sexes?" Robertson compared and contrasted males and females. When a writer compares two things, the writer looks for the similarities. When a writer contrasts two things, the writer looks for the differences. We compare and contrast things every day. We may compare how quickly the bus came this morning with how quickly it came yesterday. We may contrast the experience of walking to school with the experience of taking the bus. It is a human activity to compare and contrast. We do it in our minds, and we do it aloud with our friends. For many writers, however, the comparison-and-contrast essay can create problems.

Comparison-and-contrast essays may follow two basic patterns of organization. Both may contain the same information, but it is presented in a different manner. In the first method, the writer follows this basic pattern:

Introduction
Body Paragraph(s) A—presents all the information about A
Body Paragraph(s) B—presents all the information about B
Conclusion—sums up and makes final comparisons and/or contrasts

The second method involves alternating within each paragraph. It is organized as follows:

Introduction
Body Paragraph—about one aspect of the comparison

    Point A
    Point B
    Point A
    Point B

Body Paragraph—about another aspect of the comparison

    Point A
    Point B
    Point A
    Point B

Conclusion

Many writers find the first method, the block approach, easier to organize. In this method, all the information about one side of an issue or problem is presented, and then all the information about the other side is given. Using this method, it is also possible to present all the similarities and then all the differences. In the second method, the alternating method, a point from one side is given, then a point from the other side. This is a good method to use for longer pieces of writing because it is easy to follow. For this reason, readers may prefer this method.

The following paragraph is from an essay that uses the block form; it presents the information about women's physical superiority. We can assume that the writer will next give us all the information about the areas of male superiority.

Women, on the average, have a better sense of smell than men. Women hear better at the upper range. Women have more physical endurance than men. They generally live longer and do not usually suffer from hypertension and heart disease.

Using the alternating method, the writer of an essay about male and female differences makes the comparison within the paragraph itself. The paragraph that follows uses the alternating method to compare the health problems of men and women.

Women, on the average, have a better sense of smell than men. Men, however, have keener eyesight. Women hear better at the upper range, whereas men often have more acute hearing at the lower range. The estimated life span for men is 74 years; for women it is 78 years.

The comparison-and-contrast essay is a popular form of writing. The following student paragraph is written in the comparison-and-contrast mode. Does it follow the block pattern or the alternating pattern?

There are differences between men and women. Men usually live a shorter time than women. Women have a higher range of hearing. Men have a lower range of hearing, but they can see better for a long distance. Women have long-term strength. At night they take care of the baby and then go to work the next day. Men have short-term 5 strength. They go to work during the day and then when they get home, they complain that they are very tired. Most men spend their time outside the house. Women stay home and do the chores. Men are usually taller and women are shorter. More crimes are done by men, but women commit crimes, too. Both women and men have vices like 10 gambling and smoking. Both genders often marry more than once.

Marina Ibea, The Philippines

In comparison-and-contrast writing, we use special transition words:

To compare	To contrast
also	but
as . . . as	not as . . . as
as well as	however
likewise	nevertheless
similarly	conversely
too	in contrast

☐ ☐ ☐

EXERCISES

1. Write a paragraph comparing and contrasting the behavior of males and females in college.

2. Write a paragraph contrasting living in your native country with living in the United States.
3. Write a paragraph comparing and contrasting a book with the movie made from that book.
4. Write a paragraph comparing and contrasting the teaching methods of two teachers you have had.

Suggestions for Writing

Before you start to write your essay, try making quadrants, as shown in the "Getting Started" section below, to help you develop ideas for writing.

1. Write an essay comparing and contrasting the way girls are raised with the way boys are raised. Use your own observations and experiences as evidence.
2. Write an essay comparing and contrasting the teaching methods in your native country with those in the United States.
3. What are some of the differences between men and women? Include information from the Robertson article, as well as your own observations and experiences.
4. The characteristics that a person looks for in a friend may be very different from the ones that are important in a future husband or wife. Compare and contrast these characteristics.
5. Each language is unique, although there may be some similarities between certain languages. Compare and contrast your first language with English. Consider such characteristics as the ways in which questions are constructed, where adjectives are placed, the use of articles, how nouns are made plural, and whether or not the language is phonetic.
6. If you were a scientific researcher, what would you research and why? In an essay, explain the details of your research proposal. Imagine that your reader gives grants of money to researchers, and you are trying to convince that person that your idea is worthwhile.

Getting Started

Making Quadrants

Before you begin to write, spend some time thinking of ideas that relate to the process or pattern you are writing about. To help you come up with ideas, fold a piece of paper into four sections.

In one section, write the word *Describe*. In that section, write the following four questions:

What do you see?

What do you hear?

What do you feel?

What do you taste?

In another section, write the word *Compare*. Then write the following questions:

What is it similar to?

What is it different from?

In the next section, write the word *Analyze*. Then write the following questions:

What parts does it have?

How do they work together or not work together?

In the remaining section, write the word *Argue*. Then write the following questions:

Why is it a good idea?

Why would people think it is a bad idea?

In each of the sections, think about the process or pattern you are going to write about; then write answers to the questions. Reread these answers when preparing to write your essay.

A Student Essay

In my native country, the Dominican Republic, from the day girls or boys are born, they learn their place in society. Men are taught to be strong; as boys they are given guns to play with. The boys go with their fathers from time to time to help them on the farm, if they have one. The women are taught to do housework. As girls, they are given dolls 5
and kitchen sets to play with. The girls help their mothers while they cook by passing the foods to be prepared. Afterward, they either help cleaning or doing the dishes.

In the Dominican Republic, men are the leaders of the house. They are the ones to go out to work and bring the bread home. When they 10
are not able to, they sometimes feel less than a man because of their ego. Women stay home doing the housework and taking care of the

children. That, I believe, is because that is what they are trained to do and also because they do not get a wider education.

In the United States, more men are sharing the housework and are 15 helping out with the care of the children. Men are more liberal; they have a different perspective of their role as a man. They believe in equality and sharing decisions. Women's roles are different. They go out to work outside of the house, and they bring money home. This makes it easier on the man by having fewer financial problems. Some- 20 times the man would have a career that does not require him to go outside to work while his wife might have. In this case, he would probably be the one to have to cook more often. This, I believe, is good because there are lots of men who cook better than women.

Although I am Dominican, I do not share the belief that the woman's 25 place is at home and that the men should be the leaders of the family. I share and believe the role of the United States. I feel that women should have the same rights as men. They should have equality. Women should go out and work too. In this way, their family would have more money to manage and have a better future. 30

Nowadays things are changing in my native country—slowly, but they are. Women are getting themselves more educated, and they, too, are going outside to work. This pleases me very much because I believe that society should not tell you your place as a human being or what role you should follow but that each individual must have the right to 35 choose for herself or himself.

Rosmenia Vásquez, Dominican Republic

Revising

With a partner or in a small group, reread the student essay; then answer the following questions about it.

1. What is the main idea of this essay? How did you know?
2. Which method of comparison did the writer use in this essay?
3. What do you like about this essay? Why?
4. What would you like to add to this essay? Why?
5. What would you like to delete from this essay? Why?
6. Try to move one sentence in the essay. Which sentence did you move? Why? How does it change the rest of the essay?
7. What is the best sentence in the essay?
8. What audience do you think the writer had in mind? What in the essay told you this?

Working with a partner or in a small group, use these same questions to discuss your own draft and to help you prepare to revise it. After you have revised your writing, share it with the same classmate or group again.

Editing Strategies

Idiomatic Expressions

Each of the following paragraphs contains a context clue that will help you understand one of the idiomatic expressions used in "How Different Are the Sexes?" Underline these context clues; the first one has been done for you. Then use the expressions when you answer the questions that follow each paragraph.

1. *in other words* (line 10)

   Another way of saying that sex and gender are different is to make an analogy with something that is comparable, such as the beauty of a baby and the beauty of an elderly person. The first occurs as a gift of birth and youth; the second a person may or may not achieve because of his or her attitude or life experiences.

   Can you think of an analogy with something else in life that expresses in other words that the differences between the sexes are not purely biological?

2. *in many respects* (line 20)

   Robertson claims that the male's lack of a second X chromosome makes him in several ways weaker than the female. Male babies either die at birth or are born with physical problems more often than female babies. Males usually die earlier than females.

   In many respects, when writers report information, they present what they believe to be the most effective support for their main idea, even if others may not always agree with them. What other kinds of information would you have liked Robertson to include to convince you that males are weaker than females in many respects?

3. *in the case of* (line 43)

Many questions about sexual differences will remain mysteries because it is impossible to be sure whether certain behavior was taught or was present at birth. For example, researchers cannot be sure if the fact that girl babies smile more than boy babies is a response to inborn personality or life experience.

In the case of babies, what differences have you noticed between boy and girl babies? What do you think explains these differences?

4. *at first sight* (lines 54–55)

It may seem initially that parents teach their children the behavior that is expected of them. However, if you watch many children together and observe certain tendencies, you may begin to think that the behavior is inborn.

The Robertson article at first sight suggests that people in our world make differences between males and females. In your experience in college classes, are males and females treated differently automatically, or are they given a chance to show their individual abilities?

Learning New Vocabulary

One way to learn new vocabulary is to identify words that relate to a particular field of study. In "How Different Are the Sexes?" Robertson uses some vocabulary that relates to biology and psychology. Although each discipline has its own particular jargon or terminology, the words we shall focus on are words that you will encounter again in some of your other college classes.

Paragraph 2

species: a fundamental classification of a biological group whose members have a high degree of similarity and can reproduce among themselves

Paragraph 3

gene: the basic unit of heredity, which is a segment of the DNA molecules that transmit and determine all bodily characteristics *chromosomes:* rod-shaped bodies that carry the genes that convey the hereditary characteristics; each species has a specific number of chromosomes

malformed: abnormally formed (said of a part of the body)

malnutrition: poor nourishment resulting from insufficient food

Paragraph 4

hormones: secretions of the glands that influence most activities carried on in the body

Paragraph 5

nurturant: feeding, educating, caring for, and otherwise promoting the development of children

inborn: present at birth

sex-linked: determined by genes carried on one of the sex chromosomes and therefore linked to the sex of a person

Paragraph 6

trait: distinguishing characteristic or quality

To make the meaning of these words clearer, reread the Robertson selection, concentrating on the meaning of these words and how they are used.

Commonly Confused Words

accept/except

Read the following paragraph, observing the use of *accept* and *except*.

Many people automatically *accept* the idea that males are stronger than females. However, *except* in the area of short-term feats of physical strength, females are the stronger sex. Many men say they can *accept* the fact that males die earlier than females in almost all societies, *except* that it makes them wonder if the problem is that they are just working too hard.

From what you observed in this paragraph, can you determine the difference in meaning between *accept* and *except*? Complete the following definitions:

_____ means "agree to or receive."

_____ means "but" or "aside from the fact that."

Now use these two words in sentences of your own.

Mechanics

A Different Use for Quotation Marks

The two main uses for quotation marks were explained in Chapter Three (page 58). Quotation marks are most often used to indicate the exact words of a speaker and to set off the title of a short story or other short work.

However, the Robertson selection illustrates another use for quotation marks in writing. Notice the purpose of quotation marks in the following sentences taken from the excerpt.

All societies, however, elaborate this biological fact into secondary, nonbiological notions of "masculinity" and "femininity."
Both sexes have "male" as well as "female" hormones, but the proportion of male hormones is greater in men and that of female hormones is greater in women.

In these sentences, the quotation marks are used *to set off special words* from the rest of the sentence. When writers do this, they add extra emphasis to those words. Why do you think Robertson put the words *masculinity* and *femininity* in quotation marks in the first sentence illustrated here? Why do you think he put the words *male* and *female* in quotation marks? What effect did that have on you as a reader?

Editing Practice

The following paragraph is a first draft that contains many surface errors: one comma error, two preposition errors, four subject-verb agreement errors, one possessive error, one *the* error, two tense consistency errors, and two *there/their/they're* errors. Find and correct all the errors.

Sociologists examines how people live in groups. They examined phenomena such as peoples' behavioral patterns in relation to love and marriage. They want to know if people on Italy celebrate marriage in the same way as people on Philippines. They're studies show some customs and traditions is similar from place to place. For example people usually get married with some kind of ceremony. They usually get dressed up for there wedding. However, there are some differences. In some places marriages are arranged. In other places people meets and falls in love. In general, everyone hoped that the marriage will be happy and long-lasting.

Answers are on page 323.

Grammar Strategies

Comparatives and Superlatives

One of the most basic uses of language is to express similarities and differences, to compare and contrast. Comparisons can be expressed using adjectives, adverbs, nouns, and verbs.

1. Comparisons using adjectives:

   COMPARATIVE: Rose is *smarter than* Marie (is).

   SUPERLATIVE: Rose is *the smartest* student in the room.

   COMPARATIVE: Harry is *less competitive than* Roland (is).

   SUPERLATIVE: Harry is *the least competitive* one in his family.

2. Comparisons using adverbs:

   COMPARATIVE: Han walks *slower than* Thuy (walks, does).

   SUPERLATIVE: Han walks *the slowest* of all the students in the class.

   COMPARATIVE: Mimi talks *less frequently than* Jenny (talks, does).

   SUPERLATIVE: Mimi talks *the least* frequently of all the girls.

3. Comparisons using nouns:

   COMPARATIVE: Li has *more* books *than* Ping (has, does).

   SUPERLATIVE: Li has *the most* books of all the students.

   COMPARATIVE: Sam has *fewer* books *than* Howard (has, does). (*Books* is a countable word.)

   SUPERLATIVE: Sam has *the fewest* books of all the brothers.

   COMPARATIVE: Sam has *less* money *than* Howard (has, does). (*Money* is an uncountable word.)

   SUPERLATIVE: Sam has *the least* money of all the brothers.

4. Comparisons using verbs:

   COMPARATIVE: Hong weighs *more than* Pedro (weighs, does).

   SUPERLATIVE: Hong weighs *the most* of all the fighters.

COMPARATIVE: My school costs *more than* your school (costs, does).

SUPERLATIVE: My school costs *the most* of all the schools in this state.

The rules for using *-er* or *more* and for using *the . . . -est* and *the most* are as follows:

1. Use *-er* or *the . . . -est* with one-syllable adjectives and adverbs and with two-syllable adjectives that end in *y* (which changes to *i*), *ple, ble*, and sometimes *tle* and *dle*.
2. Use *-er* or *more* or *the . . . -est* or *the most* with two-syllable adjectives that end in *ly, ow, er*, and *some*.
3. Use *more* or *the most* with other adjectives and with adverbs of two or more syllables.

Irregular Comparative and Superlative Forms

Base Form	*Comparative Form*	*Superlative Form*
much	more	the most
many	more	the most
little	less	the least
good	better	the best
bad	worse	the worst
far	farther (literal) further (figurative)	the farthest the furthest

□ □ □

EXERCISES

1. Fill in the blanks, using the examples as your guide.

Base Form	**Comparative Form**	**Superlative Form**
cute	cuter	the cutest
nice	_____	_____
pretty	prettier	the prettiest
happy	_____	_____
ample	ampler	the amplest
simple	_____	_____

lovely	lovelier	the loveliest
manly	_____	_____
friendly	_____	_____
hollow	hollower	the hollowest
mellow	_____	_____
handsome	handsomer *or* more handsome	_____
beautiful	more beautiful	_____
intelligent	_____	the most intelligent

2. Several sentences from the selection are reproduced here with the comparatives omitted. Fill in the blanks with the words needed to make the sentences comparative. Refer to the article to check your answers.

   a. The male's lack of a second X chromosome makes him in many

   respects the _____ sex.
           (weak)

   b. The death rate for men is _____ than it is for women.
           (high)

   c. Both sexes have "male" as well as "female" hormones, but the

   proportion of male hormones is _____ in men and
           (great)

   that of female hormones is _____ in women.
           (great)

   d. Men tend to be _____ and to have _____
           (aggressive)   (great)

   mathematical ability; women tend to be _____ and
           (nurturant)

   _____.
      (emotional)

   e. Male babies are _____ than females; female babies
           (active)

   smile _____ and are _____ to warmth
      (readily)   (sensitive)

   and touch than males.

Active Voice and Passive Voice

Underline the verbs in the following sentences. The first has been done for you.

1. It <u>is known</u> by most researchers that hormones can influence both physical development and emotional arousal.
2. The male is observed by doctors to be more active than the female at birth.
3. Females are expected by most teachers to have greater verbal ability.
4. If parents are told by a nurse that the baby is a girl, they are observed to touch her more gently.

According to the first sentence, who knows that hormones can influence physical development and emotional arousal? _____

According to the second sentence, who observes that the male is more active than the female at birth? _____

According to the third sentence, who expects women to have greater verbal ability? _____

According to the fourth sentence, who tells parents that the baby is a girl? _____

All four sentences were written in the passive voice. Fill in the following blanks to change them to active voice. The first one has been done for you.

1. Most researchers *know that hormones can influence both physical development and emotional arousal.*

2. Doctors observe _____

_____

3. Most teachers expect _____

_____

4. If a nurse tells _____

_____

Compare the passive voice sentences to the active voice sentences. What differences do you observe?

PASSIVE: It *is known* by most researchers that hormones can influence both physical development and emotional arousal.
ACTIVE: Most researchers *know* that hormones can influence both physical development and emotional arousal.

In the passive construction, the verb *be* and the past participle are used. In present passive, we use *am, is,* or *are* plus the past participle. In the past passive, we use *was* or *were* plus the past participle. The preposition *by* is often used in the passive construction.

The passive voice is frequently used when the performer of the activity is unknown or unimportant. This technique emphasizes the receiver of the action rather than the doer of the action.

Both active voice and passive voice are correct forms of English. They offer the writer variety in creating sentences. You may notice that textbooks use the passive voice more frequently than newspapers. It is a more formal style. Many modern writers prefer the active voice.

☐ ☐ ☐

EXERCISE

The following paragraph is written entirely in the passive voice. Add variety to the paragraph by changing some of the sentences to the active voice.

In the past in many countries around the world, marriages were arranged by a matchmaker hired by the family. This matchmaker was expected to make a lasting match. An unhappy marriage was feared by many young people. However, the parents' wishes were respected by the children. Young people were reminded of their obligations by their family and their community. It was expected by everyone that the marriages would lead to love and mutual respect. Divorce was looked down on by most of the community and by religious leaders. Marriage was regarded as a lifetime commitment by most people in those days.

As a result, golden anniversaries were celebrated by many more couples then than at present.

Adverbial Conjunctions

In the following paragraph, connecting words such as *however, moreover, otherwise,* and *therefore* have been left out. Rewrite the paragraph, adding these words. There are many possible ways to correct this paragraph. Share your rewritten paragraph with a classmate or with your teacher.

In this chapter, we looked at some of the ways that researchers compare males and females. Women have XX chromosomes. Men have XY chromosomes. The male's lack of the second X chromosome makes him the weaker sex. Sex is determined at birth. Gender is learned throughout our lives. Robertson explained that boy and girl babies are treated differently. Boy babies and girl babies behave differently. Men are often more aggressive than women. They tend to have greater mathematical ability. Women tend to be more emotional. They often have greater verbal ability than men. These differences may be inborn or learned. No one knows for sure. Research asks questions. Research answers questions. There will always be more research needed in this field.

We can connect the sentences in this paragraph with adverbial conjunctions such as those listed here. When we use these adverbial conjunctions to connect two complete sentences, we must use a semicolon before the conjunction and a comma after it:

Men have XY chromosomes; however, women have XX chromosomes.

Here is a list of these adverbial conjunctions or joining words:

Conjunction	*Meaning*
in addition to	combined or associated with
also	in addition
furthermore	in addition
moreover	in addition
as a result	due to that fact
consequently	as a result
therefore	as a result

Conjunction	*Meaning*
hence	as a result
however	but
nevertheless	but
on the contrary	but
on the other hand	but
indeed	in fact
instead	as a substitute or an alternative
meanwhile	at the same time
otherwise	under other conditions

Let's look at some of the ways in which the sentences in the paragraph above could have been connected.

1. **Men tend to have greater mathematical ability. Women tend to have greater verbal ability.**

   We can connect these sentences using any of the words that show contrast or mean almost the same thing as *but:*

   Men tend to have greater mathematical ability; on the other hand, women tend to have greater verbal ability.
   Men tend to have greater mathematical ability; however, women tend to have greater verbal ability.

2. **Robertson explained that boy and girl babies are treated differently. Boy and girl babies behave differently.**

   We can use any of the words that mean "as a result" to connect these sentences:

   Robertson explained that boy and girl babies are treated differently; consequently, boy and girl babies behave differently.
   Robertson explained that boy and girl babies are treated differently; hence, boy and girl babies behave differently.

3. **Men are often more aggressive than women. They tend to have greater mathematical ability.**

   We can use any of the words meaning "in addition" to connect these sentences:

   Men are often more aggressive than women; furthermore, they tend to have greater mathematical ability.
   Men are often more aggressive than women; they also tend to have greater mathematical ability. (Note that *also* is treated as an adverb, not as a conjunction.)

CHAPTER NINE

Aging and Living

PREREADING ACTIVITIES

1. The following excerpt is from an autobiography written by a 93-year-old man. Before you read it, what do you expect him to write about in this piece, titled "Age and Youth"?
2. Pablo Casals, the writer of "Age and Youth," was a famous musician who traveled all over the world. Discuss your ideas about the life of a professional musician. Do you think professional musicians should retire when they reach a particular age?
3. Pablo Casals lived his last years in Puerto Rico. Where is Puerto Rico? What do you know about its land and climate?

Age and Youth

"Age and Youth" is an excerpt from Joys and Sorrows, *the autobiography of the great musician Pablo Casals. An autobiography is a nonfiction account of a person's life. This excerpt reveals Casals's feelings about his life at the age of 93.*

On my last birthday I was ninety-three years old. That is not young, of course. In fact, it is older than ninety. But age is a relative matter. If you continue to work and to absorb the beauty in the world about you, you find that age does not necessarily mean getting old. At least, not in the ordinary sense. I feel many things more intensely than 5 ever before, and for me life grows more fascinating.

Not long ago my friend Sasha Schneider brought me a letter addressed to me by a group of musicians in the Caucasus Mountains in the Soviet Union. This was the text of the letter:

°distinguished conductor, composer, or performer of music

Dear Honorable Maestro°— 10

I have the pleasure on behalf of the Georgian Caucasian Orchestra to invite you to conduct one of our concerts. You will be the first musician of your age who receives the distinction of conducting our orchestra.

Never in the history of our orchestra have we permitted a man 15 under one hundred years to conduct. All of the members of our orchestra are over one hundred years old. But we have heard of your talents as a conductor, and we feel that, despite your youthfulness, an exception should be made in your case.

We expect a favorable response as soon as possible. 20

We pay travel expenses and of course shall provide living accommodations during your stay with us.

Respectfully,
Astan Shlarba
President, 123 years old 25

Sasha is a man with a sense of humor; he likes to play a joke. That letter was one of his jokes; he had written it himself. But I must admit I took it seriously at first. And why? Because it did not seem to me implausible° that there should be an orchestra composed of musicians 30 older than a hundred. And, indeed, I was right! That portion of the letter was not a joke. There is such an orchestra in the Caucasus. Sasha had read about it in the *London Sunday Times*. He showed me the article, with photographs of the orchestra. All of its members were more than a hundred years old. There were about thirty of them—they 35 rehearse regularly and give periodic concerts. Most of them are farmers who continue to work in the fields. The oldest of the group, Astan Shlarba, is a tobacco grower who also trains horses. They are splendid-looking men, obviously full of vitality. I should like to hear them play sometime—and, in fact, to conduct them, if the opportunity 40 arose. Of course I am not sure they would permit this, in view of my inadequate age.

There is something to be learned from jokes, and it was so in this case. In spite of their age, those musicians have not lost their zest° for life. How does one explain this? I do not think the answer lies simply 45 in their physical constitutions or in something unique about the climate in which they live. It has to do with their attitude toward life; and I believe that their ability to work is due in no small measure to the fact that they do work. Work helps prevent one from getting old. I, for one, cannot dream of retiring. Not now or ever. Retire? The word is 50 alien and the idea inconceivable to me. I don't believe in retirement for anyone in my type of work, not while the spirit remains. My work is my life. I cannot think of one without the other. To "retire" means to me to begin to die. The man who works and is never bored is never old. Work and interest in worthwhile things are the best remedy for 55 age. Each day I am reborn. Each day I must begin again.

For the past eighty years I have started each day in the same manner. It is not a mechanical routine but something essential to my daily life. I go to the piano, and I play two preludes° and fugues° of Bach.° I cannot think of doing otherwise. It is a sort of benediction° 60 on the house. But that is not its only meaning for me. It is a rediscovery of the world of which I have the job of being a part. It fills me with awareness of the wonder of life, with a feeling of the incredible marvel of being a human being. The music is never the same for me, never.

°unbelievable

°enthusiasm

°opening sections of musical compositions
°type of musical composition
°Johann Sebastian Bach (1685–1750), a great German composer
°blessing

Each day it is something new, fantastic and unbelievable. That is Bach, 65
like nature, a miracle!

I do not think a day passes in my life in which I fail to look with
fresh amazement at the miracle of nature. It is there on every side. It
can be simply a shadow on a mountainside, or a spider's web gleaming
with dew, or sunlight on the leaves of a tree. I have always especially 70
loved the sea. Whenever possible, I have lived by the sea, as for these
past twelve years here in Puerto Rico. It has long been a custom of
mine to walk along the beach each morning before I start work. True,
my walks are shorter than they used to be, but that does not lessen the
wonder of the sea. How mysterious and beautiful is the sea! how 75
infinitely variable! It is never the same, never, not from one moment to
the next, always in the process of change, always becoming something
different and new.

Reading and Thinking Strategies

Discussion Activities

Analysis and Conclusions

1. What attitude does Casals have toward life? Give examples from the text to support your point of view.
2. What does retirement mean to Casals? Support your answer with examples from the text.
3. Why does Casals live by the sea? What effect does the sea have on him?

Writing and Point of View

1. Why do you think Casals included the letter in this essay instead of just telling the reader about it? What effect did reading the letter have on you?
2. The excerpt is from an autobiography. What is the difference between an autobiography and a biography? If you could meet with any famous person to write that person's biography, whom would you most want to meet with? Explain why.
3. In lines 28–33 of the essay, the pronoun *it* is used four times. What does each *it* refer to?
4. If this had been a biography, would it be written in the first person or the third person? Why? What biographies or autobiographies have you read that you would recommend to your classmates?

Personal Response and Evaluation

1. Have you ever known any older person with an especially positive attitude toward life? Describe that person.

2. Casals discusses his love of music. In Chapter Four, Khan Duong enjoys music too. How has music influenced your life? Do you like classical music, jazz, rock 'n' roll, or country and western music? If not, what kind of music do you like?

3. Some people believe that Americans do not respect older people enough and do not treat them with enough care and kindness. In your experience, does this seem to be true? Explain.

Interviewing

Ask a classmate the following questions and any others about this topic that you think would be interesting. Take notes about what your partner tells you.

1. Who is one older person that influenced your life?
2. How old was the person?
3. What memory about this person stands out in your mind?
4. What did you learn from knowing this person?
5. How would you describe this person so that I can see him or her through your eyes?

Then reverse the process, with the classmate asking you questions and taking notes. After you have finished your interviews, write a report of what you learned from your partner. Share your report with the class.

Journal Writing

The journal is an excellent tool with which the writer may begin to see his or her experience as unique in the world. Although we may focus on the same aspect of life in our journals, each of our views of the world will be personal and distinctive.

Your representation of the world differs from mine, and this is not only insofar as the world has used us differently—that is to say we have had differing experiences of it. It is also because your way of representing is not the same as mine. We are neither of us cameras. . . . I look at the world in the light of what I have learned to expect from past experiences of the world.

JAMES BRITTON, *Language and Learning*

Let us examine age and the aging process in our journals. Although we are not necessarily old, we are all constantly aging. Casals tells us that age is relative. "If you continue to work and to absorb the beauty in the world about you, you find that age does not necessarily mean getting old." He encourages us to question what it means to be old and what it means to be young. Imagine yourself as an old person. Imagine yourself as a young child. How does this make you feel? Think about this when you write in your journal.

Writing Strategies

Essay Strategies

Finding a Controlling Idea

One technique that can help focus your writing is to concentrate on a few words or a theme that illustrates the main idea of your essay. In your writing, you may not actually state this theme, but you will think about it in deciding on appropriate supporting details. For example, Pablo Casals never writes that "life is a great gift," but every example he provides about the orchestra, his music, and the beach are illustrations of this controlling idea or theme. Sometimes these controlling ideas are clichés or overused expressions, so you should not include them in your essay. However, keeping them in mind as you write can be useful to help you focus and decide on appropriate supporting details. Here are some examples of controlling ideas:

You learn from adversity.

Persistence is rewarded.

Wealth isn't always measured in terms of money.

☐ ☐ ☐

EXERCISES

1. Choose one of the themes just listed, or write your own theme that will assist you in describing a person. Make a list of supporting details that illustrate the theme and also create a picture of the person you want to describe.
2. Write a description of the person, keeping the theme in mind but never stating it. Share your writing with a classmate, and ask the classmate to tell you what your theme was.

Essay Form

Description: Writing about an Event

When Casals writes about receiving the letter, his daily routine, or walking on the beach, he is writing about important events that define who he is as a person. When you write about an event, you can focus on the *person*, the *place*, or the *feelings* associated with the event. First, you must decide what to concentrate on to describe the event from your own perspective. Once you have decided on your focus, in your first draft, practice using the four processes listed here as you write your essay. When you write your final draft, you may find that you do not need all the steps, and you may delete some or add others that work better for you.

1. *Observe.* Look closely at the event in your memory, in pictures, or in real life. Notice the specific or unusual details, the moments that stand out, so that your readers will be able to see and feel the event through your words.

2. *Describe.* Use the journalistic technique for writing described on page 72, and ask yourself the *who, what, where, when, why,* and *how* questions about the event. Write out your answers, and include in your essay as many as seem necessary to show your reader the event.

3. *Compare and contrast.* Tell the reader what event yours is similar to or different from and why. Tell your reader why this is important to understanding the event.

4. *Evaluate.* Tell your readers why this event is important to you or to others.

□ □ □

EXERCISES

1. Reread the Casals excerpt to determine which of the listed steps he used in his writing.
2. Reread another selection in the book to determine which steps the author used.
3. Reread one of your own essays describing an event to determine which steps you used. Rewrite one of your own essays, adding information using one of the steps you did not use in your earlier version. Reread both versions. Which version of your essay do you prefer? Why?

Suggestions for Writing

Choose one of the following topics that intere
begin to write, try the "Getting Started" suggestion below.

1. Describe an older person who has had an important influence on your life. Include a lot of detail so that the reader can picture the person. Tell a story about the person so that the reader can understand why this person means so much to you.

2. "Work helps prevent one from getting old," Casals writes. Do you agree or disagree? Support your point of view with your experience or observations.

3. Should people be forced to retire at the age of 65 to give opportunities to young people? Support your point of view with your experience or observations.

4. Casals says that no day passes in his life in which he fails to look with amazement at the miracle of nature. Analyze his statement and explain whether you have ever felt inspired by the "miracle of nature." Give examples from your own life.

5. "Young people in this country have been accused of not caring for their parents in the way they would have in the old country, in Puerto Rico, in the Old South, or in Italy. And this is true, but it is also true that old people in this country have been influenced by an American ideal of independence and autonomy. The most important thing in the world is to be independent. So we live alone, perhaps on the verge of starvation, in time without friends, but we are independent." Margaret Mead, a famous anthropologist, wrote this statement in an essay on grandparents. Respond to the statement on the basis of your observations and experiences.

6. There are now more people in the United States over the age of 65 than there have ever been before. What types of problems can this create? What are some ways of dealing with these problems?

Compare the way that all people are treated in the U.S. and the way all people are treated in your country.

Getting Started

Directed Freewriting

Before you begin to write your essay, take a blank piece of paper. Write the title or the main idea of your essay at the top of the paper. Close your eyes for about a minute, concentrating on those words at the top of the page. Open your eyes and begin to write anything at all that comes into your mind. Write for at least ten minutes without putting down the pen, even if what you are writing seems unrelated to the topic. Just keep writing until you have filled one to two pages with ideas. Then stop writing and read what you have written, underlining any idea that relates to your topic. When you begin to write your essay, read your freewriting again. You may find other connections with your topic, or you may decide to change your essay topic to one you find more interesting.

A Student Essay

The following student essay was written in response to suggestion 3. Read it and think about how well it answers that question.

SHOULD PEOPLE BE FORCED TO RETIRE?

People should not be forced to retire at the age of sixty-five. Even if this gives opportunities to young people, it is not fair to the elderly.

From my point of view, the United States is considering a law that affects all people at the age of sixty-five and the law is unfair. Older people should decide for themselves when it is time to retire. The   5
government or big companies should not have the right to force them to retire just to give way to the younger ones. If they are physically well enough to do their work, they should be allowed to continue. Older people are often more talented and more experienced than younger people.   10

If they are forced to retire, it could lead the old people into a forced hell of loneliness, sadness, and death. Giving them a chance will add to their lives because they love their work and enjoy what they have been doing. For some of them, their work is the only thing that keeps them from dying.   15

I think older people should be left alone by people who want them to retire. They have their own lives to lead, just as the younger generation does. The elderly should decide for themselves when they want to retire. People should not force them to do something they are not ready to do for themselves. They can still be talented and well experi- 20
enced at doing their work. They should have their own freedom, which no one should take away. They deserve some rights for all the hard work they had been doing for years. They also deserve to keep their dream and protect something that keeps them alive.

Monica Boateng, Guyana

Revising

Ask yourself these questions about Monica Boateng's essay. Then meet with a classmate to discuss what you have written. Ask your classmate to write out answers to the same questions regarding your draft. Study your classmate's responses.

1. What is the purpose of this essay? What was the writer trying to say?
2. Which ideas or examples best support the main point of the writing?
3. In which part of the essay would you have liked more information? Did you have trouble following the writing? Where?
4. Is there anything else that you would like to know about this topic that is not included? Is there anything that would make the essay more interesting to you as a reader?

After you have discussed your writing with your classmate, revise it. Then share your revision with the same classmate.

Editing Strategies

The Phrase *Used To*

Casals tells us that he used to take long walks on the beach, but now his walks on the beach are shorter. Looking back on our lives, we remember many things that we used to do that we no longer do. Write two sentences describing things you used to do that you no longer do.

I used to eat eggs for breakfast every day, but now I eat cereal and whole wheat toast.
I used to live in a houseboat, but now I live in an apartment.

Note: In the phrase *used to, used* always ends in *-d. Used to* is always followed by the simple form of the verb with no *-s, -ed,* or *-ing* ending.

☐ ☐ ☐

EXERCISES

1. Underline *used to* and the verb that follows it in each of the sentences you wrote.
2. We often follow a *used to* phrase with "but not anymore." Change each of the preceding sentences to read "but not anymore."

I used to eat eggs for breakfast, but not anymore.

_____

_____

_____

3. Write a paragraph about yourself and your family describing something you used to do but do not do anymore.

Prepositions

in/on/at (**time**)

In Chapter Three, we looked at the use of *in*, *on*, and *at* in relation to place. These prepositions are also used idiomatically in relation to time. For example, Casals begins, "On my last birthday I was ninety-three years old." It would be incorrect to use *in* or *at* in this sentence. We will examine the uses of *in*, *on*, and *at* as they are used to describe time.

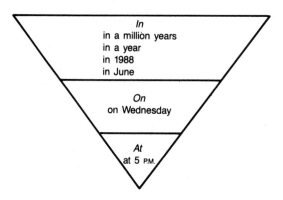

In is usually used for a large block of time:

in a million years	in the fall
in my lifetime	in the winter
in 1992	in June
in the spring	in a week
in the summer	in the second week in April

On becomes a little more specific:

on December 27	on the Fourth of July
on the eighteenth of the month	on Thanksgiving
on weekends	on Tuesday
on the weekend	on the day
on my birthday	

At is the most specific of all; it is used to pinpoint an exact time:

at midnight	at 6 P.M.
at dawn	at 10:15
at noon	at 2 o'clock

A birthday would be expressed in one of the following ways:

> I was born in 1970, in May, on the tenth of the month at 9:15 P.M.
> I was born on May 10 in 1970 at 9:15 P.M.

However, there are some special expressions using *in*. We say, "I'll be there in a minute" or "in a second" when someone asks how long we will be. If someone asks when he or she will see us again, we say:

"in a minute"	"in a month"
"in a week"	"in a year"

☐ ☐ ☐

EXERCISE   On the basis of what you have learned about prepositions so far, fill in each of the following blanks with *in, on,* or *at.*

1. Pablo Casals was born _____ 1876, _____ Vendrell, Spain,

   _____ December 29.

2. He lived _____ Puerto Rico for many years of his life.

3. _____ a typical day _____ his life, he got up _____ dawn.

4. He made his debut _____ the age of twenty-two _____ Paris

   _____ 1898.

5. Casals founded the Barcelona Orchestra _____ 1919.

6. _____ 1950, he organized and played _____ the first of the

chamber music festivals _____ Prades, France.

7. He also founded the Casals Festival _____ Puerto Rico _____
the 1950s.

Commonly Confused Words

its/it's

Notice how *its* and *it's* are used in the following paragraph. Then, on the basis of what you have observed, complete the definitions that follow.

The Casals reading is remarkable for many reasons. First, *it's* written by a 93-year-old person who is youthful in mind and spirit. *Its* main idea is work and the value of remaining busy and active. Casals writes of an orchestra and tells us that all *its* members are over 100 years old. *It's* inspiring to know that such a man as Casals and such an orchestra as the Georgian Caucasian Orchestra ever existed.

_____ means "it is."

_____ means "belongs to it."

Fill in each of the following blanks with *it's* or *its*.

1. _____ a rare opportunity to meet someone as positive as Pablo Casals.

2. Time goes by very quickly, and many people fear _____ passage.

They think that _____ too late to fulfill their dreams.

3. _____ true that music has filled Casals's life. He loves _____

sounds, _____ rhythms, and _____ beauty.

4. Casals would probably say that _____ never too late to enjoy life

and all _____ pleasures.

Now write your own sentences using *it's* and *its*.

Mechanics

The Semicolon

Lines 27–28 of "Age and Youth" contain two semicolons. Circle each of these semicolons, and copy the sentences in which they appear in the space.

_____

_____

Notice that the semicolons are used each time to connect two complete sentences. Writers use semicolons to join two sentences when the idea in the second sentence is a continuation of the idea in the first.

In the following exercise, write a second related sentence that will make sense when connected to the first.

1. Pablo Casals lived in Puerto Rico; _____

   _____.

2. His friend played a joke on him; _____

   _____.

3. Casals received a letter; _____

   _____.

4. He loved music; _____

   _____.

Editing Practice

The following paragraph is an unedited first draft that contains many surface errors: two subject/verb agreement errors, one spelling error, three *the* errors, two punctuation errors, and four preposition errors. Find and correct the errors. The answers are on page 323.

Like Pablo Casals; Marc Chagall was a remarkable man who lived a long and productive life. He was born on 1887, and he died on 1985.

Chagall lived for almost a century. His paintings makes people feel happy. They usually shows dancing figures such as flying cows and pigs, playful lovers, and bright colored flowers. Chagall was born in the Russia on Jewish quarter of town of Vitebsk. He had eight brothers, and sisters. Chagall knew he wanted to be an artist when he was a little boy. However, he did not become famous until he was on his fiftys.

Grammar Strategies

Finding and Correcting Run-ons

A run-on occurs when two or more complete sentences are joined with no punctuation or connecting word. Another type of run-on is the comma splice, in which two complete sentences are joined only by a comma. Run-ons present editing problems for many writers. In the following paragraph, there are four run-ons. Underline each one.

People in the United States are getting older, today approximately 11% of the population is 65 or over. In 1960 only 9% of the population was this old, and it is predicted that 21% of the population will be 65 or older by the year 2030. About 75% of these people live on their own another 18% live with an adult child. At least 5 million Americans are caring for a parent on any given day this can create a very stressful situation. Adult children are becoming parents to their parents, however, this can be overwhelming. The older parents also often feel the need for some independence and for the right to make decisions about their own lives.

Adapted from *Newsweek*, May 6, 1985

If you had any difficulty identifying the run-ons in the paragraph, read the following explanations.

There are five basic methods for correcting run-ons:

1. Use a period to end the first sentence and a capital letter to begin the next.

People in the United States are getting older. Today approximately 11% of the population is 65 or over.

	Subject	Verb	Complete Thought
People in the United States are getting older,	x	x	x
today approximately 11% of the population is 65 or over.	x	x	x
(This is a run-on because two complete sentences are connected only by a comma.)			
About 75% of these people live on their own	x	x	x
another 18% live with an adult child.	x	x	x
(This is a run-on because two complete sentences are linked with no sign to connect them.)			
At least 5 million Americans are caring for a parent on any given day	x	x	x
this can create a very stressful situation.	x	x	x
(This is a run-on because two complete sentences are linked with no sign to connect them.)			
Adult children are becoming parents to their parents,	x	x	x
however, this can be overwhelming.	x	x	x
(This is a run-on because two complete sentences are linked by a comma. *However* is a transition word.)			

2. Use a subordinating word such as *when, because, if, although, as,* or *since*; or a relative pronoun such as *who, which,* or *that*.

   <u>Although</u> about 75% of these people live on their own, another 18% live with an adult child.

3. Use a comma and a coordinating word: *for, or, and, yet, nor, so,* or *but*.

   At least 5 million Americans are caring for a parent on any given day, <u>and</u> this can create a very stressful situation.

4. Use a semicolon to connect two sentences when the second sentence begins with a transition word such as *however, therefore,* or *furthermore*.

   Adult children are becoming parents to their parents<u>;</u> however, this can be overwhelming.

5. Use a semicolon or a colon to connect two sentences when the idea in the second sentence is a continuation of the idea in the first sentence.

Adult children are becoming parents to their parents; this can be overwhelming.

People in the United States are getting older: today approximately 11% of the population is 65 or older.

□　□　□

EXERCISE

Correct the following run-ons, using any of the illustrated techniques. Try several approaches, as this helps to create variety in your writing.

1. He always loved music Pablo Casals learned to play the cello.
2. His friend Sasha Schneider played a joke on him Schneider sent Casals a letter inviting him to conduct an orchestra.
3. Casals liked to live near the sea he enjoyed early morning walks on the beach.
4. Looking at nature makes Casals very happy he feels connected to life in that way.
5. Some elderly people continue to work and absorb beauty around them they feel that aging does not mean getting old.
6. Casals had a routine he started every day by walking on the beach and playing the piano.
7. He went to the piano he played two preludes and fugues by Bach.
8. Casals believes there is something to be learned in jokes it was true of Schneider's joke as well.
9. All the members of the orchestra are healthy they are all over 100 years old.
10. The oldest of the group is Astan Shlarba he is a tobacco grower and a horse trainer.

Paragraph Coherence

Each paragraph should contain one basic idea that is developed by the writer. Some writers add ideas that do not belong; when they edit, they are unable to recognize these unrelated ideas. In the following paragraphs, cross out any sentences that do not belong.

1. The elderly couple sat together on the park bench. They held hands as they watched the young people pass them. Sometimes they would look at an especially affectionate young couple, and they would smile at each other as if remembering something from their own past. It was a very special day for them. It was their fiftieth anniversary, and that night they would celebrate with their children and friends. Fiftieth anniversary parties mean a lot to the families, and everyone looks forward to the parties. They had looked forward to

this event for a long time. They had discovered that as the years went by, they had grown closer together and their love had grown deeper. This love showed in their faces, and it made everyone who saw them that day feel a part of their happiness.

2. Freedom has a different meaning for each person. For one person, it might be the feeling that comes when one can say whatever one feels, whether at home or on the street, without fear of arrest. For another, it might be "a room of one's own" where no one else can enter without permission. Apartment rents are very high in most major cities right now, and it is hard to find a big apartment that is affordable, so a room of one's own is usually just a dream. For some people, freedom means the ability to love a person regardless of that person's race, sex, or religion. For others, it is the right not to love anyone and still be accepted by society. For Pablo Casals, freedom meant the right to be himself and the right to continue to play his music.

Finding a Job
and Working

CHAPTER TEN

Working with People

PREREADING ACTIVITIES

1. In a small group, discuss the characteristics of a good salesperson in the United States. Discuss whether these characteristics are different for a salesperson in a department store, a fast-food restaurant, a fruit store, and a big corporation.
2. Discuss with your group the way you expect to be treated by a college official, a government official, and a boss. Have your experiences corresponded to your expectations? Explain.
3. Discuss with your group the differences in expectations between bosses and workers in your country and in the United States. How do you explain the differences?

Trying to Be Nice: Customer Service

Jolie Solomon wrote this article for the November 29, 1990, Wall Street Journal. *It deals with treating customers in a friendly way.*

°expressions

Ten years ago, employee smile buttons, "I'm Here to Help You" name tags, and professions° of affection like, "We love to fly and it˙shows" were rare. But they have multiplied in recent years, and sometimes the results aren't as happy as they might be.

The idea sounds fine: customers deserve good feelings as much as 5
they do a quality product or competent service. And many companies are doing their best to teach and reward employee courtesy. But as companies put a big push on courtesy, they find that forced niceness can mean resentful employees and skeptical customers.

Sociologist Arlie Hochschild has coined the term "emotional la- 10
bor" to refer to the labor that goes beyond physical or mental skills. It means delivering smiles, eye contact, and friendly chitchat to a stranger with whom one's only relationship is commercial. "Part of how business works," says Ms. Hochschild, author of *The Managed Heart*, "is that it calls on people's feelings, or, more often, on people to 15
suppress their feelings."

The use of emotional labor isn't new, of course. It came naturally to mom and pop at the corner grocery and the nurse in Dr. Housecall's

°lawyers

office. And diplomats, psychologists, and litigators° are specialists in it and are rewarded for their talents. 20

But at many companies these days, much of the burden of projecting a friendly image falls on "front-line" employees, workers who are
closest to the customer but are among the lowest paid. Until recently,
many corporations simply expected front-line employees to expend
emotional labor, much as they expected their workers to arrive on 25
time. But with more and more employees on a daily "assembly line" of
serving customers, smiles have become something bosses are taking
steps to coax.

Many companies put their efforts into monitoring employees' interactions with customers and then rewarding the right behavior. Citi- 30
corp, for example, listens in on calls, then hands out prizes ranging
from quality ribbons to $1,000 checks. Some employees sign on with-
out reservations. "You have to quit thinking about yourself, put your
personal feelings aside," says Citicorp phone-bank worker Karen
Horn. 35

But some consultants recommend giving employees room for individual style and teaching them listening, negotiating, and problem-
solving techniques. If employees can react practically and personally
to what's thrown at them, the emotional part comes more naturally,
says Jennifer Cauble, director of market strategy and research at 40
Zenger-Miller, a training firm.

°routine

Avis, Inc., for one, doesn't encourage employees to give rote° responses. That "takes the creativity out of it," says Russell James, vice
president of corporate communications. In training, the car-rental
giant devotes a full day to helping employees cope with their personal 45
lives.

°angry people

With her manager listening, an Avis clerk in Washington, D.C.,
laughs comfortably about the "irates,"° as tough customers are known
to front-line staff. "You keep smiling," says Sharon Daughtry. "Then,
after they walk away, you tell each other what you'd like to do to 50
them."

°potential
°artificial

As a result, some companies are taking more care in hiring employees. Delta Air Lines puts prospective° flight attendants through
simulated° passenger contacts to gauge if they have a "kind of warmth,
a kind of pleasure to have the passengers on board," says Dennis 55
Schmidt, assistant vice president for training and security.

°goes down

As the economy slumps,° employees may find delivering service
with a smile even harder. Many companies are increasing employees'
responsibilities but expecting the same level of pleasantries. Largely
for "competitive reasons," says Delta's Mr. Schmidt, even shorter 60

°rush

flights these days have meal service, pushing attendants to scurry°
around distributing hundreds of packaged snacks.

°disks thrown in a game of
catch

Attendants call them "frisbees,"° he notes, because of the tempta-
tion to snap them out to the passengers and keep moving down the
aisle. "But," he says, "we want [attendants] to make eye contact and 65

deal individually with each passenger. One is good service, and the other is uncaring."

Reading and Thinking Strategies

Discussion Activities

Analysis and Conclusions

1. How does this article define "emotional labor"? How is emotional labor different from physical or mental labor? What kinds of jobs would you expect to require more emotional labor, physical labor, or mental labor?

2. What is the difference between being friendly and projecting a friendly image?

3. What would you expect a teacher to do in a class on listening, negotiating, and problem-solving techniques?

Writing and Point of View

1. How does the author connect her first three words, "Ten years ago," to the subject of her article?

2. What examples can you find in this article of quotations from statements made by authorities? How did these quotes affect your understanding of the article?

3. To what does *it* refer in the last sentence in the fourth paragraph?

Personal Response and Evaluation

1. Are smiles, eye contact, and friendly chitchat considered appropriate behavior in employee-customer relationships in your native country? If not, how are employees expected to behave?

2. Have you ever had an experience in which someone did not exhibit appropriate behavior when dealing with your problem? What did you do? How was the problem resolved? Would "emotional labor" have helped the situation?

3. Would you prefer getting a job in which you had regular contact with the public or not? Why or why not?

Class Presentation

1. Select an occupation that interests you, and do research on it in the library. Write one or two pages describing the education needed,

the kind of work, the beginning salary, and any other information that you think would be useful to someone interested in that job. Present your findings to the class in a short oral report.

2. Interview someone who works in a job that interests you. Ask questions to find out about both the positive and the negative aspects of the job. Present your findings to the class in a short oral report.

Journal Writing

Reading about jobs makes us think about our own future. What will we do with our lives? Is it important to make a lot of money? Is it important to help people? Is it possible to do both? How do we decide on a job for the future?

This journal entry should focus on jobs, decision making, and finding your way in the world. What jobs have you considered for yourself? Why are these jobs attractive or meaningful to you? Did any one person influence you in your ideas about a future occupation? Did any experience in your life influence you in your ideas about a future occupation?

Writing Strategies

Essay Strategies

Quoting from Other Sources

Writers use quotations for a number of purposes. Writers may use quotations to convince readers that other people have the same opinion about the subject, that the subject is important, or that the writer has read and thought about the subject before writing about it. However, the main purpose of using quotations is to persuade readers of the credibility or believability of the piece of writing.

Jolie Solomon used quotations throughout "Trying to Be Nice: Customer Service." List some of the quotations that appeared in the article, noting the source of the quotation next to it.

Look at the quotations and the sources. What do these quotations have in common? What publication did the Solomon article appear in? Who is the audience for this publication? How might the audience have affected the choice of quotations? What is Solomon's purpose for using these quotations? Which quotation is most effective to you as a reader? Which quotation is least effective? Why?

Essay Form

Persuasion: Writing to Prove a Point or to Clarify an Issue

When we write to prove a point or to clarify an issue, we are trying to persuade our readers to rethink a subject from our point of view.

The techniques for writing a persuasive essay include the following five steps:

1. *Propose.* In your first paragraph, write a clear statement or proposition that contains your main point:

   All companies should teach courtesy to their employees.
   Our relationships with our family and friends should be more important than our relationship with our jobs.
   People should not be forced to retire on the basis of age.

2. *Describe.* Describe the problem in detail. Use evidence, including facts, examples, and quotations, to convince your readers that the problem needs to be discussed or solved.

3. *Analyze.* Break your subject down into parts. Explain how the parts work together to form a whole. Include the important history or future developments relating to your problem. Review deductive and inductive reasoning on page 94 to help you decide how to organize your writing.

4. *Compare and contrast.* Compare your solution to others, and explain why your solution is the preferred way to resolve the problem.

5. *Evaluate and recommend.* Conclude your essay with a strong example or reason. Restate your proposition differently but powerfully.

□ □ □

EXERCISES

1. Reread persuasive essays that you have written to analyze your writing in relation to the five steps. Which ones did you use? What might have made your essay more effective?

2. Reread other essays in this book to decide which are persuasive and which serve other purposes. What is the author trying to persuade you about? Does the writing make you rethink your ideas? Why or why not? What advice would you give the writer to make the writing more effective?

Suggestions for Writing

Before you begin to write, look at your journal or other writing done for this chapter for ideas. If you have difficulty getting started, try the "Getting Started" activity below. Or try clustering (page 121), brainstorming (page 51), or freewriting (page 29) to help you get ideas.

1. Write a narrative that tells about an employee-customer interaction that started out with a problem and was resolved because of the employee's reaction. Think of descriptive words and the dialogue that the two people conducted.

2. Some people believe that large companies should teach courtesy to their employees who are in contact with the public and that these companies should reward courteous employees. Do you agree or disagree? Support your point of view with your own experience or your observations of others.

3. Write an essay in which you compare how employees and customers are expected to act in your native country with behavior that you have observed in the United States. How do you explain the differences in the two countries?

4. Describe a person who is very satisfied with a job. Explain why the person finds the job so fulfilling. Include enough details so that the reader will get a picture of the person you are describing and be persuaded that the job is rewarding.

5. Some people think that people work too hard in the United States. They believe that it is just as important to enjoy life as it is to work hard. Do you agree or disagree? Support your point of view with your own experience or your observations.

Getting Started

Creating a Dialogue with Yourself

Before you write your essay, write a dialogue with yourself in which you ask yourself questions about your topic. Write down your answers, and then challenge those answers with more difficult questions. Keep challenging yourself until you think you have asked and answered the difficult questions about your subject. When you have answered the difficult challenges, you will have thought about your topic, and you will be prepared to write a thoughtful and credible essay.

Revising

After you finish writing your first draft, give yourself some time to separate from your words and ideas so that you will be able to view your writing from a new perspective.

During this time, read the student essay that follows. This student was responding to writing suggestion 5. Answer the following revision questions about this essay. After you have practiced using these questions, use them to help you revise your first draft.

1. Does the introduction make you want to read more? Is it clear what the essay will be about?
2. What connects the first paragraph to the second paragraph, the second to the third, and so forth?
3. Are there enough details and information to support the ideas?
4. Is there any place in the draft where the writing seems confused or disconnected from the main idea? If so, how can it be improved?
5. Does the conclusion tie together the ideas of the essay?

After you have answered these questions, revise your essay, keeping your ideas in mind. Share your revision with a classmate.

A Student Essay

I think that all of us are supposed to have a strong relationship with our friends and families. This is a necessary thing for living in our mad world. I'm sure that human beings have already become smart enough to understand that we need each other. Our communications with friends are reduced to a minimum; at least, it is ridiculous. All people in the United States work hard and a lot. It brings money so, of course, it's not too bad. But while they are earning money, they forget about the other important side of life—relationships with others, who also think that success includes only their own house, new car, good insurance, etc.

I have been living in the United States a bit more than a year and a half. When I came to this country, I paid attention to two things, at once. First was the high level of life and second was the absolute

absence of communication with Americans. I felt it in my own experience.   15

I used to work as a truck driver in a furniture store. My salary
depended on working hours. If I worked more than eight hours per
day, I received more Sundays off. Then I could take a rest, but I worked
because it gave me extra money. At that time, I had a girlfriend. Every
day I promised her to go someplace, maybe to Atlantic City, but I   20
asked her only to give me an extra month to make more money than
I had. Each Saturday I went to bed with a firm decision that on Sunday I would go to the zoo with my little sister and then with such a
decision I slept. But in the mornings, I told myself that there would be
a lot of other Sundays and with such a conclusion, I went to work.   25

The end was too sad. My girlfriend left me and my sister moved to
her grandmother's apartment. What had I gotten? One hundred
twenty dollars per week plus my salary. I am sure that it was less than a
girlfriend and my own sister.

So I would like to add that real success is a good and strong relation-   30
ship with your friends and family. What is the sense of all the other
things if you don't have a person to share them with?

Michael Rozovsky, Russia

Editing Strategies

Learning New Vocabulary

classifying

One way to learn new vocabulary is to classify words, terminology,
or concepts in relation to a particular field. This article contains many
words that relate to business and jobs.

1. Make a list of all the words in this article that are used to describe
   people at work (for example, *employee*).
2. Make a list of the words that describe activities people do while they
   work (for example, *smile*).
3. Make a list of words that relate to "emotional labor" (for example,
   listening).

synonyms

Each of the words in column A means almost exactly the same as
one of the words in column B. Words that have almost the same
meaning are *synonyms*. Draw a line from each word in column A to its
synonym in column B. The first one has been done for you.

A	B
1. courtesy	a. angry
2. chitchat	b. uncertain
3. cope	c. measure
4. monitor	d. politeness
5. skeptical	e. conversation
6. rote	f. deal
7. irate	g. check
8. gauge	h. routine

Commonly Confused Words

Modals

may and *can*

Read the paragraph that follows. Underline *can* and *may* and the verbs that follow these words. Then fill in the blanks in the sentences below the paragraph.

If you look in the "help wanted" section of your local newspaper, you can see that there are many jobs available requiring different kinds of skills. People try to get jobs that they can do with confidence. Even though occasionally a person may find a job that involves a lot of training, this is not usually a job hunter's goal. This is a personal decision. Some people can cope with a lot of challenge in their work, but many workers want predictability. They do not feel confident thinking that their job may change from day to day. Moreover, the type of work that people want to do varies greatly. Some people may find one type of job interesting, though to someone else that job may seem boring.

Choose *may* or *can* to complete the following sentences.

_____ means "to be able to."

_____ is used to express possibility.

Now use these words in sentences of your own.

Words to Express the Future

In addition to using *will* and *be going to* to express the future, we sometimes use the simple present tense and the present continuous tense. The time context and the time expression indicate that the event is taking place in the future. Verbs such as *arrive, come, go*, and *leave* are often used in the present tenses even when they have a future meaning.

The plane arrives at 6 o'clock.
The baby-sitter comes at 7 tonight.
We go on vacation after the children finish school.
They leave for Hawaii in June.
They are arriving late tonight.
She is coming over when she finishes her homework.
We are going out tonight.
They are leaving after the third of the month.

□   □   □

EXERCISES

1. Write sentences using the present and present continuous tenses of *arrive, come, go*, and *leave* to express future time.
2. Where will you be five years from now? What will your life be like? Write a paragraph describing your future, using *will* and *be going to*.

Mechanics

The Colon

The colon is used at the end of a complete sentence for the following purposes:

1. To introduce a list:

   I bought the following items for school: a loose-leaf notebook, two pens, five pencils, computer disks, a pair of gym shoes, and books for all my classes.

2. To introduce a quotation:

   Solomon writes about employee-customer relations: "Many companies are doing their best to teach and reward employee courtesy."

3. To emphasize a word, phrase, clause, or sentence that adds emphasis to the main clause:

It means delivering smiles, eye contact, and friendly chitchat to a stranger: customer service.

4. To separate minutes from hours in expressions of clock time:

   12:30 P.M.   9:45 A.M.

5. To end the salutation of a business letter:

   To whom it may concern: Dear Ms. Daughtry:

6. To separate a title from a subtitle:

   A Writer's Workbook: An Interactive Writing Text for ESL Students

Which of these uses for the colon does the following sentence from the Solomon article illustrate?

The idea sounds fine: customers deserve good feelings as much as they do a quality product or competent service.

☐ ☐ ☐

EXERCISE   Place colons where they are needed in the following sentences.

1. According to Arlie Hochschild, "emotional labor" refers to the following skills delivering smiles, eye contact, and friendly chitchat to a stranger with whom one's only relationship is commercial.
2. Many companies are putting their efforts into monitoring employees' interactions with customers and rewarding the right behavior customer service.
3. Sharon Daughtry of Avis says "You keep smiling. Then, after they walk away, you tell each other what you'd like to do to them."

Which of the uses for the colon does each sentence illustrate?

Editing Practice

The following first draft needs editing for surface errors. Rewrite the paragraph, correcting all the errors. The errors include: one run-on, four *they're/their/there* errors, three subject/verb agreement errors, six plural errors, two pronoun reference errors, and one *live/leave* error. Answers are on page 323.

Reading about the differences between men and woman can help people learn a lot that will help them in there everyday lifes. Many scientists are conflicted about whether these differences are caused by nature or nurture. No one know for sure how much in-born genetic characteristics determine people's lifes. Man and women may be influenced by they're environment as much as there genetics. According to research, the brain changes, they can change because of many things, such as diet, the air, handedness, etc. It make sense that one should take good care of yourself by eating right, exercising, and trying to leave healthy lifes. However, despite everything people does, they're will always be some difference between the sexs.

Grammar Strategies

Indirect Speech

Sometimes when we report what another person has said, we use direct quotations, the exact words that a person has spoken. To do this, we use quotation marks and appropriate capital letters and punctuation marks.

The child said, "It is snowing."

We can also restate what the person has said without quoting the exact words. This is referred to as indirect or reported speech.

The child said that it was snowing.

The use of indirect speech has particular rules to help readers understand what they are reading.
In indirect speech, the tense changes:

1. From present to past:

Mei Mei said, "The clock *is* broken."
She said that the clock *was* broken.

2. From past to past perfect:

Jose said, "I *bought* a new television."
He said that he *had bought* a new television.

In indirect speech, the modal auxiliary changes:

1. From *may* to *might:*

   Lynn said, "It *may* rain."
   She said that it *might* rain.

2. From *can* to *could:*

   Pak said, "I *can* speak Mandarin."
   He said that he *could* speak Mandarin.

3. From *will* to *would:*

   Reinaldo said, "I *will* go to the movies."
   He said that he *would* go to the movies.

4. From *must* to *had to:*

   Estelle said, "I *must* finish my paper."
   She said that she *had to* finish her paper.

   In indirect speech, the demonstrative changes:

1. From *this* to *that:*

   Will said, "I can't carry *this* table alone."
   He said that he couldn't carry *that* table alone.

2. From *these* to *those:*

   Sonia said, "These books are overdue at the library."
   She said that *those* books were overdue at the library.

   In indirect speech, the adverbials of time and place change:

1. From *today* to *that day:*

   Leslie said, "I want to leave *today*."
   She said that she wanted to leave *that day*.

2. From *tomorrow* to *the following day* or *a day later.*
3. From *yesterday* to *the previous day* or *the day before.*
4. From *next month* or *next year* to *the following month/year* or *a month/year later.*

   In indirect speech, the word order of questions changes:

1. To a statement word order:

   Maria asked, "What time *is it?*"
   She asked what time *it was*.

2. *If* or *whether* is added if there is no question word:

   Michael asked, "Is it raining?"
   He asked if it was raining.

Using the information just given, change the following direct quotations to indirect quotations. The first one has been done for you.

1. Ms. Hochschild, author of *The Managed Heart*, said, "Business calls on people's feelings, or, more often, on people to suppress their feelings."
   <u>Ms. Hochschild, author of *The Managed Heart*, said that business</u> <u>called on people's feelings, or, more often, on people to suppress</u> <u>their feelings.</u>

2. "You have to quit thinking about yourself, put your personal feelings aside," says Citicorp phone-bank worker Karen Horn.

   _____

   _____

3. "But," Dennis Schmidt said, "we want attendants to make eye contact and deal individually with each passenger."

   _____

   _____

For additional practice, with a partner, try changing the dialogue in "A Day's Wait" on pages 113–115 from direct quotations to indirect statements. You can try this again with another article or story that uses direct quotations if you so desire.

Use of the Infinitive

In Chapter Seven, we examined verbs that are followed by the *-ing* form of the verb. In this chapter, we will look at verbs that are followed by the infinitive, which is *to* plus the simple form of the verb.
Here are some examples based on the ideas in the Solomon article:

Many employees *have to learn to deal* with irate customers. When they *decide to work* in a job in which they are on the "front line," they *choose to deal* with people and problems every day. Some employees *need to learn* how to expend emotional labor on their jobs. They *want to find out* the best way to listen to a resentful customer, negotiate the difficulty, and solve the problem without *forgetting to appear* courteous.

These are the most commonly used verbs that are followed by an infinitive:

agree	deserve	learn	refuse
appear	expect	manage	seem
ask	forget	need	try
attempt	have	plan	wait
choose	hope	prepare	want
decide	know	promise	would like

☐ ☐ ☐

EXERCISES

1. Read the following sentences, underlining each verb and the infinitive that follows it. The first one has been done for you.

   a. He <u>agreed to work</u> as a secretary during the summer, but he <u>forgot to tell</u> his boss that he was majoring in accounting.

   b. There appear to be many job openings in the fast-food industry.

   c. The recent college graduate asked to meet the president of the company.

   d. He chose to work in a big city because he wanted to meet lots of new people.

   e. The advertisement attempted to make the job sound challenging and interesting.

   f. The new driver managed to get a job as a taxi driver.

   g. The waiter deserved to get a big tip, but his customers refused to give him anything.

   h. She planned to go back to school in September even though she expected to keep her job.

2. In the following sentences, fill in each blank with a verb in the infinitive form. There are many possibilities; no one answer is right.

Decide what sounds good to you. The first one has been done for you.

a. The man decided _to ask_ for an application.

b. He knew he needed _____ a high school diploma,

   and he was prepared _____ the interviewer about the other job qualifications.

c. His friend promised _____ a copy of the records from his country.

d. He had _____ his birth certificate, his green card, and his passport for the interview.

e. Even though he knew how _____ many machines,

   he hoped _____ some training on the job.

f. In his country he had learned _____ a computer,

   and that knowledge seemed _____ important to the company.

g. As he waited _____ called for the interview, he tried

   _____ his nervousness.

h. The first thing he said to the interviewer was, "Good afternoon. I

   would like _____ for your company."

3. Fill in each of the following blanks with an appropriate verb. Choose either the infinitive or the *-ing* form of the verb.

   a. The woman learned _____ the phone right away.

   b. She enjoyed _____ to new people every day.

   c. Still she missed _____ her own language.

   d. She needed _____ with old friends at night.

   e. She tried _____ together with them, but some

      nights she had _____ the date.

f. She always appreciated _____ friends for lunch, though.

4. Write a paragraph describing a job. Use both verbs that are followed by the infinitive and verbs that are followed by the *-ing* form of the verb.

Paragraph Coherence

Each paragraph should have internal coherence; the ideas should be connected so that they flow one to the next. The sentences from paragraph 6 of the *Wall Street Journal* article are reproduced here out of order. Try to arrange them in the correct order. The first sentence has been marked for you. Then refer to the original article to check your answers.

_____ Some employees sign on without reservation.

_____ Citicorp, for example, listens in on calls, then hands out prizes ranging from quality ribbons to $1,000 checks.

_*1*_ Many companies put their efforts into monitoring employees' interactions with customers and then rewarding the right behavior.

_____ "You have to quit thinking about yourself, put your personal feelings aside," says Citicorp phone-bank worker Karen Horn.

The following sentences form a paragraph describing a person's first day in a new job. Arrange the sentences in the order that makes the most sense to you. The first sentence has been marked for you. (Some readers think this should be two paragraphs. Where would you divide it into a second paragraph?)

_____ "Mr. Western's office," I said meekly and then pushed the wrong button and lost the call.

_*1*_ When I began working for the Smith Western Company as a secretary, I was nervous.

_____ He told me that we should get acquainted and that I should begin to learn the office routine.

_____ I agreed with him and listened as he began a long series of explanations about how everything worked.

_____ I opened the glass door and stared in amazement; the office seemed enormous, and there were so many people whose names I would have to learn.

_____ There was a large computerized typewriter and a telephone with about 30 buttons.

_____ Little by little, though, it began to fall into place, and at the end of the first week, I had actually begun to like the place.

_____ My boss, Mr. Western, called me into his room right away.

CHAPTER ELEVEN

Enjoying Your Work

PREREADING ACTIVITIES

1. In a group, make a list of the qualities you would like to find in a job while you are a college student.
2. In a group, make a list of the qualities you would like to find in a job (or career) after you have completed college. What differences are there in the two lists? How do you account for the differences?
3. What do you think are the most important general qualities that make employees satisfied with their jobs?

The Work Itself: A Social Psychologist Looks at Job Satisfaction

The following excerpt is from a textbook called Applied Social Psychology *by Stuart Oskamp. It presents research exploring the variables that influence job satisfaction.*

The Work Itself

Research has shown many work attributes to be related to job satisfaction. Locke (1976) concluded that most of them have in common the element of mental challenge.

Probably the most basic attitude here is that the work must be personally interesting and meaningful to the individual in question 5
(Herzberg, Mausner & Snyderman, 1959; Nord, 1977). Obviously, this specification makes work satisfaction subject to a wide range of individual differences, for individuals with one set of values, abilities, and backgrounds may find a particular kind of work personally interesting, while people with different values, abilities, and backgrounds may 10
find the same work completely unmeaningful. A more objective aspect of meaningfulness is task significance—the impact of the work on the lives of other people (Hackman, Oldham, Janson & Purdy, 1975). For example, a worker riveting° aircraft wings has a more significant job than one riveting trash containers and is likely to feel more satisfac- 15
tion with it.

°bolting together

213

°repeated

°improvement; expansion

°mechanical; without thought

°deal with; handle

°responses

°involving relations between people

°outside the person

Application of skill is another job attribute that contributes to work satisfaction (Gruneberg, 1979). On assembly lines and other jobs that involve much repetitive° work, the amount of variety in the job has frequently been found to be positively related to job satisfaction 20 (Walker & Guest, 1952; Hackman & Lawler, 1971; Kremen, 1973). "Utility workers" and others who rotate from job to job usually show higher satisfaction than workers who perform only one operation all day long, and this finding has been the basis of many "job enrichment"° schemes. Again, individual differences are important, for not 25 all workers value more varied or challenging jobs (Hulin, 1971).

Another job aspect related to skill is job autonomy—the worker having a say in when and how to perform the job. A somewhat similar work attribute is task identity—doing a "whole" job, or at least a portion where one's personal contribution is clear and visible. Both of 30 these factors have been found to be positively related to job satisfaction (Hackman & Lawler, 1971).

Too little challenge in the work, as in completely automated° tasks, generally leads to boredom and lowered satisfaction. However, so much challenge that the worker cannot cope with° it may lead to 35 failure and frustration, also an unsatisfying state of affairs. Thus success or achievement in reaching an accepted standard of competence on the job is an important factor in satisfaction (Locke, 1965; Ivancevich, 1976), though again individual differences make this a less important factor for individuals with a low need of achievement 40 (Steers, 1975). Although success can generally be judged by workers themselves, external recognition confirms the worker's success and also provides feedback° about the level of achievement. Of course, recognition, in the form of awards, promotion, or praise, is also part of the general working conditions and of the interpersonal° aspects of 45 the job, and so it has multiple implications for satisfaction.

A final task attribute that contributes to satisfaction is the relative absence of physical strain (Chadwick-Jones, 1960). This is one major advantage of automation in heavy industrial jobs; for some jobs and some individual workers it can offset automation's disadvantage of 50 promoting boredom.

Working Conditions (Impersonal)°

Pay. Pay is one of the most important working conditions for almost all occupational groups (Smith, Kendall & Hulin, 1969; Lawler, 1981). Yet even here there is conflicting evidence, for some studies have 55 found pay to be relatively unimportant in determining job satisfaction for certain groups of workers (Opsahl & Dunnette, 1966). Gruneberg (1970) concluded:

> It appears that money means different things to different groups, and is likely to have greater importance for individuals who cannot 60 gain other satisfactions from their job. . . .

°work paid for item by item

°motivation; the more work produced, the higher the salary
°a contradiction that is nevertheless true

Another aspect of pay is the system by which wages are determined. Most studies have found that hourly pay is preferred to piecework° systems by most workers, and straight salaries are preferred to incentive° schemes (Opsahl & Dunnette, 1966; Schwab & Wallace, 1974). 65 One reason for this is that piecework systems tend to disrupt social relationships on the job, which are another major source of worker satisfactions. However, there is an interesting paradox° here, for wage incentive schemes generally result in greater productivity than does hourly pay (Warr & Wall, 1975).

Reading and Thinking Strategies

Discussion Activities

Analysis and Conclusions

1. Why is variety in the job an important factor in work satisfaction? Can there ever be too much variety?

2. Do you agree with the author that riveting aircraft wings is a more significant job than riveting trash containers? What makes one job more significant than another?

3. The author states that piecework tends to interfere with friendships on the job. Do you think this is true? Have you ever had any experiences or have you known anyone who has had experiences doing piecework? Did they have a similar experience to the one the author describes?

Writing and Point of View

1. Compare the style of writing in this excerpt with the style in "How Different Are the Sexes?" on page 154. Which did you prefer? Why?

2. What do the names and dates in parentheses mean? Why does the author include them?

3. What does the author do to help the reader understand new words and phrases? What examples of this can you find?

Personal Response and Evaluation

1. Of all the factors that the author mentions as contributing to job satisfaction, which is the most important to you?

2. What is the most satisfying job you have ever had? Discuss why this job was so satisfying. Do your reasons for liking the job correspond to the excerpt's analysis of job satisfaction?

3. Have you ever had a job that you did not like? If you have, describe the job to the class or to your group and explain in detail why this job was not satisfactory to you.

4. The author states that "success can generally be judged by workers themselves." If workers know they are doing a good job, why is external recognition so important?

Questionnaire

This textbook article is based on the findings of many different researchers (the names in parentheses). The researchers named attempted to find out what factors were most important in determining job satisfaction. It is important for you as students to examine and question such research. Most of us have had jobs or know people who have jobs. If we were to develop our own questionnaire dealing with job satisfaction, some of us might give responses similar to those given by the people surveyed for this article. Some of us, however, might have different expectations. Working is a very individual experience.

As a group, make a list of questions that you would ask in order to determine what factors people think are important for job satisfaction. Then make enough copies of the questionnaire to distribute at least five copies to everyone in the class.

To indicate which respondents are members of the class, each student should put a *C* in the top right-hand corner of his or her questionnaire. Each student should then fill out the questionnaire and ask four other people outside of class to answer the questionnaire.

As a class, add up the responses and compare the results of your survey with the findings in the excerpt. Did you find that most people thought mental challenge was the most important factor in job satisfaction? Did most people favor straight salaries? Were the responses from the class members, the *C* group, different from the other responses to the questionnaire? If so, what might explain this?

You will learn many things from doing this activity. You will learn how to create a questionnaire. You will learn how research is conducted, and you will be able to compare your results with the results of other researchers. You may then realize how interesting and often unpredictable research is.

Journal Writing

A student once wrote that the worst job she ever had was stuffing feathers into pillows in an un-air-conditioned factory in the summertime. The feathers got stuck in her mouth and her lungs, and she coughed all the time. The workers couldn't turn on a fan because the feathers would blow all over the factory. The student couldn't quit the job because she spoke very little English and needed the money. So she stayed and coughed.

The story is unforgettable. Every detail of it—the feathers, the pillows, the heat, and the coughing—remain in the mind of the reader. In your journal entry, think about the best or worst job experience you have ever had. (If you have never worked, write about an imaginary experience.) Close your eyes and recall every detail—the smells, tastes, colors, voices. When you can see a picture of the job clearly in your mind, start to write. Write everything down, not stopping to worry about grammar, spelling, or organization. Concentrate on making the experience vivid and alive.

Writing Strategies

Essay Strategies

The Conclusion

There are several ways to conclude an essay. The most basic conclusion is a summary of the essay that restates the thesis statement and the main supporting points of the essay. The concluding paragraph in this case is about three or four sentences long. For this type of conclusion, it may help to picture the essay as a clock with the introduction starting at 12 o'clock, the body of the essay moving through the hours of the day, and the conclusion arriving back at 12 o'clock to form a complete circle.

The conclusion often begins with the thesis sentence. Then some of the main points of the essay are restated in different words. All the ideas of the essay are brought together in one final summary sentence. The easiest technique for writing this type of conclusion is to reread the essay and look for the thesis sentence and the main points of the essay. Then reword them.

Another type of conclusion is one sentence long. This type of conclusion makes a strong point; it may be humorous, and it should be memorable.

"We have a date," I smile.

This is Laura Ullman's conclusion in Chapter Seven, page 133. It is effective because it corresponds so well to the introduction, in which Ullman presents the problem of asking the man for a date. The body of the essay talks about dating in general. The end of the essay returns to the original problem: she asks the man out, and he accepts. This is an example of how a conclusion can take the reader full circle.

"If I miss now, then what?" said Miss Duong, adding that in Vietnam she received high marks.

This is the conclusion to Dena Kleiman's article about Khan Duong in Chapter Four. The conclusion is effective because it leaves the reader with a question. The article describes how difficult Duong finds school in the United States, and the conclusion makes the reader reflect on Duong's problems and their questionable solutions.

□ □ □

EXERCISES

1. There is no true conclusion to the Oskamp selection in this chapter. Write a conclusion, using the thesis statement, as just described.
2. Reread the conclusions to the selections that we have read so far. Rewrite the conclusions in one of the formats described here. Read the original and your revision. Which do you prefer? Why?
3. Look through newspapers and newsmagazines to find articles that you find interesting. Examine the conclusions. Bring the articles to class, and discuss them with your fellow students. What other types of conclusions do you find?

Essay Form

Summary Writing

The summary condenses a piece of writing into its essential points. A summary can be used to include another writer's ideas in your own writing. A summary can be used to take notes from library material when doing research for term papers. The techniques for summary writing can be helpful when you take notes in class, by training you to listen for the essential points in a lecture.

What are the techniques for writing a summary? First, use your own words. Occasionally you may want to copy a few words or phrases from the original piece of writing, but in general, the most effective summary is written in your own words. Look for the main ideas in the writing and include them in your summary. Then look for the important supporting or explanatory details.

Second, you do not have to follow the exact organizational pattern of the original author. The summary is yours, and it should reflect your way of thinking and writing.

Third, even though the summary is organized by you and is written in your own words, it should not contain your ideas. You are summarizing another writer's ideas for your own use.

Finally, use your own style of writing. Do not copy the original author's writing style.

Reread the excerpt at the beginning of this chapter; then read the following summaries. Although their styles are quite different, each is a good summary. Summary writing is individual.

The author presents many work attributes that relate to job satisfaction. The main factors about the work are that it should (1) offer a mental challenge, (2) be interesting and meaningful, (3) seem significant, and (4) offer variety and autonomy. There should be little physical strain, and external recognition should be available. Pay is a factor, especially if there are not many other satisfactions from the job. In relation to pay, most people prefer a straight salary to hourly pay or piecework systems.

What makes people like their jobs? This article asks this question. People like jobs where they have some challenge but not too much. They want variety, yet they don't want to feel overtaxed. People like to feel that they have a say in their jobs and, at the same time, have the ability to see a job from start to finish. They don't want to have to work too hard; if they do, they want some recognition for what they have done. Higher pay helps, and most people would rather get a straight salary than hourly pay.

Which summary do you prefer? One is more informal and uses fewer of the author's original words. Which would you find it easier to study from? Just as in any other form of writing, you have to begin to develop your own style.

□ □ □

EXERCISES

1. Write a summary of the text selection in Chapter Two (page 21), Chapter Five (page 90), or Chapter Eight (page 154).
2. In a small group, read your summary or make a copy for each member of the group. Compare your summary with those of your classmates. Discuss what makes a good summary. Which summary in your group do you like best? Why?
3. Choose an article from a newspaper or a newsmagazine, and write a summary of its contents.

Suggestions for Writing

Before you begin to write on the topic of your choosing, try writing an outline as described in the "Getting Started" section on page 220. Many writers create outlines before doing any formal writing.

1. In essay form, write about your experiences creating the questionnaire, and discuss the results you obtained from it. How did your results compare with the findings in the article? What were the differences? How do you explain these differences?

2. Choose the three factors that are most important to you in determining job satisfaction, and write an essay explaining your choices. Support your choices with details of your own experiences and your observations.

3. Describe in detail the worst job you have ever had. Close your eyes and try to imagine how it felt to work in that place. When you begin to write, concentrate on trying to make your reader really feel what it was like to work there. Use descriptive words and dialogue, if appropriate.

4. Following the same procedure as in suggestion 3, write about the best job you have ever had.

5. Use your imagination to write an essay describing your dream job. Begin your essay with the sentence "If I could have any job in the world, I would work as a _____." Make your writing rich with details.

6. Imagine that you run a small company and have only enough money to offer your workers three of the benefits listed here. Which would you choose? In essay form, explain the reasons for your choices.

comprehensive retirement plan
good health plan
bright, cheerful cafeteria with nutritious and inexpensive food
day-care center for children of employees
end-of-year bonuses based on work output
stock in the company
employee social events such as Christmas parties and summer picnics

7. "People should be forced to change jobs every ten years. If they work at the same place for any longer than that, they begin to fall into dull routines, and their work is no longer as good as it was when the job was new and exciting." Do you agree or disagree? Write an essay supporting your point of view with your own experiences or your observations of others.

Getting Started

Outlining

Many writers find outlining helpful in their prewriting organization, and some books teach very formal outlining techniques. However, writers can spend so much time outlining that they don't have enough time to write. The outlining technique presented here is simple and effective; it will help you to think your essay through before you actually begin to write.

The outline is a guide that you will refer to as you are writing. It can be changed as you go along. Its purpose is only to help you organize and to give you the confidence that you will have something to say throughout your essay.

An outline does not have to be written in complete sentences. It is a list of ideas that you will develop more fully. The basic shape of an outline is as follows:

I. Main idea or topic sentence
   A. First supporting detail
      1. Development 1
      2. Development 2
   B. Second supporting detail
      etc.

To see how the outline works in the Oskamp selection, let's examine the second paragraph more closely.

I. Work must be interesting and meaningful to the individual.
   A. Individual variables influence what makes work satisfying.
      1. Values
      2. Abilities
      3. Background
   B. Task significance also determines work satisfaction.
      1. Impact of work on other people
      2. Importance of work to other people

This outline may be very different from the author's actual outline. You have the option of making your outline more detailed or very brief, with just a few key words to help you remember what you wanted to write about. Keep in mind that all writers are different. Some writers find outlines essential to orderly writing; others say they do all their outlining in their head. In the following exercises, you will have the opportunity to try outlining to see if it works for you.

☐ ☐ ☐

EXERCISES

1. Prepare an outline for one of the other paragraphs in the article.
2. Prepare a brief outline for the entire article.
3. Before you write your next essay, prepare a brief outline using the techniques you have just learned. See if the outline helps you to organize your essay.

Revising

Choose a partner and make a copy of your essay for that person. Each of you will have a turn being interviewer and interviewee. The interviewer will read the interviewee's essay aloud. Then the interviewer will ask the interviewee the following questions about the essay, writing down the answers as they are spoken. Practice this first with the student essay that follows.

1. What is the main idea of the essay? What is the author really trying to say?
2. If you had to leave out one line or one part, what would it be?
3. If you had to add something to one part of the essay, where would you add it and what would you add?
4. What part(s) of the essay do you like best?
5. What part(s) would you like to rewrite completely?
6. Do you think the essay says what the author wanted it to say? How could you have said it better?

When both interviews are finished, read your own interview and make any changes in your essay that you feel are necessary to improve your writing. Share your revised writing with your classmate.

A Student Essay

This student wrote this essay about his hero, who had a job that the student admired.

Roberto Clemente, My Hero

I am writing about Roberto Clemente because he had a job that fulfilled him. He achieved greatness and became a hero. But first, you should know his story.

Roberto Clemente was a good man. He was a baseball player who was born in San Anton, Puerto Rico. Roberto was only 8 years old 5 when he started to play baseball with his brothers and friends on the neighborhood team. He used to play even better with older people than with people his own age.

The bat, ball, and glove he used were handmade. The team members made them. For baseball gloves, they used coffee sacks, which 10 they cut up and filled with rags. For a bat, they used to cut pieces of wood of guava. For a ball, they took a little rock or a marble and tied rags around it. They covered it with black tape or something similar. Roberto Clemente grew up playing baseball that way.

He was 22 years old when he first came to the United States to play 15
professional baseball. Living here wasn't easy for him. He knew little
English, and it was hard for him to learn the new language.

During his years in the big league with the Pittsburgh Pirates,
Roberto became very popular as one of the best baseball players in
history. In the National League, he won four batting championships 20
and was named the best player of the league in 1966. During the years
he played baseball, he played in many all-star games.

But it all ended a few days before Christmas in 1972. There was an
earthquake in Managua, the capital of Nicaragua. The city was de-
stroyed. There were more than 6,000 people killed and 20,000 injured. 25
And there were about 3,000 people who were left homeless. At this
time, Roberto was celebrating Christmas in Puerto Rico with his
family after an excellent season of baseball.

When he heard the news, he remembered a young friend in Nicaragua who Roberto had helped some years ago here in the United 30
States. The boy had had his leg amputated. After the earthquake,
Roberto thought of his friend. Roberto felt that he should go to help
him and other people. Together with the singer Ruth Fernandez, they
asked for help on television and radio. In less than a week, the people
of Puerto Rico had donated thousands of dollars.   35

Roberto left for Nicaragua, but on New Year's Eve, his plane crashed
in the Atlantic Ocean. On that airplane was my hero. He died a hero in
baseball and a hero in trying to help people. Even though the food and
money never got to Nicaragua because of the crash, the people there
appreciated what he did.   40

Roberto Clemente was the kind of man that I would like to be one
day. He was successful in his career and successful in his private life
with his family. He cared about people and poverty, and he believed in
something important, helping other people, people who need you.

I think that if just half the people in the world would be like him, 45
the world would be an almost perfect one. I wish that the world would
read this and think about it a little bit just for a second. Believe me, it
makes sense.

Juan Carlos Rodriguez, Dominican Republic

Editing Strategies

Word Development

using context clues

When people speak to us, we have clues to help us understand what
they are saying. We can watch their faces, listen to their tone of voice,

notice their body language. In a similar way, written material often contains useful clues to help the reader understand words and special phrases. These are called *context clues*, clues that provide the meanings of words used in the piece of writing. The following sentences from the Oskamp article contain examples of such context clues.

1. A more objective aspect of meaningfulness is task significance—the impact of the work on the lives of other people. (paragraph 2)

    According to this sentence, what does "task significance" mean?

    _____

2. Another job aspect related to skill is job autonomy—the worker having a say in when and how to perform the job. (paragraph 4)

    According to this sentence, what does "job autonomy" mean?

    _____

3. A somewhat similar work attribute is task identity—doing a "whole" job, or at least a portion where one's personal contribution is clear and visible. (paragraph 4)

    According to this sentence, what does "task identity" mean?

    _____

As you read other texts, look for context clues to help you determine the meanings of difficult words without having to use the dictionary.

collective nouns

Certain nouns are collective nouns. A collective noun stands for a group of people, animals, or objects considered as a single unit. The following are examples of collective nouns: *family, class, committee, factory, government, group, majority, minority, nation, public, team.*

A collective noun used as a subject usually takes a singular verb in American English.

> The public is ruled by a system of laws.
> The committee is meeting on Thursday.

However, to emphasize the individual members of the unit, the plural verb can be used.

> The team have argued among themselves about who should be considered the best player.

In British English, the plural verb is used with collective nouns. Collective nouns are countable nouns; they can be used in the plural.

In each of the following sentences, choose the correct form of an appropriate present tense verb.

1. The class _____ to know when a test will be given.

2. That group _____ to go out together on the weekends.

3. The family that _____ together _____ together.

4. The audience _____ the performers to concentrate on the play each night.

5. The crowd _____ among themselves about who should get in the crowded train first.

Commonly Confused Words

who's/whose

Read the following paragraph, noticing the use of *who's* and *whose*.

The man *whose* wife returned to work only to find herself receiving many promotions is an interesting case. *Who's* to say that she would have responded the same way if he had started to get promotions and had to begin traveling? *Whose* problem is worse, hers or his?

Going by what you observed in the paragraph, complete the following definitions.

_____ means "who is" or "who has."

_____ means "belongs to whom."

Now use *who's* and *whose* in sentences of your own.

Mechanics

Dashes and Hyphens

the dash

The dash (—) is used for several purposes:

1. To set off a definition of a difficult or unfamiliar word or phrase
2. To indicate a pause that is longer than a comma but not as long as a period
3. To emphasize or dramatize a point

The following sentences are taken from the Oskamp selection. Decide for what purpose each dash is being used.

1. A more objective aspect of meaningfulness is task significance—the impact of the work on the lives of other people.

2. Another job aspect related to skill is job autonomy—the worker having a say in when and how to perform the job.

3. A somewhat similar work attribute is task identity—doing a "whole" job, or at least a portion where one's personal contribution is clear and visible.

the hyphen

The hyphen (·) is used for several purposes:

1. To make a compound word:

   worker-in-training, five-year-old, mother-in-law

2. To form new words beginning with the prefixes *half, self, pro, great,* and *ex*:

   half-cooked, self-confidence, pro-students, great-grandfather, ex-president

3. To join compound numbers from *twenty-one* to *ninety-nine* when you write them out

4. To break a word at the end of a line of writing. Find the two examples of words that are broken with a hyphen in the Oskamp selection. When you break a word, break it at the end of a syllable. You cannot divide a one-syllable word such as *through*. Avoid dividing short words of five letters or under. Do not divide contractions. *Always check your dictionary for the correct place to divide a word.*

□ □ □

EXERCISE

Reread some of your earlier writing, looking to see how and when you used dashes and hyphens. When you edit your first draft, make sure you have used dashes and hyphens correctly.

Substitution Words

Writers do not want to repeat the same words over and over. They often substitute words such as *one, this, that, these,* and *those*. In order for these words to be effective, the reader must know what they are replacing.

The following paragraphs from the excerpt illustrate the use of substitution words. In each paragraph, circle the substitution and underline the word or words to which it refers. The first one has been done for you.

Probably the most basic attitude here is that the work must be personally interesting and meaningful to the individual in question. Obviously, this specification makes work satisfaction subject to a wide range of individual differences. . . .

"Utility workers" and others who rotate from job to job usually show higher satisfaction than workers who perform only one operation all day long, and this finding has been the basis of many "job enrichment" schemes.

Thus success or achievement in reaching an accepted standard of competence on the job is an important factor in satisfaction, though again individual differences make this a less important factor for individuals with a low need of achievement.

A final task attribute that contributes to satisfaction is the relative absence of physical strain. This is one major advantage of automation in heavy industrial jobs. . . .

Editing Practice

The following paragraph is a first draft that contains many surface errors: one pronoun agreement error, two run-ons, one subject-verb agreement error, four *there/their* errors, and one *though/through* error. Find and correct the mistakes. Answers are on page 323.

According to Oskamp, there are many factors involved in job satisfaction. People have to feel there jobs are meaningful and interesting it has to offer the workers a mental challenge. Even through their is individual differences in what people think is important, most people agree that there jobs should offer some challenge. Pay has greater importance for individuals who cannot gain other satisfactions from there jobs. Jobs that offer external recognition, good pay, and a mental challenge are sought by most people, each person wants a feeling of fulfillment.

Grammar Strategies

Relative Pronouns

The most common relative pronouns are *who, whom, whose, that*, and *which*. *When, where*, and *why* are also sometimes used as relative pronouns. Relative pronouns are used to form adjective clauses that describe or explain a noun or noun phrase in another part of the sentence. Here are some examples of adjective clauses that Oskamp used:

1. <u>On assembly lines and other jobs</u> *that* involve much repetitive work, the amount of variety in the job has frequently been found to be related to job satisfaction.

2. <u>"Utility workers" and others</u> *who* rotate from job to job usually show higher satisfaction than <u>workers</u> *who* perform only one operation all day long, and this finding has been the basis of many "job enrichment" schemes.

3. However, <u>so much challenge</u> *that* the worker cannot cope with it may lead to failure and frustration, also an unsatisfying state of affairs.

4. <u>A final task attribute</u> *that* contributes to satisfaction is the relative absence of physical strain.

5. One reason for this is that piecework systems tend to disrupt <u>social relationships on the job</u>, *which* are another major source of worker satisfactions.

Who is used to refer to people. *Who* is used as the subject of an adjective clause (sentence 2).

Whom is also used when referring to people, but *whom* is used as the object of the adjective clause:

The employer, *whom* you prefer to work for, is aware of employee abilities and needs.

Whose is used to show possession:

The workers, *whose* needs are met, are likely to remain on the job and to work hard.

Which is used to refer to things other than people. *Which* can function as the subject or object of an adjective clause. How does *which* function in sentence 5?

That can be used to refer to people, animals, or things. *That* can function as a subject or as the object of an adjective clause.

When is used to mean "at which time":

My boss still reminds me of the day *when* I arrived late for my interview.

Where is used to mean "at which place":

In the 1990s computers and fax machines have enabled more people to work *where* they live.

Why means "for which":

Oskamp suggests many reasons *why* people prefer to work at particular types of jobs.

□ □ □

EXERCISES

1. Simple sentences can be combined with the relative pronouns just described. Fill in the blanks in the following sentences. The first one is done for you. Keep in mind that there may be more than one correct answer.

   a. Helene preferred a certain type of job.
      The job allowed her to be creative and intelligent.

      Helene preferred a job that allowed her to be creative and intelligent

   b. Helene sent out many letters to big companies.
      The big companies had room for advancement.

      _____

      _____

   c. She received one reply to her letters.
Her letters told about her background and requested an employment interview.

_____

_____

   d. The letter was sent to her home.
The letter told her the time and place of the interview.

_____

_____

   e. Helene discussed her interview with a friend.
The friend worked in the same company.

_____

_____

   f. The office building occupied a whole city block.
The building was 100 stories high.

_____

_____

2. Finish the story about Helene. What was her experience at the
interview? What was the job? Did she get the job?

Finding and Correcting Fragments

Sentence fragments (incomplete sentences) sometimes pose a big
problem for writers. During editing, it may be hard to find and correct
these errors. In the following paragraph, there are several fragments.
Read the paragraph, and underline the fragments.

In each of our lives. There are certain important passages or steps.
Such as graduating from high school, graduating from college, getting
a job, and getting married. People mature. When it is the right time for
them. They cannot just follow their friends. Because it is not right for
them. Growing into adulthood. Is not an easy process.

The paragraph contains six fragments. If you missed any of them, study the information presented next.

A complete sentence must have a subject, have a verb, and express a complete thought. We will examine several sentences to determine how we can know when a sentence is complete and how we can repair a problem sentence. The following table can serve as a guide. If an entry has an *X* in each column, it is a complete sentence. If it is missing an *X* in any column, it is a fragment.

	Subject	Verb	Complete Thought	
The baby. (This is a fragment. It has a subject, but it has no verb and it does not express a complete thought. The baby what?)	X			Fragment
The baby laughed. (This is a complete sentence.)	X	X	X	Sentence
Jumped. (This is a fragment. It has a verb, but it has no subject and it does not express a complete thought. Who or what jumped?)		X		Fragment
The horse jumped. (This is a complete sentence.)	X	X	X	Sentence
When the horse jumped. (This is a fragment. It has a subject and a verb, but it does not express a complete thought. What happened when the horse jumped?)	X	X		Fragment
When the horse jumped, the baby laughed. (This is a complete sentence.)	X	X	X	Sentence
Driving a car. (This is a fragment. It does not have a subject, it has only part of a verb, and it does not express a complete thought.)				Fragment
The teenager was driving a car. (This is a complete sentence.)	X	X	X	Sentence

	Subject	Verb	Complete Thought	
To travel to Minneapolis. (This is a fragment. It does not have a subject, it does not have a complete conjugated verb, and it does not express a complete thought.)				Fragment
I want to travel to Minneapolis. (This is a complete sentence.)	X	X	X	Sentence
If I want to travel to Minneapolis. (This is not a complete sentence because it does not express a complete thought. What do I do if I want to travel to Minneapolis?)	X	X		Fragment
If I want to travel to Minneapolis, I will have to take a plane. (This is a complete sentence.)	X	X	X	Sentence
Such as chairs, tables, and sofas. (This is a fragment. It does not have a subject or a verb, and it does not express a complete thought.)				Fragment
A furniture store has many things, such as chairs, tables, and sofas. (This is a complete sentence.)	X	X	X	Sentence

□ □ □

EXERCISE Using the criteria of subject, verb, and complete thought, decide whether each of the following is a complete sentence or a fragment. Then correct each fragment by making it into a complete sentence.

1. When I finish school.
2. I will look for a job.
3. Got married and moved to Wyoming.
4. Because he wanted to try engineering.
5. Cooking in the kitchen.
6. He cried.
7. Such as going to the movies, dancing at discos, giving parties, and eating out with friends.

CHAPTER TWELVE

Getting a Job

PREREADING ACTIVITIES

1. In a group, discuss the steps one should take to find a job.
2. Discuss your experiences on job interviews.
3. As a group, discuss and write the advice you would give to someone who has never gone on a job interview.

A Mortal Flower

Han Suyin was born and raised in Beijing. She is a pediatric physician and the author of many novels, including the well-known A Many Splendored Thing, *which was made into a movie. "A Mortal Flower" is the second of five volumes of history, biography, and autobiography, interweaving Chinese history of the past century with the experiences of the author and her family, both in and out of China. This excerpt describes the author's experience of looking for her first job.*

The day after meeting Hilda I wrote a letter to the Rockefeller Foundation, applying for a job.

Neither Father nor Mother thought I would get in. "You have to have pull. It's an American thing, Rockefeller Foundation. You must have pull." 5

°important people   Mother said: "That's where they do all those experiments on dogs and people. All the Big Shots° of the Nanking government also came here to have medical treatment, and sometimes took away a nurse to become 'a new wife.'"

It made sense to me, typing in a hospital; I would learn about 10 medicine, since I wanted to study medicine. And as there was no money at home for me to study, I would earn money, and prepare myself to enter medical school. I had already discovered that a convent-school education was not at all adequate, and that it would take me at least three more years of hard study before being able to 15 enter any college at all. Science, mathematics, Chinese literature and the classics . . . with the poor schooling given to me, it would take me years to get ready for a university.

°lower intestines   "I will do it." But clenched teeth, decision tearing my bowels,° were not enough; there was no money, no money, my mother said it, said it 20 until I felt as if every morsel of food I ate was wrenched off my father's body.

"No one is going to feed you doing nothing at home." Of course, one who does not work must not eat unless one can get married, which is called: "being settled at last." But with my looks I would never get married; I was too thin, too sharp, too ugly. Mother said it, Elder Brother had said it. Everyone agreed that I should work, because marriage would be difficult for me.

Within a week a reply came. The morning postman brought it, and I choked over my milk and coffee. "I'm to go for an interview. At the Peking Union Medical College. To the Comptroller's° office."

Father and Mother were pleased. Mother put the coffee pot down and took the letter. "What good paper, so thick." But how could we disguise the fact that I was not [even] fifteen years old? I had claimed to be sixteen in the letter. In fact, said Papa, it was not a lie since Chinese are a year old when born, and if one added the New Year as an extra year, as do the Cantonese and the Hakkas, who became two years old when they reach their first New Year (so that a baby born on December 31st would be reckoned° two years old on the following January 2nd), I could claim to being sixteen.

"You look sixteen," said Mama; "all you have to do is to stop hopping and picking your pimples. And lengthen your skirt."

What dress should I wear? I had two school uniforms, a green dress, a brown dress, and one dress with three rows of frills° for Sunday, too dressy for an interview. I had no shoes except flat-heeled school shoes, and tennis shoes. There was no time to make a dress and in those years no ready-made clothes existed. Mother lengthened the green dress, and added her voile° scarf. I squeezed two pimples on my forehead, then went to the East market and bought some face powder, Butterfly brand, pink, made in Shanghai by a Japanese firm.

The next morning, straw-hatted, with powder on my nose, I went with my father to the gates of the hospital.

"It's not this gate, this is for the sick. It's the other gate, round the corner," said the porter.

The Yu Wang Fu Palace occupied a whole city block. We walked along its high grey outer wall, hearing the dogs scream in the kennels, and came to its other gate which was the Administration building gate. It had two large stone lions, one male, one female. We crossed the marble courtyard, walked up the steps with their carved dragons coiling in the middle, into an entrance hall, with painted beams and intricate° painted ceiling, red lacquered° pillars, huge lamps. There was cork matting° on the stone floor.

"I'll leave you," said Papa. "Try to make a good impression." And he was gone.

I found the Comptroller's office easily; there was a messenger in the

Margin glosses:
°chief accountant's
°counted; calculated
°ruffles
°sheer fabric
°complicated
°shinily painted
°woven floor covering

hall directing visitors. An open door, a room, two typewriters clattering and two women making them clatter.

I stood at the door and one of the women came to me. She had the
new style of hair, all upstanding curls, which I admired, a dress with a
print round the hem; she was very pregnant, so that her belly seemed 70
to be coming at me first. She smiled. "Hello, what can I do for you?"

"I have an interview."

She took the letter from my hand. "Glad you could come. Now, just
sit you down. No, sit down there. I'll tell Mr. Harned you've come."

The office had two other doors besides the one to the corridor, on 75
one was "Comptroller." That was the one she went through and returned from.

"Mr. Harned will see you now."

Mr. Harned was very tall, thin, [with] a small bald head, a long chin,
enormous glasses. I immediately began to quiver with fright. His head 80
was like a temple on top of a mountain, like the white pagoda° on the
hill in the North Sea Park. I could not hear a word of what he said. A
paper and a pencil were in my hand, however, and Mr. Harned was
dictating to me, giving me a speed test in shorthand.

I went out of his office and the pregnant secretary sat me in front of 85
her own typewriter. I turned a stricken face to her, "I couldn't hear. I
couldn't hear what he said. . . ."

"Wait, I'll tell him." She bustled off. At the other desk was a blonde,
thin girl, who had thrown one look at me and then gone back to
clattering. The pregnant one reappeared, a pink sheet in hand: "Now 90
just copy this on the typewriter, best you can."

I hit the keys, swiftly; the typewriter was the same make as mine, a
Royal.

"My, you are fast. I'll tell Mr. Harned."

And Mr. Harned came out, benign° behind those enormous goggle 95
glasses.° "Well, Miss Chou, we've decided to take you on as a typist, at
thirty-five local dollars a month. To start Monday. Is that all right?"

I nodded, unable to speak. Had he said ten dollars I would have
accepted.

The kind secretary said: "Now take your time, and wipe your face. 100
How old are you, by the way?"

"Sixteen, nearly."

"Is that all? Why my eldest is bigger than you, and she isn't through
school yet. I told Mr. Harned you were shy and upset, and that's why
you couldn't take dictation. He's all right, just takes getting used to, 105
that's all."

"I couldn't understand his English."

"Oh, you'll get used to it. Now, I won't be around on Monday, I'm
going to have a baby. It's your letter that got them interested in you,
you wrote such good English, better than all the other letters we've 110

° sacred temple

° kindly, gentle
° large glasses that make the eyes bulge

had. Mr. Harned will give you a try." She whispered, "I put in a good word for you."

"Thanks, thanks a lot. . . . I need the money, I . . ."

°good-bye

"Yes, dear, we know." Obviously she wanted her typewriter back, and her chair. I was still sitting on it. "Well, toodle-doo° for now; hope you enjoy yourself in this job. I've been here six months and I've enjoyed every minute. Don't let Mr. Harned worry you; he's really great, once you get used to him."

I had a job, had a job, had a job.

Reading and Thinking Strategies

Discussion Activities

Analysis and Conclusions

1. What happens during the interview with Mr. Harned? Why does she get the job after all?

2. Why isn't the girl's family more helpful and supportive? Is there anything in the story that makes you believe they care for her despite their behavior?

3. Do you think the young girl has confidence in herself when she goes for the interview? Support your point of view with evidence from the story.

Writing and Point of View

1. Why do you think Han Suyin titled her story "A Mortal Flower"? How does the title relate to the story?

2. Using evidence from "A Mortal Flower," show how Han Suyin made you aware of how she felt during the job interview. What descriptive words did she use?

3. "A Mortal Flower" is excerpted from an autobiography, as is "Age and Youth" by Pablo Casals (page 175). What is similar about these two pieces of writing? What is different about the two styles? Which did you prefer? Why?

Personal Response and Evaluation

1. If you were going on a job interview, what would you do that was similar to what the girl in this story did? What would you do that was different? Why?

2. What should you do on an interview so that you make a good impression? What shouldn't you do?

3. What steps should a person take in order to find a job?

Role Playing

In a small group, write the dialogue of an interview. It can be a job interview, a school interview, an interview with a landlord, or an interview with a loan official. Two people should be talking. Read the dialogue out loud in your group to make sure that it sounds natural. Each group should act out its dialogue in front of the class.

Journal Writing

Han Suyin's story is about success. A young girl many had seen as a failure goes off on her own to a strange place, meets a kind, supportive person, and has a successful experience. She gets a job. In your journal, write about your experience with success. Have you ever had an experience like this nervous young girl's in which you were afraid of failure but, in the end, succeeded? If you have had this kind of experience, write about it.

The following quotation is taken from an article in *Self* magazine titled "Five Ways to Cash In on Your Mistakes":

Failure intimidates most people, but to the successful it is a challenge to try again. Look behind most successes and you'll find a solid foundation of failures they have learned from. Success is not something we are born to—we achieve it.

Think about this quote. What is failure? Can we learn from it? Has a failure ever led to a success in your life? For this journal entry, think about failure and success. What is the relationship between the two?

Writing Strategies

Essay Strategies

Résumé Writing

Write your résumé as though you were preparing to go for a job interview. What should employers know about you that will make them want to hire you? What special talents do you have? What

RÉSUMÉ

Carmen Perozo
116 Broadway, Apt. 4B
Madison, New Jersey 07940
(201) 377-7802
Date of birth: 10/15/70

EDUCATIONAL BACKGROUND

September 1989-present	New Jersey State College, third year Major undecided; probably accounting or business Grade point average: 2.8
April–July 1989	Riverside Learning Center, New York, New York— studied English as a Second Language
1984–1988	San Sebastian High School, Bogotá, Colombia Average: B +

WORK EXPERIENCE

| August 1989–May 1991 | Part-time bookkeeper and salesclerk
    Winston Gift Shop, Madison, N.J. |
| June 1988–August 1989 | Waitress, Three Brothers Restaurant,
    Madison, N.J. |

SPECIAL ABILITIES

I speak fluent Spanish and French. I have studied English for six years (three in
Colombia and three in the United States). I type 60 words a minute on an electric
typewriter, and I can operate a word processor and a calculator.

REFERENCES

Kay Winston, owner
Winston Gift Shop
331 Main Street
Madison, New Jersey 07940

Professor James Manley
Accounting Department
New Jersey State College
Madison, New Jersey 07940

education do you have? What job experience have you had? Your
résumé may take the following form, or your teacher may suggest
another style to you.

Name
Address
City, State, Zip Code

Telephone Number

Date of Birth (This is optional.)

Educational Background:
> (List the schools you have attended, in reverse chronological
> order, the most recent one first. If you majored in something
> special or have any unique educational experience, mention it
> here.)

Work Experience:
> (List the jobs you have had, in reverse chronological order, the
> most recent one first. You may want to explain the duties of your
> jobs if you think it will help you get the job you are applying for.)

Special Abilities:
> (List the languages you speak and any other unique abilities you
> have that may help you get the job.)

References:
> (List the names and addresses of two or three people who know
> you well enough to recommend you for a job. You should contact
> these people before using their names. A former employer and a
> teacher would be good choices.)

Type your résumé, single-spaced, making sure there are no typing
or spelling errors. Use $8\frac{1}{2}$-by-11-inch white or off-white typing paper.
Make sure your original is neat and clean; make photocopies, keeping
your original for future reference. See the sample résumé.

Transition Words

The following paragraphs, which describe how to prepare yourself
for a job interview, contain many transition words. There are transitions that indicate importance or emphasis as well as transitions that
indicate time. Underline all the transition words in the paragraphs.

The first thing you have to do to prepare for a job interview is to
write your résumé. Most of all, the résumé should emphasize all the

related experience you have had. The résumé should be clear and should be written with an awareness that the person reading it will probably be reading many other résumés. The best thing you can do is to make it obvious why you can do the job better than anybody else. Your résumé should be neatly typed.

Once you have organized your résumé, check your closet. Pay special attention to what you will wear for the interview. You don't want to be dressed up as if you were going to a party, but you also don't want to be underdressed. Consider getting your hair trimmed before the interview. Remember that neatness counts. You should be neat in your appearance as well as in your résumé.

Finally, you must keep in mind that employers do not like people to smoke or chew gum during an interview. The basic reason for this may be that you appear too relaxed. Remember, you are not visiting a friend; you are trying to get a job. If you follow all of the advice given here, you have a better chance of getting the job you desire.

Check your answers on page 324. If you had any difficulty, refer to the following lists. Transition words add a flow to your writing.

Time transitions: *first, next, then, before, after, during, now, while, finally*

Emphasis transitions: *keep in mind, remember, most of all, the most important, the best thing, the basic reason, the chief reason, the chief factor, special attention should be paid to*

☐ ☐ ☐

EXERCISE

Rewrite the paragraphs, changing them from the second person (*you*) to the third person (*he* or *she*). The first sentence should read "The first thing a person has to do to prepare for a job interview is to write his [or her] résumé."

☐ ☐ ☐

EXERCISES

1. After looking at the sample business letter and rereading the directions for writing a business letter, write the answers to the following questions on the blank lines.

     a. What are the parts of a business letter?

_____

     b. What is the purpose of the introduction?

_____

     c. What is contained in the body of the letter?

_____

     d. What goes in the upper right corner of the page?

_____

     e. Where is the date found in a business letter?

_____

     f. What is at the upper left-hand side of the page?

_____

     g. What punctuation mark is used after the salutation?

_____

     h. How do you conclude a business letter?

_____

2. With a partner or in a small group, write a formal letter applying for a job, requesting information, or complaining about a product you have bought.
3. Write a business letter applying for a job and introducing your résumé to a prospective employer.

Essay Form

Writing a Business or Formal Letter

     People write business letters to request information, to complain about a product they have bought, to explain why they haven't paid a bill on time. They write to request job interviews, to introduce their résumés. Business letters generally consist of an introduction, a body, and a conclusion. Formal essays consist of these same parts. The introduction to a business letter is usually found in the first paragraph. It is what makes the reader want to read more. It introduces the main idea that the letter will be about. The body of the letter offers specific details or examples to support the main idea that has been

116 Broadway, Apt. 4B
Madison, New Jersey 07940
May 15, 1992

Mr. Henry Walsh, Personnel Manager
Caldicott Publishing Company
177 West Vernon Boulevard
Madison, New Jersey 07940

Dear Mr. Walsh:

I am interested in applying for a weekend job as a word processor in your company. I saw your advertisement in the <u>Madison Sunday Record</u> this past Sunday, and I feel that I am qualified for this job. I have studied computers for two years at New Jersey State College in Madison. I am familiar with the WordPerfect system, which you mention in your ad. I type about 60 words a minute, and I am very accurate. I enclose my résumé, and I will be glad to send you reference letters if you so desire.

I hope that you will consider me for this job. I can be reached at the above address or at (201) 377-7802 in the evenings after school. I look forward to hearing from you. Thank you for considering me for this job.

Very truly yours,

Carmen Perozo

Carmen Perozo

presented in the introduction. The letter ends with the conclusion, in which the ideas from the rest of the letter are summarized or restated.

The form of a business letter is important. At the upper right-hand side of the page goes the writer's full address. Under the address is the date when the letter is being written. One line below this, at the left-hand side of the page, is the address to which the letter is being sent. The writer skips a line and types "Dear _____:" and skips another line, indents five spaces, and begins the introductory paragraph. The entire letter is typed, indenting for each new paragraph. After the conclusion, the writer skips a line and types "Sincerely," or "Yours truly," aligned with the address and date at the right-hand side of the page, skips five lines, and types his or her name. The writer then signs the letter, folds it into thirds, and places it in a long, rectangular envelope on which the address has been typed. The writer finally places a stamp on the envelope and mails it.

A sample letter appears on the opposite page.

Suggestions for Writing

Before you begin to write, try making a brainstorming list, as described on page 244 in "Getting Started," or try one of the prewriting techniques discussed throughout the book. You also may want to refer to your journal for ideas.

1. Describe a job interview you have been on. Create a mood so that your reader can feel what your experience was like. Use descriptive words.

2. First impressions do not always reveal the total person. Have you ever had an experience in which a first impression of a person turned out to be wrong? Describe what happened and what you learned from it.

3. Write a letter of recommendation to Mr. Harned telling him why he should hire Miss Chou.

4. Write a dialogue that takes place between the girl and her parents when she returns home to tell them that she has gotten the job. (You may want to act out your dialogue in front of the class with two other classmates.)

5. Looking for a job can be very difficult. Use this as your thesis; then give examples and experiences to support your point of view.

6. "Success is not something we are born to—we achieve it." Explain the steps that you think someone has to go through in order to achieve success. What does success mean to you?

7. Many people learn more from their failures than they do from their successes. Give examples from your own life or from your observations of others to support this point of view.

8. Imagine that you are an employer who is interviewing someone for a job. In a well-developed essay, describe what you would expect in an employee. What are the characteristics you value, and why are they important?

Getting Started

Making a Brainstorming List

Before you start to write, take out a piece of blank paper and at the top of your page, write in five words or less your main idea or thesis— what you want to write about. As soon as you finish writing this, look at it again and start to make a list of any words or ideas that come to your mind. Your list should not contain sentences or fully developed ideas. It should be fragmentary and loose, recording ideas that will lead to your future essay development. Write the list for at least five minutes. Then spend five more minutes examining the list. Star the words or ideas that seem to relate to your main idea. Cross out words or ideas that do not seem to be related. As you are doing this, other words or ideas may occur to you; put them on your list. Use this list when you get ready to start writing your essay or story.

Revising

One great aim of revision is to cut out. In the exuberance of composition it is natural to throw in—as one does in speaking—a number of small words that add nothing to meaning but keep up the flow and rhythm of thought. In writing, not only does this surplusage not add to meaning, it subtracts from it. Read and revise, reread and revise, keeping reading and revising until your text seems adequate to your thought.

JACQUES BARZUN

Jacques Barzun's advice may seem surprising after our emphasis on adding detail to your writing to make your descriptions come alive. However, there is a difference between rich, exciting language and repetitive or wordy writing. Look critically at what you have written. Every time you see the words *in my opinion*, cross them out. It is obvious that your writing expresses your opinion because you have written it. Every time you see the words *you know*, cross them out. If your reader knows, why bother to say it again? Every time you find yourself repeating something you have already said a few sentences before, cross it out. In place of those excess bits of writing, add some new and exciting ideas. Keep reading and revising until "your text seems adequate to your thought."

A Student Essay

This student is responding to writing suggestion 6. Read her essay; then discuss it using one of the revising exercises from the book that has been helpful for you.

SUCCESS

Success is achieved by people who work hard. Success is good grades, the attainment of educational degrees, and good jobs in the future.

The first definition of success is for people to get good grades in school. For instance, my boyfriend is a very smart person who gets   5 good grades in all his classes. Even though his courses are hard for other students who might get 50's and 60's on their tests, my boyfriend gets 90's. Therefore, most of his friends think he is a very successful person.

A second definition of success is for people to accomplish their 10 educational degrees. As an illustration, my older sister graduated from City College with a nursing degree. All of my family and friends thinks she is very successful for this. They don't care whether she got the highest grades in her courses; they just care about her degree.

Another definition is that most of us think that people who have 15 good jobs are also successful. For example, there is a girl in my church who doesn't know much English but has a very good job anyway. She works at New York Hospital as a medical lab technician. Once she told me that she was very satisfied with her job because she heard that all her friends admire what she does. It is true that most of our friends in 20 church think she is an achiever. Her mother's friends all admire her. They want their children to be like her.

My observations of people tell me what success means. It means the kinds of achievements that any people who work hard can attain.

Jenny Wang, People's Republic of China

Editing Strategies

Word Development

idiomatic expressions

Each of the following paragraphs contains a context clue that will help you understand one of the idiomatic expressions used in "A

Mortal Flower." Underline these context clues; the first one has been done for you. Then use the expressions when you answer the questions that follow each paragraph.

1. **to have pull** (lines 3–5)

The girl's family thinks she has to have pull before her letter of application will be considered. They think she has <u>to have influence from someone who is important</u> in order to get a job.

Have you ever needed to have pull in order to do something in your life?

2. **ready-made clothes** (line 47)

At the time Han Suyin writes of, no ready-made clothes existed. People could not just walk into a department store and buy clothes off the racks. All clothes were made by hand, usually at home.

In today's world it is rarer to find homemade clothes than ready-made clothes. Have you or has anyone in your family ever made your clothes, or are all of your clothes ready-made?

3. **make a good impression on** (line 63)

The girl's father hopes that she will make a good impression on her future boss. He wants the comptroller to think good things about her when he meets her.

It is also possible to make a bad impression on someone. Often our first impression of someone remains with us. Has anyone ever made one type of impression on you, and you later found that person to be very different from what you had first thought?

4. **to get used to** (*someone/something*) (line 118)

The secretary promises the girl that she will like Mr. Harned once she gets used to him. She has to grow accustomed to the kind of person he is.

When we meet someone for the first time, we do not know how to behave. We have to get used to the person. Can you think of any person in your life that it took you a long time to get used to? Can you think of anything else in your life that took you a long time to get used to (speaking English, perhaps)?

the

The word *the* has been omitted throughout the following paragraph. Rewrite the paragraph, adding *the* where it is necessary.

Trying to get a job at Rockefeller Foundation is difficult for a girl who does not have pull. Finally, morning postman brings letter. She is to go for an interview at Peking Medical College, to Comptroller's office. She prepares her clothes and goes to East market to buy face powder to cover her pimples. Next morning, she goes with her father to Yu Wang Fu Palace to Administration building. They cross marble courtyard and go into entrance hall. Her father leaves. She finds office and meets her future employer, Mr. Harned. His bald head reminds her of white pagoda on hill in North Sea Park. She takes required typing test and gets job.

Check your answers on page 324.

Adjective Word Order

In Chapter Six, we examined the typical order of adjectives used in English. As a review of this, the following sentences have been taken from "A Mortal Flower," but the order of the adjectives has been mixed up. In the blanks, arrange the adjectives in the correct order. If you have difficulty, refer to the chart on page 127.

1. I had _____, a green dress, a brown dress,
   (two, uniforms, school)

   and one dress with three rows of frills for Sunday, too dressy for an interview.

2. I had no shoes except _____ and tennis
   (shoes, flat-heeled, school)

   shoes.

3. We walked along its _____, hearing the
   (outer, high, wall, grey)

   dogs scream in the kennels, and came to its other gate which was the

   _____.
   (gate, Administration, building)

4. It had _____, one male, one female.

(two, stone, large, lions)

5. Mr. Harned was tall, thin, [with] _____,

(bald, small, head, a)

a long chin, and enormous glasses.

Commonly Confused Words

past/passed

Read the following paragraph, observing the use of *past* and *passed*.

In the *past*, men *passed* up being with their families so they could succeed in their jobs. Often their children grew up and their childhoods had *passed* their fathers by. A man once told me, "I got off the bus and a boy drove *past* me on his bicycle. He waved and I didn't recognize him. He was my son." Those days have *passed* for most men, and they will stay in the *past*. Nowadays fathers are as involved as mothers in their children's lives, and they are enjoying it too.

On the basis of what you observed in the paragraph, complete the following definitions.

_____ is a verb that means "went by," "handed to," or "succeeded in."

_____ is a noun or adjective that means "a time before the present."

_____ is a preposition that means "by."

Now write sentences of your own using *past* and *passed*.

Mechanics

Using Numbers in Your Writing

1. Numbers from one to nine or ten are usually written out as words. Higher numbers are usually written in numerals. However, if you use numbers very infrequently in your writing, you may choose to write out the numbers when you can do so in two or three words.

    five   seven   17   178   5,891

2. When you use the following abbreviations, use numerals.

    5′6″   2 tsp.   88°F   99%   3 in.

3. When numbers begin a sentence, write them out.

    One hundred students waited on line to get the new book.

4. Numbers that are being compared or contrasted should be kept in the same style. Look at the following excerpt from the text to see when Han Suyin wrote out the numbers and when she used numerals.

    But how could we disguise the fact that I was not [even] *fifteen* years old? I had claimed to be *sixteen* in the letter. In fact, said Papa, it was not a lie since Chinese are a year old when born, and if one added the New Year as an extra year, as do the Cantonese and the Hakkas, who became *two* years old when they reach their first New Year (so that a baby born on December *31st* would be reckoned *two* years old on the following January *2nd*), I could claim to be *sixteen*.

    What patterns do you find in Han Suyin's use of numbers in this paragraph?

Editing Practice

The following paragraph is a first draft that contains many surface errors: two fragments, one *their/there/they're* error, one *advice/advise* error, two run-ons, and inconsistent pronoun use. Find and correct the errors. Answers are on page 324.

Looking for a job can be difficult their are many different types of problems. For one thing, the interviewee is never sure what to bring on the first interview. I usually bring too much this can be confusing to the interviewer. From now on, I will bring only the necessary documents. Such as your résumé, your birth certificate, and your high school diploma. In addition, I try to impress the interviewer by dressing very neatly and never chewing gum. I always look directly into the interviewer's eyes. I want the interviewer to believe that I can be trusted. If I remember to follow my own advise. I believe I will get a job soon.

Grammar Strategies

Use of Participle Forms

A *participle* is a verb form that can function as an adjective or as a verb. The present participle ends in *-ing*; the past participle ends in *-ed* or *-en*. (Past participles are listed on pages 313–16.)

Watching a *boring* movie always puts me to sleep.

The *-ing* participle functions as an adjective describing the noun *movie*.

The *bored* student drew pictures in his notebook.

The *-ed* participle functions as an adjective describing the noun *student*.

The letter *describing* her abilities arrived at the right time.

The *-ing* participle functions as a verb because it has an object, *letter*.

□ □ □

EXERCISES

1. In the following sentences, tell whether the participle is functioning as an adjective or a verb, and explain why.

   a. The *stolen* car had been taken from 117 Main Street.
   b. A witness said he had seen a man *stealing* the car.
   c. The *confused* witness could not remember anything about the thief.
   d. The *confusing* story did not help the police very much.
   e. The victims *appealing* for help offered a reward of $50.
   f. Two weeks later, the *worried* victims found their undamaged *stolen* car *parked* in front of their building.

2. Reread Han Suyin's story, looking for participles. Notice how they are used in the story.

   The day after meeting Hilda, I wrote a letter to the Rockefeller Foundation, *applying* for a job. (*Applying* is used as a verb in this sentence.)

Contrast Transitions

Contrast transitions guide the reader to expect a change of direction or something unexpected to happen. These are some common contrast transitions:

instead of	still
but	otherwise
however	in contrast with
yet	on the contrary
even though	on the other hand
although	

In the following paragraph, underline all the contrast transition words or phrases.

John accepted a job working as a bus driver even though he often got carsick. The first few days of training were difficult, but finally he passed his road test. That first Monday morning he was beginning to feel queasy. Still, he started up the engine and backed out of the garage. A senior bus driver sat near the front of the bus and said, "Step on it, John. We have to make time. Otherwise, we'll be late." John wanted to drive slowly; however, he wanted to keep his job, so he stepped on the accelerator, and the bus lurched forward. Instead of thinking about how sick he felt, John stared out the front window and counted to ten, then twenty. When he was up to one hundred, he told the older bus driver that he had a problem with car sickness. "I used to have it too. Just relax. You're doing fine," the experienced driver responded. John believed the reassuring words; on the other hand, he worried that he wouldn't make it through the next hour, although he was trying to forget about his stomach. Yet he made it through the day and through the next two weeks. In contrast to his early fears, five years later John found himself sitting near the front of a big old bus telling a new bus driver to "just relax."

Compare your answers with the list on page 324.

□ □ □

EXERCISE

Write a paragraph in which you use three contrast transitions. Possible topics are the first day on a new job, learning how to do something new, and problems with first impressions.

Home and Finding One's Place

CHAPTER THIRTEEN

Returning Home

PREREADING ACTIVITIES

1. This essay is about a person who came to the United States from Cuba at a young age. In a small group, discuss Cuba. Where is it? What is its history? Why did some people leave Cuba and move to other countries?
2. As a class, find out what Cuba is like today. Can all people from the United States visit Cuba? If so, how? If not, why not?
3. What do you think the title of the essay "Back, but Not Home" means? In a group, discuss what you consider to be home—the United States or the country in which you were born? Why? When does a country become "home"?

Back, but Not Home

Maria L. Muñiz was born in 1958. She and her family came to the United States in 1963. In 1978 she graduated from New York University. She has written and edited many articles and books. In this 1979 essay, "Back, but Not Home," Muñiz describes her feelings about returning to Cuba.

With all the talk about resuming diplomatic relations with Cuba, and with the increasing number of Cuban exiles returning to visit friends and relatives, I am constantly being asked, "Would you ever go back?" In turn, I have asked myself, "Is there any reason for me to go?" I have had to think long and hard before finding my answer. 5 Yes.

I came to the United States with my parents when I was almost five years old. We left behind grandparents, aunts, uncles and several cousins. I grew up in a very middle-class neighborhood in Brooklyn. With one exception, all my friends were Americans. Outside of my 10 family, I do not know many Cubans. I often feel awkward visiting relatives in Miami because it is such a different world. The way of life in Cuban Miami seems very strange to me and I am accused of being too "Americanized." Yet, although I am now an American citizen, whenever anyone has asked me my nationality, I have always and 15 unhesitatingly replied "Cuban."

Outside American, inside Cuban.

°filling up

°absence of personal feelings

I recently had a conversation with a man who generally sympathizes with the Castro regime. We talked of Cuban politics and although the discussion was very casual, I felt an old anger welling° inside. After 16 years of living an "American" life, I am still unable to view the revolution with detachment or objectivity.° I cannot interpret its results in social, political or economic terms. Too many memories stand in my way.

And as I listened to this man talk of the Cuban situation, I began to remember how as a little girl I would wake up crying because I had dreamed of my aunts and grandmothers and I missed them. I remembered my mother's trembling voice and the sad look on her face whenever she spoke to her mother over the phone. I thought of the many letters and photographs that somehow were always lost in transit. And as the conversation continued, I began to remember how difficult it often was to grow up Latina in an American world.

It meant going to kindergarten knowing little English. I'd been in this country only a few months and although I understood a good deal of what was said to me, I could not express myself very well. On the first day of school I remember one little girl's saying to the teacher: "But how can we play with her? She's so stupid she can't even talk!" I felt so helpless because inside I was crying, "Don't you know I can understand everything you're saying?" But I did not have words for my thoughts and my inability to communicate terrified me.

°assigned

As I grew a little older, Latina meant being automatically relegated° to the slowest reading classes in school. By now my English was fluent, but the teachers would always assume I was somewhat illiterate or slow. I recall one teacher's amazement at discovering I could read and write just as well as her American pupils. Her incredulity° astounded° me. As a child, I began to realize that Latina would always mean proving I was as good as the others. As I grew older, it became a matter of pride to prove I was better than the others.

°disbelief
°amazed

As an adult I have come to terms with these memories and they don't hurt as much. I don't look or sound very Cuban. I don't speak with an accent and my English is far better than my Spanish. I am beginning my career and look forward to the many possibilities ahead of me.

But a persistent little voice is constantly saying, "There's something missing. It's not enough." And this is why when I am now asked, "Do you want to go back?" I say "yes" with conviction.

I do not say to Cubans, "It is time to lay aside the hurt and forgive and forget." It is impossible to forget an event that has altered and scarred all our lives so profoundly. But I find I am beginning to care less and less about politics. And I am beginning to remember and care more about the child (and how many others like her) who left her grandma behind. I have to return to Cuba one day because I want to know that little girl better.

When I try to review my life during the past 16 years, I almost feel as if I've walked into a theater right in the middle of a movie. And I'm 65 afraid I won't fully understand or enjoy the rest of the movie unless I can see and understand the beginning. And for me, the beginning is Cuba. I don't want to go "home" again; the life and home we all left behind are long gone. My home is here and I am happy. But I need to talk to my family still in Cuba. 70

Like all immigrants, my family and I have had to build a new life from almost nothing. It was often difficult, but I believe the struggle made us strong. Most of my memories are good ones.

But I want to preserve and renew my cultural heritage. I want to keep "la Cubana" within me alive. I want to return because the 75 journey back will also mean a journey within. Only then will I see the missing piece.

Reading and Thinking Strategies

Discussion Activities

Analysis and Conclusions

1. Why does the author feel awkward visiting her relatives in Miami? What does it mean to be too "Americanized"?

2. Why did the author find it difficult to grow up Latina in an American world?

3. How did she prove that her work was as good as or better than the work of the other students in her class? What is she doing now that shows that her English is excellent?

4. What is the missing piece to which Muñiz refers in the last sentence of the essay?

Writing and Point of View

1. What is this essay about? What is Muñiz trying to make you aware of? Does she make you feel what she has been through? If so, how does she do this? Are her examples good ones? Are there enough examples to convince you?

2. In what person is this essay written? Rewrite the second paragraph (lines 7–16) in the third person. ("She came to the United States with her parents when she was almost five years old," etc.) Does the meaning of the essay change when it is written in the third person? Which version do you prefer? Why?

3. Which piece of writing seems more personal, the article about Khan Duong or Maria Muñiz's essay? Why? How do you decide when your writing should be more personal or more impersonal?

Personal Response and Evaluation

1. Compare Muñiz's experience with her teachers to your own experiences and those of your classmates.

2. Many people experience disappointment when they return to a place they left when they were children. Places change, and so do people. What kind of experience do you think the author will have in Cuba? Have you ever returned to a place that you left years before? What was your experience?

3. Is it important to hold on to the customs and cultural patterns of your native country? Is it important to maintain your first language when you are living in a new country?

Collaborative Story Writing

In a group of no more than five students, work together to write a story beginning with one of the following lines.

1. When Maria arrived in Cuba one sunny morning, the first thing she did was . . .

2. Maria talked to a friend who visited relatives that she hadn't seen in many years. Her friend said . . .

3. Maria receives a letter from an old friend who has just moved to the United States. The letter begins . . .

After your group has agreed on which story to write, one student writes the first line of the story and then passes it to another student, who writes the next line. Pass the story around, each person adding a line, until you reach a satisfying ending. Each group then shares its story with the class.

Journal Writing

The theme of this chapter is going home, returning to a way of life that still lives in memories. The upheaval of confronting a new country, a new language, and a new way of life is probably one of the most emotionally charged experiences a person can have in life. By this time, you have made many adjustments to your new life; there is probably a part of you, however, that thinks of the past with sadness, joy, or a bit of both.

In this journal entry, you may want to think about home. A famous American writer, Thomas Wolfe, wrote a book titled *You Can't Go Home Again*. Do you agree with the title? Do you ever think about returning to your home country? Do you still have friends and family in your country? Where do you feel your real home is?

If you have difficulty writing about this, you might want to try the clustering technique, using *home* as the nucleus word.

Writing Strategies

Essay Strategies

Time Transitions

In the essay in this chapter, Maria Muñiz tells a story about the last 16 years of her life. She makes transitions between various paragraphs using phrases that signify time, including these:

when I was almost five years old

as a little girl

as a child

as I grew older

as an adult

The essay begins when Muñiz is almost 5 years old and arriving in the United States and continues until she is 21 years old and writing the essay. Using time phrases to make transitions between ideas is an effective way of connecting ideas. Time transitions are particularly useful for telling a story in which the sequence of events is important.

Time indicators help the audience to follow the story from the beginning to the present or even into the future. Here are some of the time indicators Muñiz uses:

I came to the United States when I was almost five years old. (lines 7–8; past tense)

I began to remember how as a little girl . . . (lines 25–26 past tense)

As a child, I began to realize . . . (line 46; past tense)

As I grew older, it became a matter of pride. . . (line 47; past tense)

As an adult I have come to terms . . . (line 49; present perfect tense)

When I try to review my life during the past years, I almost feel as if . . . (lines 64–65; present tense)

You can use these time phrases to create your own paragraph, for example:

I came to the United States when I was almost 9 years old. I began to remember how as a little boy I had to try extra hard to do well in school. I was left back in the fourth grade because I was shy and my English was not good. As I grew older, I began to do better in school than a lot of the students who were born in this country. As an adult, I feel proud of my accomplishments. When I try to review my life, I realize that there were many difficult moments, but there were also many great times.

Use these time phrases to create a paragraph about yourself or someone you know.

Details make stories rich. And, as we have observed in Muñiz's writing, a sense of time, a chronology that we can follow, makes a story easier to understand.

In the Hemingway story we read in Chapter Six (page 113), we followed one day in the life of a family. The story began in the morning, continued into the afternoon, and ended later that day. That time framework made the story easy to follow. In the writing exercises for this chapter, keep in mind the elements that make a story work for you. You may want to go back to the stories you wrote in the last chapter and revise them, keeping in mind detail and chronology.

□   □   □

EXERCISE

Read the following poem and then read it again, thinking about the Muñiz essay.

These Days

whatever you have to say, leave
the roots on, let them
dangle

And the dirt
　　　just to make clear
　　　where they have come from.

CHARLES OLSON

1. Why do you think this poem has been included in this chapter? What is this poem about?
2. Poems are condensations of emotional feelings into a short, tight form. In a few words, they can say many things. Therefore, each word must be selected very carefully. The words resonate—like the sun, their meaning beams out in many directions. Poems are often symbolic. What might *roots* refer to other than roots of plants in the soil? What might *dirt* symbolize?
3. Do Charles Olson and Maria L. Muñiz have similar ideas? If so, what are these ideas?

Essay Form

Writing a Process Essay

On page 259, we discussed the importance of a sense of time or chronology in a narrative. Another type of writing in which order is important is the process or step-by-step ordering of a task, an event, or a realization. In Muñiz's essay, she takes us step by step through the process of making a decision to return to Cuba to find a part of herself that is still missing.

When you write about a process, you are making clear to your readers the steps that are involved in doing something, in coming to a decision, or in experiencing something. Try some of the writing strategies described in the following five steps as you organize your process writing.

1. *Look around* and carefully observe the specific details of the way you or other people behave while going through the process you are writing about. If you are writing in the classroom, use your memory. Think about the step-by-step details of the process before you begin to write.

2. *Define* or narrow your subject. Some writers use the dictionary or other source book to help them define the process they wish to describe. Others narrow the process down after step 1, once they have recognized the detail that will be needed in the final essay.

3. *Describe* in detail the steps that are needed to understand the process or pattern. Readers see the picture through your words, so make them clear and direct. What specific steps did Muñiz describe that helped her make the decision to return to Cuba for a visit? How do the specific details add to the overall effectiveness of the essay?

4. *Analyze* the parts or steps of the pattern or process you are explaining. Then tell how these steps work together. Tell the reader about the history and the future of your subject. What does Muñiz include about her personal history to help the reader understand her decision? What does she tell the reader about the history of her country? How does knowing something about the history of Cuba help you understand her decision?

5. *Evaluate* the reasons why the pattern or process you are explaining is important to the reader. What does Muñiz write that convinces you that the issue she is explaining is important to you as a reader?

You will not need to use all five steps in every process essay that you write, but keeping them in mind can help you write a clear and effective essay.

□ □ □

EXERCISES

1. In the first paragraph, Muñiz asks two questions: "Would you ever go back?" and "Is there any reason for me to go?" In the rest of the essay, she explains her process for making the decision to return to Cuba for a visit. Reread her essay, listing the steps leading to her decision. Are the steps in any particular order?

2. In the story on page 233, Han Suyin tells the steps that Rosalie Chou takes to get her first job. Reread that story, listing the steps leading to her job. How does she order these steps?

Process writing enables the reader to understand us better or to do something that we have done before. When we look at Casals's "Age and Youth" (page 175), we learn something about him from the step-by-step outline of his day-to-day routine.

Casals gets up each morning and goes to the piano. He plays two preludes and fugues of Bach. Then he takes a walk along the beach. He observes the nature that surrounds him.

What do we learn about Casals from this?

There are many uses for the process type of writing, but the most common example is the recipe. The writer attempts to tell the reader, with sufficient detail and in the right order, the way to prepare a dish. The following is a recipe for "Grandma Robbins's Potato Latkes (Pancakes)":

To make 18 to 20 potato latkes or pancakes, first peel 6 large potatoes and then grate them into a colander. With your hands, squeeze some of the liquid out and put the potatoes in a bowl. Then grate 1 medium-sized onion into the same bowl and add two beaten eggs, ½ cup flour, and ½ teaspoon of salt. Mix this together well. Next heat oil in a skillet and drop the potato batter by spoonfuls into the hot oil, forming small pancake shapes. Let the latkes fry until they are crisp at the edge and brown. Then turn and cook the other side in the same way. Drain the pancakes on brown paper or paper towels. Then keep them warm in the oven while you cook the others. Finally, serve them to your hungry guests. These are delicious served with sour cream or applesauce.

If a recipe is well written, the reader should be able to follow each step and make the dish. Reread the recipe, underlining all the transition words.

We also use process writing when we want to explain to someone how to do something. If someone asks us how to register for a class or get a passport, for example, we will give the steps that are required to do the activity. In the following example, a student describes the way to eat a slice of pizza:

First, you order the pizza by walking up and looking the counterperson straight in the eye and saying, "A slice, please." The slice comes on a thin, waxy piece of paper. Next you grab a napkin and quickly slip it under the paper, so you don't spill hot oil all over. Then you put your index finger in the middle of the crust and try to bend it in half. This way you can hold the slice in one hand without dropping it. At this point, you have to be careful because you can burn your finger on the hot cheese. Slowly bring the slice close to your mouth. Breathe in as you do this. Then your mouth begins to water in anticipation of the taste. Take a bite at the tip of the triangle and chew carefully because the first taste, believe it or not, is always the best. Eat slowly and enjoy. Always remember to save a little of the cheese and sauce at the end so the crust will not be too dry. Finally, finish it all, even though it is probably cold.

Reread this description, underlining the transition words.

□ □ □

EXERCISES

1. Write a step-by-step explanation of how to get from school to the front door of your home.
2. Write a step-by-step recipe.
3. Write a step-by-step explanation of your decision to attend your college.
4. Write a step-by-step explanation of your realization of the importance of a certain subject.

Suggestions for Writing

Take some time to think about your ideas before you start to write. You may want to look at your journal for ideas, or you may want to try reminiscing, as described in the "Getting Started" section that follows. Choose one of the following topics to write about.

1. "Outside American, inside Cuban." What does Muñiz mean by these words? Have you ever felt this way in relation to your country? If you have, describe your feelings and experiences in a narrative. Keep in mind the order of the events.

2. Write a letter to Muñiz telling her how her essay affected you. Offer her advice about whether she should return to Cuba. Explain your reasons.

3. "Like most immigrants, my family and I have had to build a new life from almost nothing. It was often difficult, but I believe the struggle made us strong." How can struggle make someone strong? Tell a story about yourself or about someone you know or have heard of who has grown stronger through struggle.

4. Many people feel confused about how much of their cultural heritage they should keep in America and how much they should give up in order to become more "Americanized." How have you resolved this question? Tell a story describing how you or someone you have heard of dealt with this issue.

5. Do you think that we all have a responsibility to be political? Should we be familiar with what is going on in other countries of the world? Or do you believe that our responsibility should be only to ourselves, our families, and our neighborhoods? Explain and give examples supporting your point of view.

Getting Started

Reminiscing

In Maria L. Muñiz's essay, she wrote about her own past and the past of her family. In doing this, she reminisced about her family history. This helped to make her writing more powerful and real to her readers.

As you prepare to write one of the essays from the "Suggestions for Writing" above, think about your past and your family history. Focus on the personal experiences or observations that relate to the question you will answer. Jot down a few words that will help you recall these events. Write down as many events or memories as you can recall in five to ten minutes. Then, before you write your essay, look through these reminiscences or memories and choose the ones that, developed more fully, will enrich your writing.

A Student Essay

The following student essay was written in response to suggested topic 3.

MY FATHER

Like most immigrants, my family has had to build a new life by working hard. Watching my father as he does this shows me what it means to be strong. He is 5 feet 9 inches tall, has light brown skin color, short black-and-white hair, and brown eyes, and weighs roughly 180 pounds. My father is now 59 years old, and I am truly one of his secret admirers.

The first of seven children, my father was born in Haiti in a town 20 miles away from the capital of the country. He then proceeded to Port-au-Prince, the capital of Haiti, for his schooling, which he finished before he left the city.

My father became a minister at about the age of 30 or 31. From that time on, he went through some traumatic experiences in his life. At the age of 32, he was married to a woman and had two children with her. A year and a half later, his wife was suddenly attacked by a sickness. She succumbed to the sickness and died. There was no indication what caused the sickness or even the name of the sickness.

Two years after the death of my father's first wife, my father married my mother. She conceived seven children with him, which gives him a total of nine children. The first two were sons. They are now married and have children of their own. They are now living with their wives, three blocks from our house.

My father went through a lot in Haiti, and finally my whole family moved to the United States. My father has always played a very important role in my life. If it weren't for him, I don't think I would be sitting here in school writing about him. My father is a very diligent man. He works 12 hours every day to support the family. Sometimes when there is an emergency such as the gas bill, the electric bill, or the telephone bill, he has even worked on Saturdays to make the extra money to pay the bills.

My father works every day except Sunday. He works in the summer as well as in the winter. He wakes up at 5 o'clock in the morning and goes to wait for the bus, which is two blocks away from where he lives. Sometimes when it's really cold, below zero, I feel like crying thinking about my father waiting in the cold weather to catch a bus. It is even worse when he has finished working inside in the heat, and he is exhausted, tired, hungry, and yet he must go back through the same process again.

He has shown me what it means to be strong, and one day I want to be the strong one. One day, I will make sure that all his hard working will stop. That's a promise.

Nickso Marcellus, Haiti

When you finish reading Nickso's essay, review some of the other student essays in this book. What have you learned from reading these essays and doing revision exercises on them? How has their writing influenced your writing? What are you more careful about when you write now that you were not aware of earlier in the term?

Revising

After discussing Nickso Marcellus's essay with your classmates, review the draft of the essay you wrote as you prepare to revise it. Put away the pen you used to write the essay; use a different pen or pencil now. Read your essay aloud, and ask yourself questions about it; you may want to write these questions on a separate piece of paper. Some possible questions are these:

1. What is the writer trying to say in this essay?
2. Does it make sense?
3. Are there enough examples, and are they clear?
4. Are there enough details?
5. Is the essay interesting to read?

Use these questions to help you during the rewriting process. Try to be a helpful critic. Focus on the organization of the essay. Does one idea lead to the next? Are there enough details so that you can form pictures in your mind? How can this piece of writing be made to come alive to its readers?

Editing Strategies

Word Development

word forms

A useful way to increase vocabulary is to learn new forms of words that you already know. In this way you more than triple the number of words that you can understand and use.

The underlined forms of the following words appear in "Back, but Not Home." They are all words that are commonly used in college-level material.

Adjective	*Adverb*	*Noun*	*Verb*
sympathetic	sympathetically	sympathy	sympathize
communicative	communicatively	communication	communicate
persistent	persistently	persistence	persist
hesitant	hesitantly	hesitation	hesitate
hesitating	(un)hesitatingly		

□ □ □

EXERCISE   Use the correct word form in each of the following sentences. If the word form is a verb, be sure to use the appropriate ending.

sympathetic   *sympathetically*   *sympathy*   *sympathize*

1. The teacher should have treated the small child more

   _____.

2. Because of her experiences, she is _____ to others.

   communicative   *communicatively*   *communication*   *communicate*

3. In this essay, Maria L. Muñiz _____ her feelings about Cuba.

4. Writing is a _____ process.

   persistent   *persistently*   *persistence*   *persist*

5. Her _____ in learning English may have helped her to succeed in her career as a journalist.

6. If one does not _____, one will not succeed in this world.

   hesitant   *hesitantly*   *hesitation*   *hesitate*
   hesitating   *(un)hesitatingly*

7. Muñiz _____ before she made the difficult decision.

8. Her _____ gave her time to think through all the positives and negatives.

   These words will become part of your active vocabulary if you use them. Write sentences using these words in each of their forms. In addition, try to use some of them in your next essay.

Commonly Confused Words

where/were
Read the following paragraph, observing the use of *where* and *were*.

Sometimes our response to bad news is affected by *where* we hear it. If we *were* at home, we might allow ourselves to cry and feel grief. If we *were* out on the street, we might find ourselves trying to hold back our tears and deep feelings until we got to a place *where* we felt safe.

On the basis of what you observed in the paragraph, complete the following definitions.

_____ is the plural past tense of the verb *be*.

_____ asks in what place something is.

Wear and *ware* are also sometimes confused with *where* and *were*. *Wear* means "to have on," as clothing. ("She *wears* a suit to work every day.") *Ware* means "piece of goods to be sold." ("A peddler was selling his *wares*.")

Fill in the blanks in the following sentences with *where, were, wear,* or *ware(s)*.

1. She didn't know what to _____ because she didn't know

   _____ they _____ going on their date.

2. The peddler sold his _____ on the street corner.

3. They _____ not sure _____ to go after they heard the news.

Now write your own sentences using *where, were, wear,* and *ware*.

Mechanics

Parentheses

The first rule to remember about using parentheses is to avoid using them as much as possible. They are distracting to the reader. However, writers do use parentheses to separate explanatory or supplementary material from the body of the main text when necessary.

Parentheses are also used in research papers when a writer reports or rephrases what another writer has written. In that case, the parentheses enclose the name and date of the source of research. Look at the Oskamp selection on page 213 to see how writers use parentheses to credit the source of research findings being discussed.

When quoting someone's exact words, a writer uses quotation marks around the words and follows them, in parentheses, with the original author's name, the date of the publication, and the page number, for example, "Quotation" (Rose, 1989, p. 17).

This is a general description of the use of parentheses. The exact format for documenting research and other writing can vary, depending on your teacher's style requirements. Check this with your teacher before writing a research paper.

Editing Practice

The following paragraph is an unedited first draft. Read it and edit the paragraph, looking for errors of any kind. If you have difficulty, discuss it with a classmate. To check your answers, turn to page 324.

The essay "Back, but Not Home" by Maria L. muñiz made me think about returning to my country. I grown up thinking that their was no reason to go back, but now I am not sure. Its interesting for me to think about the world that I left behind, I feel mixed emotions. Such as happiness, sadness, and regret. My aunts and uncle still lives in my country. They still live in the same town; in the same house. I have never seen most of my cousins, the youngest one is five month old and I would like to know him to. My brother visited my family last year, and he told me all the news. Its strange hearing about my best girlfriends which are getting married and one even has a baby. The Muñiz essay, my brother's visit, and my dreams makes me: want to return to my country for a visit.

Grammar Strategies

Parallelism

Words in a pair or in series should have a balanced or parallel structure. The following examples of parallel structure are taken from the Muñiz essay.

> I am still unable to view the revolution with *detachment* or *objectivity*. (Both these words are nouns.)
> I cannot interpret its results in *social, political,* or *economic* terms. (These words are all adjectives.)

The following examples of parallel structure are taken from the Han Suyin story on page 233.

> But with my looks I would never get married; I was *too thin, too sharp, too ugly.* (These adjectives are all modified by *too.*)
> "You look sixteen," said Mama; "all you have to do is to stop *hopping* and *picking* your pimples." (Both words end in *-ing.*)

☐ ☐ ☐

EXERCISES

1. Fill in the blanks with appropriate words in parallel structure. Many answers are correct, so share what you have written with a partner.

Muñiz explains that some of the steps that she went through to make a difficult decision included talking with others, _____, and _____. She decided to return to Cuba so that she could visit her old house, _____, and _____. She wants to know, to _____, and to _____. After living in the United States for many years, she still thinks about her grandmother, _____, and _____. She has letters, _____, and _____ to remind her of her family, but that is not enough. She wants to return to the place where she was born, _____, and _____ until she moved to the United States. She thinks it is time to _____ and to _____.

2. Combine the following sentences, making sure to use parallel constructions and commas between the items in a series. The first one is done for you.

a. She came to the United States.
   She moved to Brooklyn.
   She entered school.

   She came to the United States, moved to Brooklyn, and entered school.

b. She learned English by talking.
   She learned English by listening.
   She learned English by thinking.

   _____

   _____

c. Her grandmother remained in Cuba.
   Her aunts remained in Cuba.
   Her uncles remained in Cuba.

   _____

   _____

d. She wanted to speak English.
   She wanted to fit in.
   She wanted to be accepted.

   _____

   _____

CHAPTER FOURTEEN

Establishing an Identity

PREREADING ACTIVITIES

1. In a small group, decide on the ten historical events that have most influenced the world we live in today. Discuss your list with the rest of the class. In what ways are the lists in your class similar? In what ways are they different? How did you resolve conflicts in your group about what should be on the list?

2. In a small group, decide on the ten historical events that have occurred during your lifetime that have most influenced the world we live in today. Discuss in what ways this list differs from the list you made in response to activity 1. Share your list with the rest of the class.

3. Many people say that it is important to study history because it helps us understand our world better. In a group, discuss the ways in which knowing history has influenced your understanding of the world.

The Social Context of Identity Formation

This excerpt from the textbook Human Development *by Kurt W. Fischer and Arlyne Lazerson examines the effects of the Great Depression of the 1930s on a group of young people growing up in California. The authors conclude that cultural or social changes have a broad effect on people's daily lives. However, most people are able to adapt to such major social changes by altering but not losing their sense of identity.*

°ten-year period

°pertaining to Queen Victoria's time (1837–1901), which was characterized by modest behavior and manners

The decade° of the 1920s—the Roaring 20s—was a period of social revolution in the United States. After World War I (and in some ways because of it), there was a dramatic shift from strict Victorian° prewar standards of behavior to more relaxed standards in regard to dress, drink, male-female relations, and much more. The 20s were also 5 a very prosperous time. After World War I the economic balloon expanded until 1929, when it burst and the Depression began. The stock market crashed; banks and businesses failed; thousands of men lost their jobs and their life savings. Many families that had been comfortably middle class in the 20s became poor in the 30s. 10

In 1931, the Berkeley Institute of Human Development began a longitudinal study of adolescent development, called the Oakland

°thoroughly

(California) Growth Study. The children, 84 boys and 83 girls, were in fifth grade when the study began, and they and their families were studied intensively° and continuously from 1931 until 1939. Follow-up 15 surveys of this group were conducted through the 1960s, by which time many of these Depression adolescents had adolescent children of their own.

Glenn Elder (1974, 1980), a sociologist, analyzed the data from this study in an effort to determine how the Depression had affected 20 people who had been adolescents during those hard times. He was particularly interested in families that had suffered a major loss of income and status. Statistics show that average family income in Oakland declined about 40 percent between 1929 and 1933. Small businessmen lost their businesses, and workmen lost their jobs. Most 25 investments became worthless, and savings disappeared. Parents were unable to feed and clothe their families without charity or government

°something new

assistance—a Depression innovation° that many people found hard to accept. Many men, raised to believe that any man who could not support his family was worthless, suffered a shattering loss of self- 30 esteem.°

°belief in value of self

In many such families, Elder found, there was a shift of power from the father to the mother. As the father's role declined, the mother's role grew more important. Often the mother both worked at odd jobs to bring income into the household and served as the main decision 35 maker and emotional resource. Because the mother was so busy and the family so poor, the adolescent children were given important adultlike responsibilities. This shift of responsibilities had major effects, which differed greatly for girls and boys.

Adolescent girls were given many housekeeping duties. Because 40 they had not even a slight hope of education beyond high school (who could afford it?) and because jobs were so scarce, they concentrated on a domestic future. Middle-class girls whose families had suffered severe losses tended to marry early. In the Roaring 20s, the feminist movement had flowered. The great prosperity and liberal social norms 45 of that decade had encouraged young women to think of their future in terms of education and career. The Depression greatly constricted°

°reduced, shrank

these possibilities. Young women were forced by social circumstances to adopt a more traditional female identity as homemaker and mother.

The father's loss of status in the family and the mother's extra 50 burdens had a different effect on boys, serving to liberate them from parental controls at an early age. Teen-age boys took jobs, if they could

°on top of things, not sinking under debt

find them, to help keep the family afloat.° In their work or search for work, these young adolescents dealt as one adult to another with many men and women outside the family. The circumstance of the Depres- 55

°speeded up

sion thus accelerated° the development of these boys toward adult roles as breadwinners and achievers. In fact, as adults, men whose

°severe

families had suffered a drastic° loss of income when they were boys showed higher motivation to achieve than men whose family incomes had not dropped so much. 60

The effects of social circumstances on the identities of the men and women in this study continued to be evident in later life. As adults, the women continued to be family-centered, viewing care of their children as their most significant responsibility. The men did not appear to have suffered from delay or lack of higher education. Their early 65 entrance into the life of work and their need to achieve were enough to make them generally successful in their adult vocations. The men were also more family-oriented as adults than were Depression adolescents whose families had not suffered major financial losses. In the 1920s, when these people were born, their parents did not intend to 70 bring them up as they did. Most parents did not plan to place the major burdens of housekeeping on their daughters or to send their sons out to earn money for groceries and rent. But when the Depression came, the parents had to adapt their ways of socializing their children to the unexpected hard times. 75

Elder's work illustrates two points that had previously been difficult to document. First, the historical context of growing up has important effects on the course of human development, including the personal identity formed in adolescence and early adulthood. Second, within the identity they choose, most people have the flexibility to 80 adapt to major social changes during their adult years, to modify rather than to lose their sense of identity.

Any great cultural or social changes—in fact, all broad influences— are experienced by individuals through what happens in their daily life. Adolescents learn about life's possibilities—and impossibilities— 85 from their relationships with parents and friends and from the adults and books they encounter in high school. These influences all make important contributions to an adolescent's self-image.

Reading and Thinking Strategies

Discussion Activities

Analysis and Conclusions

1. According to Glenn Elder's findings, why was there a shift of power from the father to the mother after the Depression began?

2. How did life change for the adolescent girls studied? For the boys studied? Why did these kinds of changes occur?

3. How did the changes affect the lives of these young people as they grew to be men and women? Many of these people became parents

in the 1950s. What kind of parents do you think they became? How do you think they brought their children up? On what did you base your answer?

Writing and Point of View

1. The authors of this excerpt are trying to convince the reader that "the historical context of growing up has important effects on the course of human development." What evidence do they use to support this point of view? Is there sufficient evidence to persuade you as the reader?

2. The fifth sentence in paragraph 1 contains two semicolons. Why did the authors use semicolons to connect these sentences? Could the sentences have been connected in some other way? Which do you prefer? (If you are confused about semicolons, review page 187.)

3. Compare the description of family in this article with the Bergers' description of family on page 21. How do the styles of the two pieces differ? Which piece did you prefer reading and why?

Personal Response and Evaluation

1. Have you known anyone who "suffered a major loss of income and status"? How did that person deal with the situation?

2. The authors claim that "people have the flexibility to adapt to major social changes during their adult years, to modify rather than lose their sense of identity." Do you think that adults are more flexible and change more easily than adolescents? Support your opinion with your own observations or experiences.

3. Gail Sheehy in her book *Passages* writes, "The work of adult life is not easy." In what ways is adulthood more difficult than childhood?

Writing the Survey

The selection in this chapter described a longitudinal study of a large group of people to find out how the Depression had affected their lives. Each part of the study probably included some type of survey in which questions were asked of individual members of the group to determine group response. As a class, prepare a survey containing ten questions that will provide information about your class members. Decide on the questions, and then conduct the survey. As a follow-up, you might want to conduct this survey at one-month intervals throughout the semester. If you decide to conduct follow-up surveys, you may want to consider questions whose answers might vary, such as "What is your biggest problem adjusting to life in the United States?" or "What is the easiest part about learning English?" (Answers to questions such as "How tall are you?" would probably not change in the follow-up surveys.)

Journal Writing

A student wrote in her journal, "I may look different in five years, and I may be living a very different life. I expect I will be married by then, or at least I will have found someone to love. But deep down inside I will be the same person. Deep down inside people really don't change very much at all." This journal entry would seem to be in agreement with the article we have read. On the basis of your own experience, do you agree or disagree?

What event in your life has had the greatest influence on you? Is there any event that has made a change in where you live or how you live? Do you feel that you are a very different person today from the person you were five years ago?

Writing Strategies

Essay Strategies

Getting Information from Your Textbook

One important skill for college students is being able to get information from various sources. One source is your textbook. When you read a textbook, you cannot expect to remember every detail. However, the text itself is constructed in a way that can help you find and remember the most important ideas. Some students highlight these important ideas with specially colored pens; other students copy them into their notebooks or onto index cards. Copying the main ideas and supporting details is a good idea because most people find it easier to remember material that they have written down than material that they have simply read and underlined.

In your classes, when you read textbook material, you should make notes that you will refer to later. One way to break down the notes into a usable form is to label them with the authors' names, the title, and the page number. If you write down the authors' exact words, put them in quotation marks, and record the page number. This will help you if you need to find this information again. It will also help if you are writing a research paper and want to quote or paraphrase the material.

The following exercises will help you break down and analyze the selection at the start of this chapter. Although you will not go through all of these steps when you read your textbooks, these exercises will give you experience in analyzing the structure of textbook writing. When you take notes for your classes or research papers, you should concentrate on finding the main idea or theme and the most important supporting details.

◻ ◻ ◻

EXERCISES

1. The selection has two introductory paragraphs. Reread the first two paragraphs, and note here the events that a reader needs to know to understand the historical context the authors will analyze in their writing.

   _____

   _____

2. The authors developed their selection with facts that led them to a general conclusion. This is deductive reasoning (see page 94 for an explanation of this). Their general conclusion or main idea is found in the last two paragraphs on page 274. What is the main idea of "The Social Context of Identity Formation"?

   _____

3. Reread paragraphs three to seven. List the details that support the main idea.

   _____

   _____

   _____

   _____

4. Reread what you have listed in Exercise 3. Put an *F* next to the details that are based on fact and an *O* next to the details that are based on opinion. In what types of writing would you expect to find more facts? In what types of writing would you expect to find more opinions?

Summary Writing

Students often write short summaries of textbook material. These summaries include the names of the writers, the title of the piece, and the pages on which it occurs. The summary should contain the most important ideas from the original piece of writing, expressed in your own words. Your summary should be no longer than one-third or one-fourth of the original piece of writing. You may include a quotation from the original selection, but if you do this, put it in quotation marks so that you will remember that this is not your own writing.

When you write your summary, look for key words or phrases. Be sure to include important names, places, dates, and facts. Answer the *who, what, where, when, why*, and *how* questions as clearly and concisely as possible.

□ □ □

EXERCISES

1. Write a summary of "The Social Context of Identity Formation."
2. Write a summary of another selection from the book, and share it with a classmate.

Essay Form

Writing a Cause-and-Effect Essay

The authors of the textbook excerpt use *cause-and-effect* reasoning to convince their readers that the events of the 1920s in the United States affected the lives of the adolescents of that time period. When you organize your writing using cause and effect, you are clarifying the connections between events for your reader. The following steps are useful in establishing cause and effect:

1. *Define* the cause. Put the event or occurrence in a historical context—tell what happened immediately before, and briefly outline the steps that led to the major event. Tell your readers why it is important for them to know about and understand this event. Which event do the authors define in their selection? How do they set it in a historical context?

2. *Describe* in detail what followed the event or occurrence you define in step 1. Readers follow your reasoning through your words, so make them clear and direct. What specific descriptive details did the selection authors use? How do they add to the overall effectiveness of the essay?

3. *Analyze* the details you are explaining. Tell in what ways these details are direct responses to the cause you have defined in step 1. Explain the history and the future of your subject to your readers. What do the textbook authors tell their readers about U.S. history

in their selection? How do they relate the histo_____
effect they describe?

4. *Evaluate* why the cause led to the effect you describ____
about what this can mean to others or to the future. Co____
reader that your subject is important for them to kn____
generalizations do the textbook writers present to concl____
selection? Do they convince you that their subject is impor____
you as a reader?

Suggestions for Writing

Before you begin to write, choose one of the topics that follow. Discuss some of your ideas about this subject with a classmate, or use the "Getting Started" suggestions on page 280 (or others found in this book) to help you find ideas. You may also decide to look at your journal for ideas. Always spend some time thinking before you start to write.

1. The historical events that occur in a country can have profound effects on the lives of the people of that country. Describe a situation in which a historical event markedly changed someone's life. Write about the cause and the effects that followed it. Explain to your readers how the person coped with the changes. Generalize about what this meant to the person or what it might mean to society at large.

2. Write an essay in which you analyze the effect of a tuition increase at your college. Imagine that students are faced with double the tuition they are presently paying. Describe the effects that such an event might have on students. Generalize about how this could affect students' educational experiences and educational future.

3. Some people believe that a bill should be passed in the United States making English the official language of the country. People would be required to learn English to survive in this country. Write an essay in which you analyze the effect of making English the only language used in public institutions in this country. Generalize about how this could affect life in your community and in the United States as a whole.

4. Write an essay in which you analyze the effect of legalizing the sale of drugs in the United States. Describe the effects that such an event might have on individuals and on society in general. Generalize about how this could influence life in the United States as you know it.

5. The authors of the excerpt in this chapter state: "Adolescents tend to follow in their parents' footsteps, taking on values, beliefs and

ablishing an identity

to the general

Generalize

vince your

ow. What

de this

ant to

279

ire very much like those of their parents." How do people

is right for themselves? Describe how you make these

ng examples from your experience or observations.

o be individual and unique. At the same time,

ant to be accepted by their peers, so they conform

olain how you or someone you know has resolved

ites, "The best part of growing up is freedom. And the

part of growing up is freedom." What do you think this

dent means? How can one deal with the responsibilities and
freedoms of adult life? Use your experiences and observations to
support your point of view.

8. "Young people should move away from home as soon as they are
able to support themselves because it is important for them to be
independent and self-sufficient before making a commitment to
anyone else." Do you agree or disagree? Support your point of view
with your own experience or your observations of others.

Getting Started

Freewriting with a Purpose: Creating Your Own Context

The article's authors write that "any great cultural or social
changes—in fact, all broad influences—are experienced by individuals through what happens in their daily life." According to this, all of
us live in the context of what happens around us that affects our lives.
For the next ten minutes, write about the context in which you live. To
do this, think about the place you live in, the people you see on the
street, the newspaper you read, the television programs you watch, the
music you listen to, and the school you attend. Describe as many of
these and any other influences that occur to you. Look at the world
that surrounds you, and write about how it has affected your values,
ambitions, and daily life.

A Student Essay

This student responded to writing suggestion 8.

Sooner or later all teenagers grow up. And usually, when the crucial
moment comes, the moment to take the big step from being a teen to
being an adult, the majority of teenagers make a lot of mistakes. These
kinds of mistakes cannot be caused by anyone around them, but by life
itself. In order to be prepared for the "adult life," meaning all the   5

difficulties and problems that are usual for an adult, but might be extremely difficult for a teenager, teenagers should learn to make their own decisions.

Young people should move away from home as soon as they are able to support themselves. It is important for them to be independent and 10 self-sufficient before making a commitment to anyone and anything else in life.

Making the right decision is the first and most important step for teenagers to learn. As soon as teenagers move out, they learn that now they have to make decisions by themselves. There are no parents and 15 brothers or sisters around to make decisions for them. No, they are on their own. By making their own decisions, they grow more mature and intelligent.

By living separately from their parents, young people learn about the problems they never had at home. Household problems were 20 always taken care of by their parents. On their own, they have to face the problems. At that time, young people realize the difficulties their parents had but they never noticed before.

All these new experiences that young people will face as soon as they become independent are excellent lessons in life. Before young 25 people make the commitment to someone else, they should necessarily experience the task of life. This way they will have more chances that their future life and family will work out for the best.

Margaret Nesterovskya, Poland

Revising

Here are some questions to ask yourself about Margaret Nesterovskya's essay. After you have reviewed her essay, meet with a classmate to discuss the essay you have written. Write out the following questions, and ask your classmate to write out answers for you about your draft.

1. What is the purpose of this essay? What was the writer trying to say?

2. Which ideas or examples best support the main point of the writing?

3. In which part of the essay would you have liked more information? Where did you have trouble following the writing?

4. Is there anything else that you would like to know about this topic that is not included? Is there anything that would make the essay more interesting to you as a reader?

Revise what you have written, and share this with the same classmate.

Editing Strategies

Word Development

words relating to research

As you continue your studies and as you read more newspapers and newsmagazines, you will encounter various types of research. In this selection, many of the vocabulary words relate to the conduct of research. These words will be useful to you throughout your college career and during your everday life.

1. **standards** (line 4)

   After World War I (and in some ways because of it), there was a dramatic shift from strict Victorian prewar standards of behavior to more relaxed standards in regard to dress, drink, male-female relations, and much more.

   standard: anything accepted by general agreement as a basis of comparison; a model.

   Are standards in the United States today strict or relaxed? Compare the standards in your native country (in relation to dress, smoking, drink, and so on) with those in the United States.

2. **longitudinal study** (line 12)

   In 1931, the Berkeley Institute of Human Development began a longitudinal study of adolescent development, called the Oakland (California) Growth Study. The children, 84 boys and 83 girls, were in fifth grade when the study began, and they and their families were studied intensively and continuously from 1931 until 1939.

   longitudinal study: a study in which the same group of subjects is repeatedly tested as they grow older or over a long period of time.

   Another type of study commonly used is a *cross-sectional study*, in which groups of people of different ages are studied and observed at the same time and measured in the same way. If, for example, the groups are similar in all important respects except age, differences can be assumed to be due to developmental changes due to aging. In this type of study, people are measured at one time, not over a period of time.

   If all the members of your class filled out a questionnaire about their favorite music, would it be a cross-sectional study or a longitudinal study? If class members filled out the questionnaire every two months for two years, would it be a cross-sectional study or a longitudinal study?

3. **follow-up** (line 15); **survey** (line 16)

Follow-up surveys of this group were conducted through the 1960s, by which time many of these Depression adolescents had adolescent children of their own.

follow-up: the recontacting of a person for business or study purposes.

survey: a study of the particular facts about some thing in order to determine its condition or character.

A cross-sectional study in which questions are asked of a group, such as the members of your class, is a survey. If you were to return to this group and ask the same questions again, that would be a follow-up survey.

If you could do a survey about one aspect of your class members, what would it be? Would you also do a follow-up survey?

4. **data** (line 19)

Glenn Elder (1974, 1980), a sociologist, analyzed the data from this study in an effort to determine how the Depression had affected people who had been adolescents during those hard times.

data: facts or information, often in the form of numbers, used in reaching conclusions or in doing studies.

What data would you need in order to know which language is spoken by the majority of students in your class?

5. **average** *(line 23);* **statistics** (line 23)

Statistics show that average family income in Oakland declined about 40 percent between 1929 and 1933.

average: an arithmetic mean found by adding up all the data on a particular group and then dividing by the number of quantities added. The average of $3,000, $4,000, and $8,000 is $5,000 ($3,000 + $4,000 + $8,000 = $15,000 ÷ 3 = $5,000).

statistics: the numerical facts or data that have been collected, classified, and used to explain a certain subject.

As a class project, ask how many brothers and sisters each member of your class has. Add up the numbers, and divide by the number of class members who contributed information. You will then have the average number of siblings (brothers and sisters) of the members of your class. What can you determine from these statistics?

synonyms

Each word in column A means almost the same thing as one of the words in column B. A word that has almost the same meaning as another word is a synonym. Draw a line from each word in column A to its synonym in column B. The first one has been done for you.

A	*B*
1. prosperous	a. growth
2. adolescents	b. modify
3. development	c. teenagers
4. liberate	d. rich
5. drastic	e. bring up
6. adapt	f. change
7. shift	g. severe, forceful
8. raise	h. release, free

Fill in each of the following blanks with a synonym from column B (in its appropriate form).

1. The postwar period of the 1920s was a _____ time in

   which there was great financial _____.

2. The stock market crash brought about a _____ change in the lives of most Americans.

3. A study was conducted to determine how _____ had to

   _____ their lifestyles because of their family's lack of money.

4. Boys who had been _____ to seek higher education

   took jobs that served to _____ them from their family's control.

Now use these words in sentences of your own.

Commonly Confused Words

affect/effect

Glenn Elder analyzed the data from this study in an effort to determine how the Depression had *affected* people who had been adolescents during that time period.

Is *affect* used as a verb or as a noun? Does it mean "influence" or "bring about"?

After the Depression, there was a shift of responsibilities that had major *effects* on the lives of the boys and girls.

The father's loss of status in the family and the mother's extra burdens had a different *effect* on boys.

The *effects* of social circumstances on the identities of the men and women in this study were evident all their lives.

The historical context of growing up has *effected* changes in the course of human development.

Is *effect* used as a verb or as a noun in each of the preceding sentences? If you had to use a synonym for *effect* in these sentences, what would it be?

Examine how *affect* and *effect* are used in the following paragraph. Then complete the definitions.

The *effects* of becoming an adult are varied. Your younger brothers and sisters can be *affected* because they can see the positive things you are doing with your life. The *effect* may be that they will grow up and try to be like you. You can *effect* real changes in their lives.

_____ is a noun that means "result."

_____ is a verb that means "to influence."

_____ is a verb that means "to bring about."

Fill in the blanks in the following sentences with either *affect* or *effect*.

1. The birth of her first child had a big _____ on her life.

2. It _____ed the way she related to her own mother.

3. The _____ was very positive. She was able to

   _____ some changes in her family relationships.

Now write your own sentences using *affect* and *effect*.

Mechanics

Abbreviations

An abbreviation is a shortened form of a word. In general, most writers avoid most abbreviations in the formal writing that is required of college students. However, some abbreviations are acceptable in college writing.

Acceptable abbreviations followed by a period: Mr., Mrs., Ms., Dr., Jr., Sr., a.m. *or* A.M., p.m. *or* P.M., B.C., A.D.

Acceptable abbreviations that do not need a period: FBI, CIA, FM, AM, NBC, CBS, ABC, NASA, VISTA, radar, laser, sonar

Do *not* abbreviate the names of months, days, countries, states, units of time, or names of courses in your writing. Do not abbreviate the words *street, road, avenue, company,* or *association* or other words that are part of a proper name. Do not use signs such as @, #, or & in your writing. The $ sign is acceptable when you are writing a number that contains both dollars and cents.

□ □ □

EXERCISES

1. As part of your editing process, review essays that you have written earlier in the semester, noting how you handled the words and abbreviations described above.
2. When you write, check this list to make sure that you have used abbreviations appropriately.

Editing Practice

The paragraph below is an unedited first draft that contains many errors. Find and correct as many as you can. If you have difficulty, discuss the paragraph with a classmate. The answers are on page 324.

Although getting engaged has changed Samia's life. But she doesn't want to marry now. Ahmed, her boyfriend, want to get married right away, but she disagree. For now, she like showing her girlfriends her diamond ring. She also enjoy discussing her future wedding with them. When she is in school. Even through she is knowing that she make her friends jealous, but she enjoys showing off. The other day her best friends did a real effort not to review there homeworks with her in the cafeteria as they usually did every afternoon after class. She is realizing they envied her, yet she is continuing the same behavior. Samia claim that she is liking being engaged, but she doesn't want to get married right away. Being housewives doesn't sound like to much fun to her.

Grammar Strategies

Modal Auxiliaries with *have* + Past Participle

In Chapter Seven on page 146 we discussed modal auxiliaries (*can/ could, have to, may/might, must, shall, will/would, should, ought to*). These words are followed by the simple form of the verb (*I can swim* or *He can swim*). Modal auxiliaries are not usually indicators of time and tense, although most users of English agree that *I can swim* has a different time meaning than *I could swim*.

When we combine the modal auxiliary with *have* and the past participle (a list of past participles appears on pages 313–16), the meaning of the modal auxiliary is altered. The modal with *have* and the past participle can be used in the following ways:

1. To indicate that the action referred to was not accomplished:

   He could have gotten a better job by now (but he hasn't).
   They should have graduated from college by now (but they haven't).
   You would have been rich if you had taken the opportunity (but you didn't).

2. To infer something:

   He must have missed the train (because he isn't here yet).
   She might have decided to go by bus (because she wasn't on the train).

3. To show advisability or a social obligation:

   They should have visited her when she was in the hospital.
   She must have called her mother to tell her about the baby.
   He could have paid for half the taxi ride.

4. To show possibility:

   Thuy might have lived in Hong Kong when she first left Vietnam.
   Jaime could have studied English in his country.

Who can that have been?
What could have caused that much noise?

5. To predict (*will* and *shall* only):

In the year 2000, she will have lived in San Francisco for ten years.
She will have been living in San Francisco for ten years in the year 2000.
By 2000, I shall have repaid my school loan.
By the year 2000, we shall have lived in the United States longer than we lived in Ecuador.

□ □ □

EXERCISE   Write your response to the following situations using the modal auxiliary with *have* and the past participle of the verb that you think makes the most sense. Because there is more than one correct answer for each, discuss your answers in a small group in class.

1. A student fails a course that she thinks she should have passed. She sees her teacher in the hall, and she turns away to avoid talking to her teacher. Later, she feels angry and upset. What could this student have done so she wouldn't have felt angry and upset about this situation?

2. Two good friends had an argument about who should have paid for dinner at an expensive restaurant. One person thinks that he should have paid because it was his friend's birthday. The other person thinks that he should have paid because he invited his friend to join him. Who should have paid? Why?

3. A student moves her desk and finds a book that she borrowed from the library one year ago. She doesn't say anything and just puts it in the return book slot. When the library sends her a letter telling her that she cannot get her grades, she goes there and claims that she doesn't know anything about the book. Afterward, she feels guilty and goes back to tell the truth. What might she have done in the beginning that would have saved her embarrassment?

4. Two cars are parked at a red light. A third driver suddenly appears and smashes into one of the cars. The driver is not hurt, but his car is badly damaged. When the police arrive at the scene, they question the other car waiting at the light. The driver is in a hurry, and he doesn't want to get involved. The police say that he must have seen what happened, and they insist on taking his name. Although he saw everything, he tells them that he was looking the other way. Did he make the right decision? Why? What could he have done to help the other driver but still not lose time?

CHAPTER FIFTEEN

Responding to Change

PREREADING ACTIVITIES

1. This story is about a person who left Iran to come to the United States. In a small group, discuss Iran. Where is it? What is its history? What do you know about the relationship between the United States and Iran?
2. The main character in the story is returning to Iran after being away for 14 years. What do you expect her to feel when she returns to her country, home, and family?
3. What do you think the title of the story "Foreigner" means? In a group, discuss the feeling of being a foreigner in a country. Do you think you might feel like a foreigner if you returned to your home country? Have you ever felt like a foreigner in the United States?

Foreigner

This excerpt is from the novel Foreigner *by Nahid Rachlin, an Iranian woman who now lives and writes in the United States. It is about a woman returning home to Iran after 14 years. She has to learn to deal with changes in herself, her family, and her country.*

As I boarded the plane at Logan Airport in Boston I paused on the top step and waved to Tony. He waved back. I pulled the window curtain beside me and closed my eyes, seeing Tony's face falling away, bitten by light.

In the Teheran airport I was groggy° and disoriented.° I found my valise° and set it on a table, where two customs officers searched it. Behind a large window people waited. The women, mostly hidden under dark chadors,° formed a single fluid shape. I kept looking towards the window trying to spot my father, stepmother, or step-brother, but I did not see any of them. Perhaps they were there and we could not immediately recognize each other. It had been fourteen years since I had seen them.

A young man sat on a bench beside the table, his task there not clear. He wore his shirt open and I could see bristles of dark hair on his chest. He was making shadow pictures on the floor—a rabbit, a bird— and then dissolving the shapes between his feet. Energy emanated°

°dazed, half awake
°confused
°suitcase

°Iranian women's clothing

°flowed

289

from his hands, a crude, confused energy. Suddenly he looked at me, staring into my eyes. I turned away.

I entered the waiting room and looked around. Most people had left. There was still no one for me. What could possibly have hap- 20 pened? Normally someone would be there—a definite effort would be made. I fought to shake off my groggy state.

°handmade wares

A row of phones stood in the corner next to a handicraft° shop. I tried to call my father. There were no phone books and the informa- tion line rang busy, on and on. 25

I went outside and approached a collection of taxis. The drivers stood around, talking. "Can I take one of these?" I asked.

The men turned to me but no one spoke.

"I need a taxi," I said.

"Where do you want to go?" one of the men asked. He was old with 30 stooped shoulders and a thin, unfriendly face. I gave him my father's address.

"That's all the way on the other side of the city." He did not move from his spot.

"Please . . . I have to get there somehow." 35

The driver looked at the other men as if this were a group project.

"Take her," one of them said. "I would take her myself but I have to get home." He smiled at me.

"All right, get in," the older man said, pointing to a taxi.

In the taxi, he turned off the meter almost immediately. "You have 40

°Iranian money

to pay me 100 tomans° for this."

"That much?"

"It would cost you more if I left the meter on."

There was no point arguing with him. I sat stiffly and looked out.

°yellowish
°trees

We seemed to be floating in the sallow° light cast by the street lamps. 45 Thin old sycamores° lined the sidewalks. Water flowed in the gutters. The smoky mountains surrounding the city, now barely visible, were like a dark ring. The streets were more crowded and there were many more tall western buildings than I had remembered. Cars sped by, bouncing over holes, passing each other recklessly, honking. My taxi 50 driver also drove badly and I had visions of an accident, of being

°physically harmed

maimed.°

°Moslem place of worship
°dirty and neglected

We passed through quieter, older sections. The driver slowed down on a narrow street with a mosque° at its center, then stopped in front of a large, squalid° house. This was the street I had lived on for so 55 many years; here I had played hide-and-seek in alleys and hallways. I had a fleeting sensation that I had never left this street, that my other life with Tony had never existed.

I paid the driver, picked up my valise, and got out. On the cracked blue tile above the door, "Akbar Mehri," my father's name, was writ- 60 ten.

I banged the iron knocker several times and waited. In the light of the street lamps I could see a beggar with his jaw twisted sitting against the wall of the mosque. Even though it was rather late, a hum of prayers, like a moan, rose from the mosque. A Moslem priest came out, 65 looked past the beggar and spat on the ground. The doors of the house across the street were open. I had played with two little girls, sisters, who had lived there. I could almost hear their voices, laughter. The April air was mild and velvety against my skin but I shivered at the

°nearness

proximity° to my childhood. 70

A pebble suddenly hit me on the back. I turned but could not see anyone. A moment later another pebble hit my leg and another behind my knee. More hit the ground. I turned again and saw a small boy running and hiding in the arched hallway of a house nearby.

I knocked again. 75

There was a thud from the inside, shuffling, and then soft footsteps. The door opened and a man—my father—stood before me. His cheeks were hollower than I had recalled, the circles under his eyes deeper, and his hair more evenly gray. We stared at each other.

°making a twisted facial
expression

"It's you!" He was grimacing,° as though in pain. 80

"Didn't you get my telegram?"

He nodded. "We waited for you for two hours this morning at the airport. What happened to you?"

I was not sure if he was angry or in a daze. "You must have gotten the time mixed up. I meant nine in the evening." 85

My father stretched his hands forward, about to embrace me but, as though struck by shyness, he let them drop at his sides. "Come in now."

I followed him inside. I too was in the grip of shyness, or something like it.

"I thought you'd never come back," he said. 90

"I know, I know."

"You aren't even happy to see me."

"That's not true. I'm just . . ."

"You're shocked. Of course you are."

He went towards the rooms arranged in a semicircle, on the other 95

°porch

side of the courtyard. A veranda° with columns extended along several of the rooms. Crocuses, unpruned rosebushes, and pomegranate trees filled the flower beds. The place seemed cramped, untended. But still it was the same house. Roses would blossom, sparrows would chirp at the edge of the pool. At dawn and dusk the voice of the muezzin would 100 mix with the noise of people coming from and going to the nearby bazaars.

We went up the steps onto the veranda and my father opened the door to one of the rooms. He stepped inside and turned on the light. I paused for a moment, afraid to cross the threshold. I could smell it: 105 must, jasmin, rosewater, garlic, vinegar, recalling my childhood. Shut

°lazy

doors with confused noises behind them, slippery footsteps, black, golden-eyed cats staring from every corner, indolent° afternoons when people reclined on mattresses, forbidden subjects occasionally reaching me—talk about a heavy flow of menstrual blood, sex inflicted by force, the last dark words of a woman on her death bed. 110

My father disappeared into another room. I heard voices whispering and then someone said loudly, "She's here?" Footsteps approached. In the semidarkness of a doorway at the far end of the room two faces appeared and then another face, like three moons, staring at me. 115

"Feri, what happened?" a woman's voice asked, and a figure stepped forward. I recognized my stepmother, Ziba. She wore a long, plain cotton nightgown.

"The time got mixed up, I guess." My voice sounded feeble and hesitant. 120

A man laughed and walked into the light too. It was my stepbrother, Darius. He grinned at me, a smile disconnected from his eyes.

"Let's go to the kitchen," my father said. "So that Feri can eat something."

°one in front of another

They went back through the same doorway and I followed them. We walked through the dim, intersecting rooms in tandem.° In one room all the walls were covered with black cloth, and a throne, also covered with a black cloth, was set in a corner—for monthly prayers when neighborhood women would come in and a Moslem priest was invited to give sermons. The women would wail and beat their chests in these sessions as the priest talked about man's guilt or the sacrifices the leaders of Islam had made. They would cry as if at their own irrevoca- 130

°unchangeable

ble° guilt and sorrow.

We were together in the kitchen. Darius, Ziba, my father—they seemed at once familiar and remote like figures in dreams. 135

Reading and Thinking Strategies

Discussion Activities

Analysis and Conclusions

1. Do you think Feri is wearing a chador, or is she dressed in Western style? Do you think this affects the way she is treated by the men at the airport and the little boy throwing the pebbles?

2. What are some of the details from the story that suggest that Feri feels like a foreigner in her own country?

3. Her father stretches his hands forward as though to embrace her, and then he drops his hands. Why does he drop his hands? How does this make her feel?

Writing and Point of View

1. Writers try to create moods by their choices of words and images. This story is dreamlike. What words and images does Rachlin use to make this story dreamlike?

2. Like Hemingway, Rachlin uses dialogue throughout the story. Do you enjoy stories in which there is dialogue? Why or why not?

3. "A Mortal Flower" in Chapter Twelve is excerpted from an autobiography; "Foreigner" is excerpted from a novel. Are there differences in the styles of writing? Are there any indications that "Foreigner" is fictional? If so, what are they?

Personal Response and Evaluation

1. Rachlin says that the veranda seems "cramped and untended." Sometimes when we return to a place that we knew as children, it seems cramped and smaller than we remember it. Have you ever had that experience? Why do you think this occurs?

2. Do you think Feri will remain in Iran or return to her life in the United States? What in the story helps you to decide?

3. Have you ever had an experience similar to Feri's? How did it make you feel?

Response Paragraph

After you have read "Foreigner," write a paragraph about how this story made you feel and what you thought about as you read it. Share your paragraphs with your classmates.

One student wrote the following paragraph:

After I read "Foreigner," it made me think about me visiting my country after I had been gone for four and a half years. I'd been gone only four and a half years, but I understand her feeling that she thought she hadn't gone anywhere. Everyone was strange, even my friends, but the places and streets were the same. I talked about our past with my friends. After a few hours, I could feel that they were my friends and they still are. Then I felt I really had come to my hometown. It was hard to catch up to the distance made by four and a half years that we'd been apart, but I believe it was more difficult for Feri. It will take time for her to fit in her family as she was before.

Sohyung Kim, South Korea

Did you feel any of the same feelings as Sohyung felt when she read "Foreigner"?

Journal Writing

> What is writing, if it is not the countenance of our daily experience: sensuous, contemplative, imaginary, what we see and hear, dream of, how it strikes us, how it comes into us, travels through us, and emerges in some language hopefully useful to others.
>
> M. C. RICHARDS, *Centering: Poetry, Pottery and the Person*

Journals let us record our impressions of the world and make sense of them with our words. Sometimes we record dreams and sometimes real events; regardless, we try to use our journal entries to deepen our understanding of ourselves and, at the same time, to improve our writing.

When you write this time, think of dreams, of returning to places that you have thought about and had mixed feelings about. Before you write, you might want to cluster around the word *foreigner* or *dream*. You may want to write a story, a poem, or prose (writing that is not a poem). A short poem by the Russian poet Olga Berggolts may help you to reflect on these ideas and stimulate your mind and pen.

TO MY SISTER

I dreamt of the old house
where I spent my childhood years,
and the heart, as before, finds
comfort, and love, and warmth.

I dreamt of Christmas, the tree,   5
and my sister laughing out loud,
from morning, the rosy windows
sparkle tenderly.

And in the evening gifts are given
and the pine needles smell of stories,   10
And golden stars risen
are scattered like cinder above the rooftop.

I know that our old house
is falling into disrepair
Bare, despondent branches   15
knock against darkening panes.

And in the room with its old furniture,
a resentful captive, cooped up,
lives our father, lonely and weary—
he feels abandoned by us.   20

Why, oh why do I dream of the country
where the love's all consumed, all?
Maria, my friend, my sister,
speak my name, call to me, call . . .

Writing Strategies

Essay Strategies

Setting the Mood in Your Writing

images

To understand how images can create a feeling or understanding on the part of the reader, let's examine some of the images Rachlin uses.

In the Teheran airport, Rachlin tells us about the relationships between men and women.

The women, mostly hidden under dark chadors, formed a single fluid shape.

What does this sentence tell us about the women in the airport?

Do you think Feri is wearing a chador? Why would Rachlin want the reader to know if Feri were wearing a chador?

A young man sat on a bench beside the table, his task there not clear. He wore his shirt open and I could see bristles of dark hair on his chest.

Contrast these two descriptions. What is Rachlin telling us about the differences between men and women in Teheran?

The April air was mild and velvety against my skin but I shivered at the proximity to my childhood.

There is an interesting contrast of images in this sentence. What does it tell the reader about Feri's childhood?

---

mood

Rachlin creates a dreamlike mood with her choice of descriptive words.

We seemed to be floating in the sallow light cast by the street lamps.

"Floating" creates a very dreamy feeling. "Sallow light" is a shadowy light, as contrasted with bright, sunny light.

The smoky mountains surrounding the city, now barely visible, were like a dark ring.

"Smoky mountains" conveys an image that is vague, cloudy, and dreamy. "Barely visible" gives the reader the same feeling.

Read through the story, looking for other images that suggest dreams.

Rachlin has used many delicate poetic images to convey strong feelings. What do you think Rachlin wants the reader to think about Feri?

_____

What do you think Rachlin wants the reader to think about Feri's family?

_____

What do you think Rachlin wants the reader to think about Teheran?

_____

Similes and Metaphors

Writers use comparisons to enrich their writing. One type of comparison is the *simile*—a comparison of unlike things, usually using the word *like* or *as:*

In the semidarkness of a doorway at the far end of the room two faces appeared and then another face, *like* three moons staring at me. (Moons are known to us yet they are remote and mysterious.)

Writers also use *metaphors* to describe feelings and events. A metaphor uses a word or term that usually stands for one thing to stand for another:

I pulled the window curtains beside me and closed my eyes, seeing Tony's face falling away, bitten by light. (This implies that Tony is disappearing, being eaten up by the light.)

The women, mostly hidden under dark chadors, formed a single fluid shape. (This suggests that the women look the same and seem to melt into each other, to form a liquid mass.)

The April air was mild and velvety against my skin . . . (This implies a softness in the air.)

Poets use words very carefully. They are always looking for exactly the right word to convey meaning. Poets work with fewer words than prose writers do; however, prose writers must also be concerned with finding the right word. The examples illustrate some of the ways in which Rachlin was able to influence the reader's view of her characters and the city she describes. When you write, keep in mind the power of words. Search for the right word to help your reader understand what you have written.

Essay Form

Describing a Person

In "Foreigner," Nahid Rachlin describes a young man at the airport.

> A young man sat on a bench beside the table, his task there not clear. He wore his shirt open and I could see bristles of dark hair on his chest. He was making shadow pictures on the floor—a rabbit, a bird—and then dissolving the shapes between his feet. Energy emanated from his hands, a crude, confused energy. Suddenly he looked at me, staring into my eyes. I turned away.

This choice of the young man as the first person described in Iran helps the reader to share the main character's feelings about arriving as a foreigner in her own country. Later, Rachlin describes Feri's father, whom the woman has not seen for 14 years:

> The door opened and a man—my father—stood before me. His cheeks were hollower than I had recalled, the circles under his eyes deeper, and his hair more evenly gray. We stared at each other.

Rachlin could have just written that the father had gotten older, but instead she describes his cheeks, his eyes, and his hair. How does this description make you feel as a reader?

In "A Mortal Flower" in Chapter Twelve, Han Suyin describes Mr. Harned:

> Mr. Harned was very tall, thin, [with] a small bald head, a long chin, enormous glasses. I immediately began to quiver with fright. His head was like a temple on top of a mountain, like the white pagoda on the hill in the North Sea Park. I could not hear a word of what he said. A paper and a pencil were in my hand, however, and Mr. Harned was dictating to me, giving me a speed test in shorthand.

This description helps the reader to see Mr. Harned and to feel the terror the young girl feels during her job interview. We picture a person who is cold and unfriendly. If she had wanted him to appear warm and cuddly, she could have described him as "short and chubby." We read that he wears "enormous glasses." His glasses probably magnify his eyes and make him seem even more frightening and forbidding. She continues, "His head was like a temple on top of a mountain, like the white pagoda on the hill in the North Sea Park." A temple on top of a mountain is something far away and not easily approached, and a pagoda is a holy temple that in some cases women are not even allowed to visit. Han Suyin uses similes, comparisons that use the word *like* or *as*, to create a mood of distance and fear.

"I could not hear a word of what he said." Once again, the girl is removed from Mr. Harned. They cannot communicate. "A paper and a pencil were in my hand, however, and Mr. Harned was dictating to me, giving me a speed test in shorthand." Han Suyin does not tell us that Mr. Harned handed her the paper. He does not even smile at her. There is no connection between the two of them. He dictates to her; he does not speak to her or talk with her. Throughout the paragraph, Han Suyin creates a mood of aloofness on the part of Mr. Harned and perceived isolation on the part of the girl. She is alone and frightened during the interview. In fact, we find out later in the story that Mr. Harned is benign (kindly or gentle), but we do not get this feeling in our first impression of him. Han Suyin has used description to create a mood and a feeling about a character.

The following excerpt from *Sleepless Nights* by Elizabeth Hardwick illustrates how description can make us feel about a character.

> For a time she had a lover, Bernie. He was terrible to look at. Very short, and if not fat, with too many muscles and bulges. Bernie was put together like a pumpkin, or two pumpkins, one placed on top of the other. The top was his merry, jack-o'-lantern face with its broken teeth.

The reader is told that Bernie is terrible to look at. In the next lines, however, Hardwick tells us that he looks "like a pumpkin, or two pumpkins, one placed on top of the other." A pumpkin is a big, round, orange fruit that makes us think of Halloween. Moreover, Hardwick goes on to say, "The top was his merry, jack-o'-lantern face with its broken teeth." A jack-o'-lantern is a pumpkin that is cut to look like a face; sometimes a candle is put inside it as a decoration. It has a holiday mood and feeling. Hardwick tells us that Bernie's face is "merry." Santa Claus is "merry." Overall Hardwick has written a short description that creates a fun, holiday mood and that makes us feel that Bernie is a likable fellow even if he is "terrible to look at."

In one of her letters, Katherine Mansfield says:

> The old woman who looks after me is about 106, nimble and small, with the loveliest skin—pink rubbed over cream—and she has blue eyes and white hair and one tooth, a sort of family monument to all the 31 departed ones.

The images are soft and gentle. Words like *nimble* and *small* begin to suggest a picture of a child. Mansfield describes the woman's skin as "pink rubbed over cream," a very poetic but also lovely image. The one tooth, which could have made the woman frightening and witch-like, is described in a humorous way. The reader likes the old woman and feels she is beautiful in a very special way.

Description makes us feel something about a person or a place. By our choice of words, we can make a person or a place seem inviting or forbidding, kindly or hostile. It is up to us as writers to choose the words that best convey what we are trying to express.

Writing about a Person

When you write about a person, the following four steps will help you think about and organize your writing.

1. *Observe* and reflect on the person before you start to write. Make notes about the stories that tell you something about the person's character and behavior patterns.

2. *Describe* the person so that your reader can visualize him or her clearly. Use picture words that are specific and vivid. Avoid words like *nice, cute, sweet,* and *great.* Show your reader how the person looks, sounds, moves, and smells.

3. *Analyze* the person's weaknesses and strengths, and explain how they make the person unique and interesting to know.

4. *Evaluate* why you have chosen to write about this person and why a reader should want to read about the person. Why is this person important to you and to others?

Keep these steps in mind when you describe a person in your next piece of writing.

☐ ☐ ☐

EXERCISES

1. Write a description in which you make the person being described seem frightening and forbidding. Use similes (comparisons that use *like* or *as*).

2. Write a description in which you make the person being described seem friendly and gentle. Use similes to create your image.

3. Rewrite Han Suyin's description of Mr. Harned so that he seems to be a warm and friendly man.

4. Write a description of someone in your class, and read it aloud to the class. See if anyone can recognize the individual you have written about.

Suggestions for Writing

Before you begin to write, choose one of the following topics listed here. Discuss some of your ideas about this subject with a classmate, or use one of the "Getting Started" exercises in this book to help you find ideas. You may also decide to review your journal for ideas. Always spend some time thinking before you start to write.

1. Feri is a foreigner in her own land. Have you ever felt this way? Have you ever felt foreign and strange anywhere? Write an essay in

which you analyze what people did that made you feel this way. What effect did your feeling have on your behavior and your self-image? What would you do to help someone who feels like a foreigner in your neighborhood or school?

2. Write a description of a person that will help your reader to imagine the person, your feelings about the person, and your relationship with each other.

3. Feri describes the feeling of going home. In Chapter Thirteen, Maria Muñiz writes of returning to Cuba. Do you think Muñiz's experience will be similar to Feri's? Imagine that you are Muñiz returning to Cuba. What will your experience be like? Compare it to Feri's. (If you prefer, you can visualize yourself returning to your own country.)

4. Imagine that you are Feri and it is your first night home in Teheran. Write a letter to Tony in Boston telling him about your experiences. Describe in detail the people and events that you experience.

5. "Childhood is not always the happy, peaceful time it is usually pictured to be." Do you agree or disagree? Support your point of view with your experiences or observations.

6. In the poem by Olga Berggolts on page 294, the poet describes dreaming of Christmas in the old house where she spent her childhood years. Visualize returning to your childhood house at holiday time. Describe in detail what you see, smell, hear, and taste. What about it seems different now that you are no longer a child?

Getting Started

Visualization

In this chapter, we will examine another way to stimulate interesting and creative writing. Using this technique, the writer visualizes or sees what is going to be written about. The writer totally enters the life or the world of the piece of writing.

New Zealand writer Katherine Mansfield describes her writing process:

When I write about ducks, I swear that I am a white duck with a round eye, floating on a pond fringed with yellow-blobs and taking an occasional dart at the other duck with the round eye, which floats beneath me. . . . In fact the whole process of becoming the duck . . . is so thrilling that I can hardly breathe, only to think about it. . . . I don't see how art is going to make that divine spring into the bounding outline of things if it hasn't passed through the process of trying to become these things before recreating them.

LETTERS OF KATHERINE MANSFIELD

Mansfield describes a process similar to the one you will use. Once you have decided on the topic you will write about, close your eyes and try to enter the world of that topic. You can use experiences that you have had in your life to help you see more clearly. Mansfield wrote about the duck because when she was a little girl, she witnessed the killing of a duck that she had loved. The duck was to be made into dinner, but young Mansfield was unaware of this as she went down to the water's edge with some other children. The duck's head was chopped off in front of the impressionable child, and the duck ran around headless until it died. Mansfield never forgot this moment, and she was able to use her feelings for the duck to make her writing come alive.

When you visualize, use any experience or observation you have had, and try to bring it alive inside your head. By the time you actually begin to write, you should have the sights, sounds, smells, and feelings inside your head. If you are writing a comparison-and-contrast essay, visualize the ideas until they come alive inside you. If you are writing a persuasive essay, persuade yourself first by totally immersing yourself in the topic.

If you have trouble getting started, use the clustering technique. Begin to cluster around a word, and when an image starts to come to you, close your eyes and try to make the image as vivid as possible.

□ □ □

EXERCISES

1. Visualize someone or something else's world. Mansfield visualizes being a duck. You can visualize yourself as your sister, your father, a dog, a cat, or a tree on the street. Try to re-create in its entirety the world of that person, creature, or thing.
2. Visualize as completely as possible your first day in this country or any other important day in your life. Re-create your experience, and then write down as much of it as you can in the next 20 minutes. Don't worry about spelling or grammar for this exercise.
3. By yourself or with a classmate, create your own visualization exercise.

Revising

Using the questions in this section to guide you, discuss the essay that follows, by Wan Ping Wu. Then, using the same questions, reread your writing and have a classmate read it. Keep in mind that your writing is not in its final form. As you read now, you may want to make changes. You may add or delete ideas. You may want to move or remove sentences or paragraphs. You may decide that other words express your meaning better.

Ask your partner the following questions about your writing, and write your answers on a separate piece of paper that you will refer to when you revise.

1. Does the paper have a clear beginning that makes the reader want to read more?
2. What is the main idea that the entire piece of writing holds together?
3. What are the supporting details—facts, observations, and experiences that support the main points?
4. Are the details specific—can the reader understand, see, hear, smell, and feel what this piece of writing is about?
5. Does the draft have a clear ending so that the reader knows the piece is completed?

After revising your essay, share it with your partner.

A Student Essay

A student wrote this description of a woman she would never meet.

One day I saw an old wooden trunk on the street. I went over to it and when I opened it, a beautiful woman's eyes looked into my eyes. The picture was old and dusty. And the woman was dressed in a long, low-cut dress. She looked very rich because she wore a necklace, a ring, and a tiny hair clip shaped like a butterfly in her upswept hair. But I   5
didn't know the color of her hair because the picture was colorless.

I forgot the other things in the trunk, but I think there was an old comb, old clothes, and many old letters. They seemed to have belonged to a man, maybe an old man. But there was a little box in the corner of the trunk. Inside, there was a tiny elaborate hair clip; it   10
looked like it was made from the yellow gold of a butterfly. I wanted to keep it.

I thought this trunk had been dumped by an old man at least eighty years old, and the things inside had been very important to him. Maybe the woman in the picture had been the old man's lover when   15
they were young. I closed the trunk and I knew I had to leave it because I could feel the old man looking at me from a long time ago. When I saw him, I felt guilty, so I hurried home.

When I got home, I told my mother all these things. I told her I wanted to keep the tiny yellow gold butterfly hair clip. But my mother   20
told me it was an unlucky thing, and she didn't let me keep it. So now the tiny yellow gold hair clip will be in my memory forever.

Wan Ping Wu, People's Republic of China

Editing Strategies

Word Development

words relating to Iran and Islam

"Foreigner" introduces us to the special vocabulary of the country of Iran and the religion of Islam. As you read about different countries and peoples, you will be exposed to such new vocabulary.

chador: a dress that Iranian women wear, which is draped around the body, across the shoulders, over the head, and across the lower part of the face

tomans: Iranian money

mosque: a Moslem place for the worship of God

muezzin: a crier who calls faithful Moslems to prayer

Islam: the religion taught by the Prophet Mohammed in the 600s (Mohammed, who was born in Mecca in 570, taught the worship of one God, Allah, and proclaimed that he, Mohammed, was Allah's messenger. *Islam* is an Arabic word that means "submission." Islam is the faith of approximately one-fifth of the world's population.)

Moslems (Muslims): Believers in Allah who accept Mohammed as God's messenger (In Arabic, *Moslem* means "one who submits to God.")

☐   ☐   ☐

EXERCISES

1. If there is a Moslem student in the class, that student might inform the other class members about the Islamic religion and traditions.
2. You might want to consult your library to find out more about Islam or about other religions. Write a short paper to hand in to your teacher or present to the class.

Commonly Confused Words

cloth/clothes

Read the following paragraph, noticing the use of *cloth* and *clothes*.

Cloth is a piece of fabric. You make *clothes* out of *cloth*. *Cloth* is not singular for *clothes*. *Clothes* are the items that we put on our bodies when we dress. Men's and women's *clothes* are very different in some parts of the world. In Iran, for example, women wear very different *clothes* from those that men wear. In the United States, by contrast, some *clothes* that men and women wear are very similar.

Fill in each of the following blanks with *cloth* or *clothes*.

1. I bought some _____ to make some _____.

2. A designer buys beautiful _____ to put together a new

   line of _____.

3. Because there was no door, the heavy dark _____ hung in

   front of the _____ closet.

   Write two more sentences using these words.

Sentence Skills: Tense Review

Simple Past Tense

In the following sentences from "Foreigner," the past tense verbs have been removed. Fill in the correct form of the verb. If you have difficulty, see pages 313–16 for a list of irregular verbs. Refer to the story to check your answers.

1. I _____ my valise and _____ it on a table,
       (find)   (set)

   where two customs officers _____ it.
             (search)

2. I _____ looking towards the window trying to spot my
    (keep)

   father, stepmother, or stepbrother, but I _____ not see
             (do)

   any of them.

3. A row of phones _____ in the corner next to a handi-
       (stand)

   craft shop.

4. I _____ outside and _____ a collection of taxis.
    (go)   (approach)

5. I _____ the driver, _____ up my valise, and
    (pay)   (pick)

   _____ out.
    (get)

6. A pebble suddenly _____ me on the back.
            (hit)

7. I _____ nine in the evening.
      (mean)

8. My father _____ his hands forward, about to em-
              (stretch)

   brace me but, as though _____ by shyness, he
                              (strike)

   _____ them drop at his sides.
           (let)

Past Perfect Tense

Fill in the following blanks. If you have any difficulty, see Chapter Three, page 61.

The past perfect tense is used when we want to write about more than one event that occurred in the _____. We use the

_____ tense to describe the event that happened first and

we use the _____ tense to describe the event that hap-

pened next. The past perfect tense is formed with _____

plus the past _____.

Examine the following examples from the story.

I entered the waiting room and looked around. Most people had left.

Which happened first—Feri entered the room or people left?

_____

Why did Rachlin use the past perfect tense for the second sentence?

_____

The streets were more crowded and there were many more tall western build-ings than I had remembered.

Why does Rachlin use "had remembered" in this sentence? _____

_____

His cheeks were hollower than I had recalled. . . .

When had Feri last seen her father? _____

Why does Rachlin use "had recalled" in this sentence? _____

_____

Combining Sentences

Using some of the techniques from earlier chapters, combine these short sentences into longer ones. Keep in mind that there are many correct ways to create new sentences. Try several combinations, and share them with a classmate.

1. I boarded the plane at Logan Airport in Boston.
   I paused on the top step.
   I waved to Tony.

   _____

2. I found my valise.
   I set it on the table.
   Two customs officers searched it.

   _____

3. I kept looking towards the window.
   I was trying to spot my father, stepmother, or stepbrother.
   I did not see any of them.

   _____

4. We went up the steps.
   The steps led to the veranda.
   My father opened the door.
   The door led to one of the rooms.

   _____

5. A man laughed.
   He walked into the light.
   He was my stepbrother.
   His name was Darius.

   _____

Indirect Speech

In Chapter Ten, on page 206, we examined indirect speech—expressing what someone has said or written without using quotation marks or the exact words. This is also called reported speech.

"I need a taxi," she said. (line 29)	Direct quotation
She said that she needed a taxi.	Indirect speech

Notice the pronoun change from direct quotation to indirect speech. *I*, the person speaking, changes to *she*.

"Where do you want to go?" one of the men asked. (line 30)	Direct quotation
One of the men asked where she wanted to go.	Indirect speech

Notice the pronoun change from *you* to *she*.

Her father said, "We waited for you for two hours this morning at the airport." (lines 82–83)	Direct quotation
Her father said that they had waited for _____ for two hours that morning at the airport.	Indirect speech

Notice the change from *this* in the direct quotation to *that* in indirect speech.

"Feri, what happened?" a woman's voice asked. (line 116)	Direct quotation
A woman's voice asked her _____.	Indirect speech

Notice that the speaker is identified before the reported speech begins.

"You have to pay me 100 tomans for this," said the taxi driver. (lines 40–41)	Direct quotation
The taxi driver said that _____ had to pay _____ 100 tomans.	Indirect speech
Feri asked, "Didn't you get my telegram?" (line 81)	Direct quotation
Feri asked if they had _____ telegram.	Indirect speech

Notice how the question form changes in reported speech.

☐ ☐ ☐

EXERCISES

1. For more practice, change the following direct quotations to indirect or reported speech.

    a. "I am happy to see you," she said to her father.
    b. "Things have really changed here," he told her.
    c. "Do you have a phone?" Feri asked her brother.

2. For extra practice, change other direct quotations in the story to indirect speech.

Transitions of Place

Rachlin moves her reader by using transitions of place, which she locates at the beginnings of the paragraphs. To illustrate, we will examine the first lines of several of the paragraphs. As we examine the words of transition, think about why Rachlin might want to make the reader very conscious of place.

As I boarded the plane at Logan Airport in Boston . . . (paragraph 1)
In the Teheran airport I was groggy and disoriented. (paragraph 2)

What happens between paragraph 1 and paragraph 2? _____

_____

Does the author tell the reader much about Boston? _____

Which place do you think will be more important in this story—Boston or Teheran? Why do you think this?

_____

A young man sat on a bench beside the table. . . .
I entered the waiting room and looked around.
A row of phones stood in the corner next to a handicraft shop.
I went outside and approached a collection of taxis.

Where has Rachlin taken us in these paragraphs? _____

_____

What do we know about Teheran at this point? _____

_____

How do you think Feri feels about Teheran? What does Rachlin say

that makes you think that way? _____

_____

We passed through quieter, older sections.
I followed him [her father] inside.
He went towards the rooms. . . .
We went up the steps onto the veranda. . . .
My father disappeared into another room.
They went back through the same doorway and I followed them.
We were together in the kitchen.

Is Feri happy to be home? How does the reader know?

_____

Did Feri have a happy childhood? How does Rachlin use words about
place to let the reader know the answer to this question?

_____

   Rachlin has taken us on a tour of Feri's life using the transitions of
place. We have followed her from Boston to Teheran. We have followed her through the confusing airport to the expensive taxi that
drove her through streets familiar yet strange. We have arrived at her
street and seen the mosque, the house of old playmates, and finally
her old home, which looks frighteningly similar to the way it had
looked when she left 14 years before. Once in the house, Rachlin leads
us through a maze of a veranda, into the "rooms." Finally we end up in
the kitchen.

   Why do you think the author used these transitions of place? How
does reading them make you feel?

_____

According to the story, how does Feri see her world?

_____

   Look back at the other stories we have read. Do any of them use
place in the way that Rachlin does?

Mechanics

Underlining

When you are putting an essay on your computer or writing an essay by hand and you do not have *italics* (the slightly slanted print in which the word *italics* appears), you underline. How do you know which words need to be underlined? Follow these guidelines:

1. Underline the names of books, plays, movies, magazines, newspapers, pamphlets, radio and television programs, recordings and videos, legal cases, and ships and aircraft.
2. Underline foreign words that are not commonly used in English.
3. Do *not* underline or put in quotation marks sacred writing (including books from the Bible, the Koran, the Talmud, or the Torah).

□   □   □

EXERCISES

1. Reread or review any of your earlier writing assignments this semester to make sure that you used underlining correctly.
2. When you edit your next draft, check to make sure that you have used underlining correctly.

Editing Practice

The following paragraph is a first draft. It contains many surface errors. Edit and rewrite the paragraph, correcting the errors.

Returning home can be very difficult. As we see in Nahid Rachlin's story *foreigner*. People return to their home countries they often find many changes. The streets may not look the same. People they remember may not recognized them. If they go back to there own childhood house. The house may look very different. It may appear small and cramped. One women wrote that she returned to her neighborhood and their house was gone. In it's place was a little store. No one remembers her. She is extremely depressed. It is also possible to return to a place where everyone remember you. That makes a person happy inside; on least you where not forgotten.

For the answers, turn to page 325.

Grammar Strategies

Conditionals Using *if*

Conditionals are used in English for a number of reasons and in a number of forms:

1. To express relationships that are true and unchanging:

   If you lower the temperature of water to 0°C, it freezes.
   If you boil water, it vaporizes. (Notice the present tense is used in both clauses. This kind of conditional is often used in scientific writing.)

2. To express relationships that are habitual:

   If I wash the car, it rains.
   If I had washed the car, it would have rained.

   Note: In 1 and 2, it is possible to substitute *when* or *whenever* for *if* without changing the meaning of the sentence:

   When (*whenever*) you lower the temperature of water to 0°C, it freezes.

   Try using *when* or *whenever* with the other examples.

3. To express inferences:

   If the police can't solve that crime, no one can solve it.
   If you'll go to Pierre's party, I'll go too.
   If you act happy, the baby will stop crying.

4. To express a condition in the future:

   If it snows, I'll wear my boots.
   If you do your homework, you'll pass the course.
   If you call me tonight, I'll call you tomorrow. (The first clause uses the present tense and the second clause uses the future tense.)

5. To express unlikely but possible events:

   If I had the energy, I would jog tonight.
   If he had left work early, he would be home by now. (Notice that the first clause uses *had* and the second clause uses *would*.)

6. To express impossible events:

> If I had your face, I would become a model.
> If Gandhi were alive today, he would make peace in the world.

Using *were* in Conditionals

English uses *were* to indicate unlikely or impossible circumstances. "If I were a genius" means that the writer is not a genius. *Were* is used with all subjects (*I, you, we, he, she it, they*) to indicate an unlikely or untrue situation:

> If he were to win the lottery, he would buy his parents a new house. (He does not expect to win the lottery.)
> If they were to quit their jobs, they would go to Hawaii.
> (They do not expect to quit their jobs.)
> If I were you, I would study harder. (I am not and could never be you.)

Notice that the independent clause that follows the *were* part of the sentence uses *would* and no ending on the verb that follows. You can also use *should, could, ought to*, and *might* in this structure.

☐ ☐ ☐

EXERCISE

Complete the following sentences using the structure just described.

1. If he were to win the contest, he ought to _____

   _____.

2. If I were you, I might _____.

3. If a student were to fail a course, she might _____.
4. If schools were to give automatic passing grades to all students,

   students could _____.

5. If I were to win the lottery, I would _____.

Principal Parts
of Irregular Verbs

Base	Past	Past Participle
awake	awoke, awaked	awoken, awaked
be	was, were	been
bear	bore	borne
beat	beat	beat, beaten
become	became	become
begin	began	begun
bend	bent	bent
bet	bet	bet
bind	bound	bound
bite	bit	bit, bitten
bleed	bled	bled
blow	blew	blown
break	broke	broken
breed	bred	bred
bring	brought	brought
build	built	built
burst	burst	burst
buy	bought	bought
catch	caught	caught
choose	chose	chosen
come	came	come
cost	cost	cost
creep	crept	crept
cut	cut	cut
deal	dealt	dealt

Base	Past	Past Participle
dig	dug	dug
dive	dived, dove	dived
do	did	done
draw	drew	drawn
dream	dreamed, dreamt	dreamed, dreamt
drink	drank	drunk
drive	drove	driven
eat	ate	eaten
fall	fell	fallen
feed	fed	fed
feel	felt	felt
fight	fought	fought
find	found	found
fit	fit, fitted	fit, fitted
flee	fled	fled
fly	flew	flown
forbid	forbade	forbidden
forget	forgot	forgotten, forgot
freeze	froze	frozen
get	got	gotten, got
give	gave	given
go	went	gone
grind	ground	ground
grow	grew	grown
hang (an object)	hung	hung
hang (a person)	hanged	hanged
have	had	had
hear	heard	heard
hide	hid	hidden, hid
hit	hit	hit
hold	held	held
hurt	hurt	hurt
keep	kept	kept
kneel	knelt, kneeled	knelt, kneeled
knit	knitted, knit	knitted, knit

Base	*Past*	*Past Participle*
know	knew	known
lay (put)	laid	laid
lead	led	led
lean	leaned, leant	leaned, leant
leave	left	left
lend	lent	lent
let (allow)	let	let
lie (recline)	lay	lain
light	lighted, lit	lighted, lit
lose	lost	lost
make	made	made
mean	meant	meant
pay	paid	paid
prove	proved	proved, proven
quit	quit, quitted	quit, quitted
read	read	read
rid	rid, ridded	rid, ridded
ride	rode	ridden
ring	rang	rung
rise	rose	risen
run	ran	run
say	said	said
see	saw	seen
seek	sought	sought
sell	sold	sold
send	sent	sent
set	set	set
shake	shook	shaken
shine	shone, shined	shone, shined
shoot	shot	shot
show	showed	shown, showed
shrink	shrank	shrunk
shut	shut	shut
sing	sang	sung
sink	sank	sunk

Base	*Past*	*Past Participle*
sit	sat	sat
sleep	slept	slept
slide	slid	slid, slidden
speak	spoke	spoken
speed	sped, speeded	sped, speeded
spend	spent	spent
spin	spun	spun
split	split	split
spread	spread	spread
spring	sprang	sprung
stand	stood	stood
steal	stole	stolen
stick	stuck	stuck
sting	stung	stung
strike	struck	struck, stricken
swear	swore	sworn
swim	swam	swum
swing	swung	swung
take	took	taken
teach	taught	taught
tear	tore	torn
tell	told	told
think	thought	thought
throw	threw	thrown
wake	woke, waked	woken, waked
wear	wore	worn
weave	wove	woven
weep	wept	wept
win	won	won
wring	wrung	wrung
write	wrote	written

Models for Tenses

Active Voice

SINGULAR	PLURAL	SINGULAR	PLURAL
Simple Present Tense		*Present Continuous Tense*	
I go	we go	I am helping	we are helping
you go	you go	you are helping	you are helping
he goes		he is helping	
she goes	they go	she is helping	they are helping
it goes		it is helping	
Simple Past Tense		*Past Continuous Tense*	
I lived	we lived	I was sleeping	we were sleeping
you lived	you lived	you were sleeping	you were sleeping
he lived		he was sleeping	
she lived	they lived	she was sleeping	they were sleeping
it lived		it was sleeping	
Simple Future Tense		*Future Continuous Tense*	
I will learn	we will learn	I will be playing	we will be playing
you will learn	you will learn	you will be playing	you will be playing
he will learn		he will be playing	
she will learn	they will learn	she will be playing	they will be playing
it will learn		it will be playing	

Active Voice

SINGULAR	PLURAL	SINGULAR	PLURAL
Present Perfect Tense		*Present Perfect Continuous Tense*	
I have seen	we have seen	I have been trying	we have been trying
you have seen	you have seen	you have been trying	you have been trying
he has seen		he has been trying	
she has seen	they have seen	she has been trying	they have been trying
it has seen		it has been trying	
Past Perfect Tense		*Past Perfect Continuous Tense*	
I had jumped	we had jumped	I had been running	we had been running
you had jumped	you had jumped	you had been running	you had been running
he had jumped		he had been running	
she had jumped	they had jumped	she had been running	they had been running
it had jumped		it had been running	
Future Perfect Tense			
I will have left	we will have left		
you will have left	you will have left		
he will have left			
she will have left	they will have left		
it will have left			
Future Perfect Continuous Tense			
I will have been getting	we will have been getting		
you will have been getting	you will have been getting		
he will have been getting			
she will have been getting	they will have been getting		
it will have been getting			

Passive Voice

SINGULAR	PLURAL	SINGULAR	PLURAL
Simple Present		*Present Continuous*	
I am given	we are given	I am being taken	we are being taken
you are given	you are given	you are being taken	you are being taken
he is given		he is being taken	
she is given	they are given	she is being taken	they are being taken
it is given		it is being taken	
Simple Past		*Past Continuous*	
I was brought	we were brought	I was being carried	we were being carried
you were brought	you were brought	you were being carried	you were being carried

Passive Voice

SINGULAR	PLURAL	SINGULAR	PLURAL
Simple Past		*Present Continuous*	
he was brought		he was being carried	
she was brought	they were brought	she was being carried	they were being carried
it was brought		it was being carried	

SINGULAR	PLURAL
Simple Future	
I will be found	we will be found
you will be found	you will be found
he will be found	
she will be found	they will be found
it will be found	
Present Perfect	
I have been offered	we have been offered
you have been offered	you have been offered
he has been offered	
she has been offered	they have been offered
it has been offered	
Past Perfect	
I had been loved	we had been loved
you had been loved	you had been loved
he had been loved	
she had been loved	they had been loved
it had been loved	
Future Perfect	
I will have been seen	we will have been seen
you will have been seen	you will have been seen
he will have been seen	
she will have been seen	they will have been seen
it will have been seen	

Answers to Exercises

page 16

Having a Little Brother

I have lived in the United States for six years and my brother has lived here for two years. He came here last because my parents thought he was too young to travel. When we left my country, he was a baby. I studied hard, but it has taken me a long time to learn English. For my brother, it has been different. He speaks English so well already. He talks to all his friends in English, and he is an *A* student in the second grade. I believe I can learn a lot from watching and talking to him. I hope there are things he can learn from me, too.

page 34

The Bergers are writing about the family from a sociological point of view. They are defining the two major types of family structures in most of the world: the nuclear family and the extended family. In the extended family, the larger family lives together, and they help each other, too. The nuclear family, however, consists of the parent(s) and the children. They usually have to handle difficulties on their own. When there are problems in the nuclear family, then they can ask for help from schools and religious institutions, but this is not always easy. Some of these families would rather solve their own problems than ask outsiders for advice. However, small families of parents and children alone often do not have the family support they need.

page 59

"The Last Word Was Love" describes a family at a critical point in time. The oldest brother in the family decides to leave the family and move to San Francisco. He feels disappointment with the way his parents live. The younger brother wants to know why his brother wants to move away from home. Their mother seems to understand, but she is quiet and does not discuss the problem with her younger son. Although the members of the family seem to love each other, they do not communicate well.

page 81

Thousands of men, women, and children have left Vietnam to come to the United States. They have had to leave their parents, friends, and families behind. When these people arrived, they suffered many crises; often they found their lives were difficult. They had to attend classes to learn the new language, and they usually had to move to overcrowded cities in order to get job opportunities. Traditionally, people have come to the United States from countries all over the world. Despite the many difficulties of adjusting, these immigrants give a vitality to the country, and the country offers many possibilities to these newcomers.

page 85

One part of learning a new language involves learning to use the language with others. Recently, a researcher in the way people learn languages wrote that if people want to learn how to talk in a second language, they should not be afraid to make mistakes. They should make contact with speakers of the new language. They should ask for corrections, and they should memorize dialogues.

If students want to learn to read, they should read something every day. They should read things that are familiar. They should look for meaning from the context without always looking at the dictionary. To gain confidence, they should start by reading books at the beginner's level.

page 103

Sung Hee moved to Massachusetts from Korea. She attended Boston University and lived in a dorm with her cousin. She began to work on Saturday nights at Filene's, a big department store, and she practiced English with her customers. On Sundays Sung Hee usually rented a little Chevrolet from Avis. Carrying a tourist book called *Inside Massachusetts*, she visited such historic sites as Plymouth Rock and the Old North Church. She spent hours at the Boston Public Library looking at the John Singer Sargent murals. She met Tony at a midnight showing of *Casablanca*, and last Christmas they said "I do." Now she is teaching Tony Korean and planning to travel home to introduce him to her family.

page 105

When Mikhail and Fatima volunteered to work one afternoon in the Western College Post Office, they were in for a surprise. In one corner, there were many boxes piled high. They found three heavy cartons of French language tapes addressed to Professor Maude Cousteau, now of the Ford Foundation. She had left the school back in February and had moved to New Mexico. Fatima accidentally opened a box filled with the Lotus 1-2-3 programs needed for the college IBM computers. "Mr. Smith, this post office is a mess," Mikhail told the postmaster. "I know it, son. We just have to get a little more organized. The U.S. mail has to go through, and we will do it. Soon." Mikhail and Fatima left there wondering if the college mail would ever get through.

page 105

Marie learns languages very easily. She was born in Haiti and has spoken French and Creole all her life. Now Marie also knows English, Spanish, and Italian. She has a special technique that always works for her. At night she goes to sleep by hypnotizing herself as she stares at a poster of the stained-glass window of Notre Dame Cathedral in Paris. Her Sony Walkman tape deck is on her head, and she listens to a different language tape each night.

page 111

Once upon a time there was a smart young man who decided to trick a wise old man. He caught a little bird and held it in one hand behind his back. The boy approached the wise man and said, "Sir, I have a question for you. I want to see how wise you are. I am holding a bird in my hand. Is it alive, or is it dead?"

The boy thought that if the man said the bird was dead, he would open his hand to reveal the live bird, but if the man said the bird was alive, he would crush the bird, killing it. The old man stared into the boy's eyes for a long time. Then he said, "The answer, my friend, is in your hands."

page 126

Ernest Hemingway's story "A Day's Wait" tells about a young boy who is afraid of dying. He hears the doctor say, "His temperature is one hundred and two degrees." He remembers his friends at school in France saying, "Schatz, you can't live with a temperature over forty-four degrees." The boy's temperature is very high. "You don't have to stay in here with me," he tells his father, "if it bothers you." His father doesn't know what's really bothering the boy. When he finds out, he says, "Schatz, it's like miles and kilometers." Schatz believes his father, but still he doesn't relax for several days.

page 127

My sister, Hilda, lives in an apartment on the top of a high hill in San Francisco. She works as a computer operator in a big bank there, and when she looks out her window, she sees the Golden Gate Bridge. She loves heights. She even flew in a private airplane over the Rocky Mountains. Once she said to me, "I saw both the Pacific and the Atlantic Oceans in one day." She would like to travel around the world someday.

page 143

March 14, 1992

5516 Buena Vista Avenue
Miami, Florida 33158

Dear Aunt Millie,

I think you should sit down before you read this letter, and I think you should have your handkerchief handy. I am sitting here in Santo Domingo with Luis, your favorite nephew. He was happy to see me, and he wants you to know how much he misses seeing you and the rest of the family. Luis said to give you 10,000 kisses when I get home, so I know I will be busy. I am sure you want to know how everyone else is, but I have not traveled out to see the rest of the family yet. Well, Luis says they are all fine. By the way, he is married, and he has a little girl. Just like that you are a great-aunt. Even though you have never seen her, her name is Millie. Standing there with her short curly hair, she looks just like you. Millie, your new 4-year-old niece says, "Hi!" I will bring you a picture of her, some homemade candy, and a crocheted scarf. I guess I will see you soon, won't I?

Always,

Carmen

Carmen

page 146
Traveling to a different country, whether it is returning home or going to a new destination, is exciting. When the airplane arrives in the airport safely, even people who travel often are glad. Suddenly, they are in a new, exciting world. Feeling tired, they get off the plane, and they head for their destination. They convert their money, wait in line for taxis, and spend too much money on foolish things. On the way home, they feel mixed emotions, but, overall, most of them are glad they took the chance and traveled.

page 167
Sociologists examine how people live in groups. They examine phenomena such as people's behavioral patterns in relation to love and marriage. They want to know if people in Italy celebrate marriage in the same way as people in the Philippines. Their studies show some customs and traditions are similar from place to place. For example, people usually get married with some kind of ceremony. They usually get dressed up for their wedding. However, there are some differences. In some places, marriages are arranged. In other places, people meet and fall in love. In general, everyone hopes that the marriage will be happy and long-lasting.

page 187
Like Pablo Casals, Marc Chagall was a remarkable man who lived a long and productive life. He was born in 1887, and he died in 1985. Chagall lived for almost a century. His paintings make people feel happy. They usually show dancing figures such as flying cows and pigs, playful lovers, and bright colored flowers. Chagall was born in Russia in the Jewish quarter of the town of Vitebsk. He had eight brothers and sisters. Chagall knew he wanted to be an artist when he was a little boy. However, he did not become famous until he was in his fifties.

page 205
Reading about the differences between men and women can help people learn a lot that will help them in their everyday lives. Many scientists are conflicted about whether these differences are caused by nature or nurture. No one knows for sure how much in-born genetic characteristics determine people's lives. Men and women may be influenced by their environment as much as by their genetics. According to research, the brain changes. It can change because of many things, such as diet, the air, handedness, etc. It makes sense that one should take good care of oneself by eating right, exercising, and trying to live a healthy life. However, despite everything people do, there will always be some differences between the sexes.

page 227
According to Oskamp, there are many factors involved in job satisfaction. People have to feel their jobs are meaningful and interesting. They have to offer the workers a mental challenge. Even though there are individual differences in what people think is important, most people agree that their jobs should offer some challenge. Pay has greater importance for individuals who cannot gain other satisfactions from their jobs. Jobs that offer external recognition, good pay, and a mental challenge are sought by most people. Each person wants a feeling of fulfillment.

page 239　　　　　　　　The first thing, Most of all, The best thing, Finally, The basic reason

page 247　　　　　　　　Trying to get a job at the Rockefeller Foundation is difficult for a girl who does not have pull. Finally, the morning postman brings the letter. She is to go for an interview at Peking Medical College, to the Comptroller's office. She prepares her clothes and goes to the East market to buy face powder to cover her pimples. The next morning, she goes with her father to Yu Wang Fu Palace to the Administration building. They cross the marble courtyard and go into the entrance hall. Her father leaves. She finds the office and meets her future employer, Mr. Harned. His bald head reminds her of the white pagoda on the hill in North Sea Park. She takes the required typing test and gets the job.

page 249　　　　　　　　Looking for a job can be difficult. There are many different types of problems. For one thing, the interviewee is never sure what to bring on the first interview. I usually bring too much. This can be confusing to the interviewer. From now on, I will bring only the necessary documents such as my résumé, my birth certificate, and my high school diploma. In addition, I try to impress the interviewer by dressing very neatly and never chewing gum. I always look directly into the interviewer's eyes. I want the interviewer to believe that I can be trusted. If I remember to follow my own advice, I believe I will get a job soon.

page 251　　　　　　　　even though, but, Still, Otherwise, however, Instead of, on the other hand, although, Yet, In contrast to

page 269　　　　　　　　The essay "Back, but Not Home," by Maria L. Muñiz, made me think about returning to my country. I grew up thinking that there was no reason to go back, but now I am not sure. It's interesting for me to think about the world that I left behind. I feel mixed emotions such as happiness, sadness, and regret. My aunts and uncles still live in my country. They still live in the same town, in the same house. I have never seen most of my cousins; the youngest one is five months old, and I would like to know him, too. My brother visited my family last year, and he told me all the news. It's strange hearing about my best girlfriends who are getting married, and one even has a baby. The Muñiz essay, my brother's visit, and my dreams make me want to return to my country for a visit.

page 286　　　　　　　　Although getting engaged has changed Samia's life, she doesn't want to marry now. Ahmed, her boyfriend, wants to get married right away, but she disagrees. For now, she likes showing her girlfriends her diamond ring. She also enjoys discussing her future wedding with them when she is in school. Even though she knows that she makes her friends jealous, she enjoys showing off. The other day her best friends made a real effort not to review their homework with her in the cafeteria as they usually do every afternoon after class. She realizes they envy her, yet she continues the same behavior. Samia claims that she likes being engaged, but she doesn't want to get married right away. Being a housewife doesn't sound like too much fun to her.

page 310

Returning home can be very difficult, as we see in Nahid Rachlin's story "Foreigner." When people return to their home countries, they often find many changes. The streets may not look the same. People they remember may not recognize them. If they go back to their own childhood house, the house may look very different. It may appear small and cramped. One woman wrote that she returned to her neighborhood and her house was gone. In its place was a little store. No one remembered her. She was extremely depressed. It is also possible to return to a place where everyone remembers you. That makes a person feel happy inside; at least you were not forgotten.

Index